W0006110

PASTORAL MINISTRY
– AN ESSAY IN PASTORAL THEOLOGY

Pastoral Ministry
– An Essay in Pastoral Theology

David J. Oakley

Pentland Books
Durham · Edinburgh · Oxford

First published in 2001 by
Pentland Books
1 Hutton Close
South Church
Bishop Auckland
Durham

British Library Cataloguing in Publication Data.
A catalogue record for this book is available
from the British Library.

ISBN 1 85821 896 9

Typeset by George Wishart & Associates, Whitley Bay.
Printed and bound by Antony Rowe Ltd., Chippenham.

Contents

Foreword

I welcome this book. Pastoral Theology is the concern of all who serve the People of God, particularly those directly involved in parish ministry.

This book is a thorough and systematic study of themes central to the pastoral work of the Church. Even though the approach is scholarly, the topics covered by the book are those of everyday. Every parish seeks to announce the Gospel, nurture faith, cultivate prayer, celebrate the liturgy of the Church. And every priest, together with those who work with him, muses over the issues involved. Sometimes that musing turns to puzzlement over real tensions and conflicting ideas.

This book develops its reflections round central themes: the centrality of liturgy in Christian living, a clear understanding of the role of the ordained priest, the importance of the parish in the life of the Church and the need to be attentive to a wide variety of sources.

Even though parish life is demanding of time and energy, I hope that every priest and co-worker makes time for serious reading and thinking. There is no doubt that this book can be an important contribution to that task. It is helpful and thought provoking. It will bring deeper understanding and clarity to the task of pastoral ministry. It will serve the life of the Church well.

✠ Vincent Nichols
Archbishop of Birmingham

Acknowledgements

I wish to acknowledge the countless fellow pilgrims who have travelled with me along the path of discipleship. In some instances, their journey of faith ended, more than a few of them have now gone to their eternal rest. Some are no longer walking along the same road of faith. Despite their doubts and fears, a multitude of others still struggle to remain faithful. It is with enormous respect that one remembers the response that pastoral ministry found in their lives. During the past twenty years, it has been a privilege to serve a number of parishes in the Archdiocese of Birmingham. It is amongst these communities, above all, that the truth about pastoral ministry became most evident: the practice of ecclesial pastoral ministry has the potential to become an experience that is revelatory of the saving mystery of our redemption in Christ.

I want to express my gratitude to the staff and students of Oscott College. Furthermore, I wish to acknowledge the parishioners I presently serve in the Staffordshire Moorlands. These good people have been very patient with me!

Finally, and leaving the best wine until last, I want to thank Professor V. Alan McClelland. This study first saw the light of day as a persistent and gnawing thought that would not go away. Without his encouragement, advice and gentle patience, it would never have first become a research project and then a Ph.D. thesis. To Professor McClelland, above all, I offer my sincere gratitude and appreciation.

Preface

The fruit of theological reflection is the bringing to birth and nurturing of that awe and wonder which gives praise to the living God. This investigation of contemporary pastoral theology was originally situated in a context of formation of students for priestly ministry. This is a challenging time for those involved in pastoral ministry formation programmes. Above all, there is a need to protect inherited traditional values and, at the same time, to be open to necessary change. The study of pastoral theology provides an essential theological understanding of pastoral care practice. It also enables the ongoing development of authentic theological reflection upon that practice. In many respects, this present study attempts a response to the great challenge of discovering an authentic theological understanding of pastoral ministry.

The ecclesial references and theological statements in this study are situated within a Roman Catholic context. Indeed, this tradition and theological perspective provide the framework for the whole investigation. However, there is an attempt to learn from the witness and testimony of theologians from other backgrounds. It is hoped that this study will have something to offer those who exercise pastoral ministry in other denominational communions. Although there is an obvious focus on the ministry of ordained priesthood, this study may have much to offer those who are involved in other pastoral ministries within the communion of disciples.

The Second Vatican Council took place between 1962 and 1965. The Roman Catholic Church believes this Council to be the twenty-first Ecumenical Council. This Council was particularly concerned with the presentation of doctrinal matters within a pastoral context. It sought the renewal of Church life and an open dialogue with other religious and philosophical traditions. Since the Second Vatican Council, pastoral theology has found a renewed integrity and maturity of purpose. However, there are still those who wonder whether pastoral theology is an authentic theological discipline.[1] The problem is exacerbated to some extent by those involved in formation for ministry. Concern with speculative theological conundrums can too easily become more important than a theological preparation for practical ministry. It is hoped that this investigation will provide some response to this concern.

The present writer is particularly aware of the implications and dominant influence of non-theological methodologies in the discipline of pastoral theology. The inheritance of ancient Christian tradition is an important source material. This study strives to discover anew the relevance of this material for contemporary pastoral studies. I believe that this is very much the approach of the bishops at the Second Vatican Council. The conciliar documents testify to the new openness to the human sciences. They also suggest that there is an exciting re-discovery of pre-scholastic source material.

This preface must, then, acknowledge a second influence on the choice of research into pastoral ministry. The patristic mystagogia was a school that was developed in a time of cultural ambiguity and theological pluralism. Pastor theologians who undertook serious theological reflection within a particular pastoral context crafted the mystagogical method. Mystagogy was essentially a pedagogical tool. It invited the newly baptized to learn more about the Christian life by a systematic reflection on their involvement in liturgical celebration. This sacramental participation enabled the newly initiated disciple to experience Christ's saving love. The contemporary potential of the mystagogical technique is explored in the final two chapters of this inquiry. It is assumed in this part of the investigation that authentic pastoral ministry contains the same intrinsic dynamic as liturgical celebration. This means, within a mystagogical interpretation, that the Church's pastoral ministry is a Trinito-Christological revelation of divine saving action.

A further point must be made in this preface. Pastoral theology is truly a broad field, and has been widened even more since the publication of texts from the Second Vatican Council. It is inconceivable that this inquiry should plough every furrow within the field. Therefore, the guiding principle of the pages that follow is the

1. Cf. Oster H. *The Paschal Mystery in Parish Life* (London: Burns & Oates, 1967) p.48

application of this theological reflection to the ministry of sacramental priesthood within the life of the Church today. This seems particularly appropriate in the light of certain insecurity in some circles. Daniel Donovan, Professor of Systematic Theology at the University of St Michael's College, Toronto, suggests that 'at the present time there is obviously no single Roman Catholic theology of the ministerial priesthood.'[2] A ministry that is essentially exercised within the communion of disciples demands consideration of those with whom the priest relates and collaborates, in particular, this includes the episcopal order, the specific community in which the priest exercises his ministry, and the wider society of all human communities.

The first seven chapters of this study are historical and thematic investigations of important pastoral theological material, with a specific reference to the ministry of ordained priesthood. This material is not presented as an anatomical dissection of disparate themes, but rather, an analysis of one particular movement known as pastoral theology. The first chapter, then, seeks to situate the origin of academic pastoral theology within a Catholic tradition. Tridentine definitions (found in the decrees of the Council of Trent 1545-63) and subsequent developments are analysed within the context of evolving social, philosophical and political influences. The chapter concludes with a reflection on local pastoral ministerial concerns in the latter part of the nineteenth century.

The second chapter is an examination of ministry in the documents of the Second Vatican Council. This necessarily demands the investigation of an evolving ecclesiology during the course of the Council. Within a broader understanding of pastoral ministry, the episcopal office is seen to provide the paradigm for all pastoral ministries. In particular, this concerns the Council's emphasis on the rediscovered patristic notion of episcopal collegiality. The underlying theme of this chapter is the Council's attempt to achieve theological renewal through a retrieval of scriptural and biblical sources. The post-conciliar developments are investigated in the next chapter. In particular, there is a focus on three important themes for contemporary presbyteral ministry: configuration to Christ, communion and the 'signs of the times'.

2. Donovan D. *What are they saying about the ministerial priesthood?* (New York: Paulist press, 1992) p.138

The next four chapters explore the nature and importance of the parish in the life of the Church today. This particular structure forms a specific context of ecclesiological communion in the exercise of pastoral ministry. The institution of the parish is offered as an important model for the practice of pastoral care amongst the communion of disciples. This does not suggest that the parish is the only place where pastoral ministry is given and received. The fourth chapter investigates the institution of the parish and its contemporary development. This inquiry also introduces the sociological phenomena which impact on parish life today. The next chapter is a consideration of liturgical celebration and its importance within pastoral ministry. Many earlier themes find an important integration in the liturgical and sacramental life of the Church. At the end of the chapter, the recently established *Rite of Christian Initiation of Adults* provides an acute forum for an analysis of strengths and weaknesses in post-conciliar liturgical renewal.

An authentic pastoral theological reflection necessarily promotes the missionary dynamic of pastoral ministry. This is the subject of the next chapter. Liturgical celebration finds fullness of life only when those who participate in the liturgy are evangelized. This evangelization then leads to a desire to become involved in ecclesial mission. However, there are many ways in which this vision of the Second Vatican Council's liturgical constitution is thwarted. Above all, this is seen in the cultural influence and effects of an increasing secularism. Secularism is presented in this study of contemporary pastoral theology as a challenge to the practice of authentic pastoral ministry. Nevertheless, there must be a creative response to this situation. Mission, then, is considered as the necessary inter-face between pastoral theology and contemporary socio-cultural forms. Chapter seven is an examination of the developing theology of the lay faithful and the ministry of all believers. Significant post-conciliar developments in this area have led to the burgeoning of diverse models in collaborative ministry. These have created new pastoral opportunities, but also some tensions and the need to re-examine the nature of sacramental priesthood.

The final two chapters of this study bring together these themes in the development of a paradigmatic methodological model for pastoral ministry. There is a clear attempt to frame this methodology within the theological programme of the Second Vatican Council and subsequent developments. This exercise also involves the investigation of mystagogy as an appropriate model for contemporary pastoral theological reflection. This involves an examination of the two focal elements of practical pastoral care and theological reflection within pastoral ministry. The model enables the proposal of an authentic understanding of pastoral ministry practice. Then, the model is used in the establishment of a mystagogical form of theological reflection.

CHAPTER ONE

The Foundations of Pastoral Theology

1.0 Introduction

This is a study of the important themes in contemporary pastoral theology. It acknowledges a rich theological inheritance within Christian life and practice. The historical tradition suggests that our theological discipline belongs to an ecclesiological taxonomy. At the beginning of this work, however, we also want to affirm the Christological foundations of theological reflection on pastoral practice. John of the Cross, the sixteenth century Spanish reformer of the Carmelite Order, indicates his fundamental understanding of theological inquiry in the language of poetic imagery:

> And then we shall go forth
> to the lofty caverns of the rock which are well hidden.[1]

The words 'which are well hidden' are explained by his commentary on the poem. This mystic is convinced that 'despite all the mysteries and wonders which have been discovered by holy doctors and understood by holy souls in this estate of life, there has remained much to be said, and even to be understood, and thus there are great depths to be fathomed in Christ'.[2] These 'great depths' are to be found in Jesus Christ. Four centuries later, Hans Urs von Balthasar has inherited the Christocentric focus of John of the Cross. Balthasar's theological reflection was forged in the context of a dialogue between theology and culture. This dialogue is very much at the heart of contemporary pastoral theological reflection. Indeed, Balthasar suggests that there is an essential need for a Christological foundation to current ecclesiological developments.[3]

Definition is only a small part of our investigation of pastoral

1. Tr. and ed. Allison Peers E. *The Complete Works of Saint John of the Cross, vol.2*, (Wheathampstead: Anthony Clarke, 1953) p.364
2. Tr. and ed. Allison Peers E. (1953) op.cit. pp.365-366
3. Cf. Balthasar H. *Explorations in Theology vol.2* (San Francisco: Ignatius Press, 1991) pp.15, 20 and 22

theology. Hermeneutics defines the inquiry more accurately. This focus on interpretation is essential to the search for an understanding of this discipline. Authentic pastoral ministry is an appropriation of systematic doctrine. Within a reciprocal dynamic, the practice of ministry then influences theological concern and expression. Thus, there is a mutual interest and the possibility of development in both doctrine and pastoral care. The Second Vatican Council's *Dogmatic Constitution on Divine Revelation* states that 'the Church, in her doctrine, life and worship, perpetuates and transmits to every generation all that she herself is, all that she believes. The tradition that comes from the apostles makes progress in the Church, with the help of the Holy Spirit. There is a growth in insight into the realities and words that are being passed on.'[4] This issue of development is generally accepted and has been explored in numerous places. However, there is little theological exploration of the reciprocal relationship between doctrine and the practice of pastoral care. Indeed, this relationship is often unacknowledged and remains on the agenda for future consideration.[5] The complementary relationship between theoretical doctrine and pastoral practice is largely a result of the influence of pastoral theological reflection. Contemporary theologians are beginning to discover that theological hypothesis is largely concerned with the examination of empirical data alongside textual source analysis.[6] It is possible to understand theological inquiry as the Church's reflection on the practice of pastoral ministry. In turn, then, pastoral practice may determine the vortex of authentic theological research.

1.1 The Origins and Definitions of Pastoral Theology

Tradition constitutes an integral aspect of identity within the Roman Catholic Church. Hence, some historical perspective is necessary for an understanding of contemporary Catholic pastoral theology. The origins of Christian pastoral ministry are to be found in the initial proclamation of the Gospel. The academic discipline of pastoral theology is a much more recent business. The discipline of pastoral theology was

4. *Dei Verbum* (1965) art. 8. In footnotes only, references to conciliar decrees and other teaching documents will be given by their Latin titles.
5. Geffré acknowledges the place of pastoral practice within theological reflection. Nevertheless, despite this 'veritable transformation', he believes that 'we have not yet taken all its consequences fully into account.' Cf. Geffré C. *The Risk of Interpretation* (New York: Paulist Press, 1987) p.19
6. Cf. Chirico P. *Infallibility: The Crossroads of Doctrine* (London: Sheed & Ward, 1977) p.46

introduced into German-speaking universities during the Maria Theresa reforms of 1777.[7] The new discipline was a fruit of theological concern with the Enlightenment and the nascent secularism of the eighteenth century. Pastoral theology was conceived as the practical application of doctrine to situations encountered within pastoral care. Alex Blochlinger, a Swiss theologian, offers a definition of our subject within this original context: 'pastoral theology is fundamentally an ecclesiology dealing with the Church's mediating action.'[8] The diversification of pastoral care and the involvement of non-ordained practitioners have both contributed to a development of the original concept. The advent of the secular social sciences, and their influence upon the study of theology, created further tensions for pastoral theologians. This has led to the re-naming of the subject as 'practical' theology in many circles. The influence of non-theological methodologies is a fundamental problem for pastoral theology today. The search for academic respectability may imply that pastoral theology can easily renegotiate its theological nature.[9] There are problems. Pastoral theology must inevitably employ empirical data as a raw material of theological analysis. The reconciliation of historical theological tradition with contemporary social analysis is a particular problem for pastoral theology. This work has been described as the 'transforming of events and words of a time now past into the realities and needs of the present.'[10] There is a clearly defined sociological content to the ecclesial community and its programme of pastoral care. However, the important and legitimate use of pastoral sociological data cannot detract from the fundamentally theological nature of our subject.

The very nature of the Church has been defined as 'a mystery of faith'.[11] There is a need, then, for pastoral theology to adopt a disciplined approach that is fully aware of its theological nature. Furthermore, if this discipline is to be faithful to the insights of the Second Vatican Council, it must find renewal in the scriptural and

---

7. The date is taken from the appointment of the first professor of pastoral theology at the University of Prague. Although, it may be argued that the pastoral theological work was published in 1749 (cf. Lapsley J. *Practical Theology and Pastoral Care* in ed. Browning D. *Practical Theology* (San Francisco: Harper & Row, 1983) p.186

8. Blochlinger A. *The Modern Parish Community* (London: Geoffrey Chapman, 1965) p.8

9. Cf. Imbelli R. and Groome T. *Signposts towards a Pastoral Theology in Theological Studies* vol.53 no.1 March 1992, p.131

10. Ratzinger J. *Principles of Catholic Theology* (San Francisco: Ignatius Press, 1987) p.9

11. Cf. Balthasar H. (1991) op.cit. p.15

patristic sources of the Christian tradition. This is the theological method employed by the bishops at the Second Vatican Council. Otherwise, pastoral theology will drown in the 'sterile side by side system of mere theories and pragmatic recipes.'[12] The essential nature of pastoral theology must be concerned with that soteriological event in which pastoral concern and doctrinal exposition are united together. Hence, the need for firm Christological foundations. Within this perspective, pastoral theology demands an ever-renewed analysis of society and culture. There are two theological reasons for this critical study. First of all, the Kingdom of God is revealed to the world within a constantly unfolding history. Secondly, and within this historical context, the Church is not a static institution. It can be asserted that the communion of disciples exists within an inconstant social milieu. If pastoral theological reflection needs to be informed by empirical data, gathered by scientific means, then the discussion must always be recognized within an ecclesial community of faith. Hence, this definition of pastoral theology as 'that branch of theology which deals with the Church's self-fulfilment in the ever new contemporary situation.'[13] In this tradition, pastoral ministry has been defined as 'the activity of the Church whereby moved by the Holy Spirit she visibly fulfils the mission that Christ has entrusted to her and pursues the realization of the Father's saving purpose for creation.'[14] One systematic theologian defines our subject even more succinctly: 'A fundamental theology of ministry is ultimately a theology of grace.'[15]

Pastoral theology, then, is that reflection within a communion of faith that informs and directs pastoral ministry. It employs a method of mediation between the fulfilment of genuine care needs and the insights of revelation. The principal concerns of pastoral theology are the various ministries within the Church, in particular, the development of mission as evangelization and catechesis. Within the communion of faith, this leads to the development of liturgical celebration and a mature life of faith. The task of pastoral theology is

12. Ratzinger J. *The Pastoral Implications of Episcopal Collegiality in Concilium* vol. 3 no. 1 *The Pastoral Mission of the Church* (New Jersey: Paulist Press, 1965) p.7

13. Schuster H. *The Nature and Function of Pastoral Theology in Concilium* vol. 3 no. 1 *The Pastoral Mission of the Church* (New Jersey: Paulist Press, 1965) p. 7. Heinz Schuster was heavily influenced by the theological work of his teacher, Karl Rahner.

14. Dingemans L. *La Pastorale et ses buts généraux* in *Evangéliser* 17 (1962), p.247

15. O'Meara T. *Theology of Ministry* (New York: Paulist Press, 1983) p.14

to challenge and interpret other theological disciplines within a developing historical context. The unity between theological definition and pastoral practice will always lead to a deeper understanding of the transcendent nature of the human being. This fundamental element of Christian anthropology provides a forward-looking dimension to theological reflection. It enables pastoral theological reflection to suggest a renewed vision of pastoral care in ever-new situations. The Church cannot behave as if new situations 'were but a change of décor in front of which she plays her invariable act, untouched by it all, according to eternal rules and always with the same texts.'[16] The notion of constant change is an abiding tenet of pastoral theological method. However, genuine developments in pastoral ministry are never arbitrary. They are situated within an eschatological system that considers the communion of disciples to have a teleological purpose. The pastoral ministers and those receiving their ministry are all involved in a pilgrim journey of faith. True pastoral renewal takes place, like any other ecclesial renewal, when conversion of life lies at the heart of the theological reflection. This context suggests that renewal is enabled when the focus is redirected towards the life-giving and life-changing realities of the Gospel.

1.2 Within a Tridentine Perspective

From a Catholic viewpoint, pastoral theology was initially established within a Tridentine context. Indeed, the theological definitions of the Council of Trent are still influential four hundred years later. The Council of Trent began in 1545 and continued for the next eighteen years. It had a convoluted historical development and a varied number of participants, depending on the political stability of the European regions. Doctrinal and disciplinary issues were treated together in an inter-dependent fashion.

Some scholars hold a somewhat negative view of pastoral practice in the late medieval period. Paul Bernier, who teaches theology in the Philippines, is a good example of this school of thought. He suggests that pastoral ministers were so identified with the structures of feudal government that they were unable to deal with abusive practices.[17] There were serious problems. Nevertheless, it is possible to take a

16. Schuster H. (1965) op.cit. p.7
17. Bernier P. *Ministry in the Church* (Mystic: Twenty-Third Publications, 1992) p.151

kinder view of the situation. There were many unemployed priests. These men were ill-prepared for pastoral ministry and had no clear means of support. Many others had entered into Holy Orders in the hope that it would bring them high social status and material benefits. Eamon Duffy, the Cambridge historian, confirms all these problems within English ecclesiastical life. However, he has also amassed an enormous body of evidence that suggests pastoral attempts to deal with the situation.[18] There were signs of a vibrant devotional life and a pastorally sensitive parochial clergy in medieval England. There were many attempts to educate the clergy, and through their ministry, to engage in catechesis of the faithful. Indeed, Duffy suggests that the Tridentine decree establishing the seminary system of presbyteral formation is based on a model established by Cardinal Pole in 1555.[19]

The Protestant Reformation provided the catalyst for debate and action. The thirteenth century saw the development of a number of anti-clerical groups. Their heterodox theological positions were pseudo-mystical in character and contrary to ecclesiastical authority. The Protestant Reformation, however, went much further in its rejection of Catholic programmes of pastoral renewal. Bernier is right to suggest that the protest was against the 'localization of God's activity in the human and created'.[20] Various Protestant theologians developed this protest in a variety of forms. It is, then, not possible to define a typical 'Protestant' position. However, the Council of Trent attempted a response to the variety of doctrinal positions collectively known as Protestantism. The Protestant understanding of pastoral ministry can be framed within the context of vocation and election. The vocation to service is divine, whereas the authority to enter ministry is bestowed by the election of the Christian community. It is this notion of popular election that was particularly repugnant to Catholic theologians at the Council of Trent.

The Council of Trent dealt with the Sacrament of Orders during its twenty-third session. The Council's definition of the Catholic Church's solemn teaching about the priesthood was made on 15 July 1563. This doctrine is closely related to Trent's understanding of sacramental theology. The solemn definition of Holy Orders was also closely

18. Cf. Duffy E. *The Stripping of the Altars* (New Haven: Yale University Press, 1992)
19. Ibid. p.525
20. Bernier P. (1992) op.cit. p.151

connected with an important disciplinary decree on clerical reform. It may be argued that this doctrinal definition, and its practical application, did not advance the medieval scholastic position any further. Too much criticism in this area is not entirely fair. The bishops at Trent attempted a synthesis and the universal application of local initiatives. It can be asserted that theological definition was rooted in a very real pastoral context. Trent did not seek the development of a specific pastoral theological discipline. Nevertheless, the Council's understanding of pastoral ministry was certainly influenced by a theological understanding of the sacramental economy.

It is important to note that speculative theological development was not within Trent's brief. This was an age of polemical argument between Catholic and Protestant theologians. Firmly held viewpoints became entrenched and often closed to negotiation and dialogue. The bishops at Trent had to face the need for clear and precise definition. They chose the concept of 'sacramental character' as the most important feature of their theology of Orders. Some present-day commentators have set up a controversy between two possible interpretations of this doctrine. One position understands ministry within the context of a personal power that is given in Holy Orders, for example, the power to celebrate the Eucharist and to absolve sin. This is named the ontological perspective. It is based on a restricted understanding of sacramental character. An alternative viewpoint begins with the perceived needs of the Christian community and may be termed functionalist. This perspective can lead to a very fluid understanding of pastoral ministry depending on the situation of the particular community. There is a tension between these two viewpoints of pastoral ministry. Nevertheless, it is possible to combine the insights of both positions. Furthermore, we should not readily accept the suggestion that the bishops at Trent were prejudiced in favour of the first position. The Council of Trent was concerned with authentic pastoral renewal. The bishops introduced seminaries for the formation of the parish clergy. Priests and bishops were instructed to reside in their parishes and dioceses. They were given instruction on the celebration of the sacraments. The jurisdiction of bishops was clearly defined.[21] There is a clear zeal in these reforms of pastoral practice.

21. Cf. Olin J. *Catholic Reform from Cardinal Xinenes to the Council of Trent 1495-1563* (New York: Fordham University Press, 1990) p.30

These areas of renewal also suggest a theological attempt to bring the ontological and functionalist viewpoints together.

There is always a tension within Council debate between a number of theological positions and nuances. The Council of Trent was no different. It is difficult to accept the view, however, that the theological notion of sacramental character ignored the needs of pastoral care. Furthermore, contemporary commentators sometimes have a tendency to work with an anachronistic view of community. Schillebeeckx, for example, wants to suggest that Trent isolated priestly ministry from the Christian community and that after the Council, priesthood and ministry were firmly defined in cultic language.[22] This is not entirely fair to the evidence of Tridentine debate and text. It is important to focus on the actual conciliar texts and their constant use of Gospel imagery. The pastoral model of the Good Shepherd was employed in the discussion of Holy Orders. The bishops determined in the first chapter of the twenty-third session decree that, 'it is enjoined on all to whom is entrusted the care of souls to know their sheep (John 10: 1-16, 21:15-17; Acts 20:28).' The relationship between pastors and their communities is developed further. They are 'to offer sacrifice for them, and to feed them by the preaching of the divine word, the administration of the sacraments, and the example of all good works, to exercise a fatherly care in behalf of the poor and other distressed persons, and to apply themselves to all other pastoral duties.' These sixteenth century bishops certainly wanted to enable the pastoral effectivity of their doctrinal decrees. They declared, in chapter eighteen of the decree on ministry, that 'it is highly desirable for the salvation of souls that they be directed by worthy and competent parish priests.' The Council Fathers responded to this need during the twenty-fourth session. A decree of 2 November 1563 ordered the preparation of a catechism to be used by parish priests in their pastoral ministry.

The *Catechism of the Council of Trent for Parish Priests* was not completed by the close of the Council. Pius IV appointed his nephew, Charles Borromeo, as president of the catechism commission. Borromeo was a doctor of canon law and the Archbishop of Milan. He was especially noted for his abilities as a pastor. The work was published some three years after its conception, during the pontificate

22. Cf. Schillebeeckx E. *The Priest and the Synod of 1971* in *Doctrine and Life vol.22* February 1972, p.59. Cf. also, Bernier P. (1992) op.cit. p.193

of Pius V. This document is pertinent to our investigation and an important text, as it contains a distillation of Tridentine theological reflection. It was presented as a work in which parish priests, 'on whom the duty of imparting instruction devolves, may be able to seek and find reliable matter for the edification of the faithful'.[23] It may be suggested that the Tridentine Catechism is like a diptych, in which the story of salvation is presented as divine initiative and human response. This Catechism presents pastoral ministry within a Christological perspective. It states that, 'as our Saviour was sent by His Father, and as the Apostles and disciples were sent into the whole world by Christ our Lord, so priests are sent daily with the same powers, for the perfecting of the saints, for the work of ministry, and the edifying of the body of Christ.'[24] In addition, this explanation of Catholic faith taught that ministry 'is to be conferred on those only who by their holiness of life, their knowledge, faith and prudence, are able to bear it.'[25] The Catechism also suggests an 'internal priesthood' in which all Christians share by virtue of their baptism. The theme of ministerial priesthood is then introduced within this context. This is given 'to certain men who have been ordained and consecrated to God by the lawful imposition of hands and by the solemn ceremonies of holy Church, *and who are thereby devoted to a particular sacred ministry*.'[26] The theological vision of the Tridentine Catechism indicates a more integrated understanding of pastoral ministry than may be suggested by Trent's critics.

It is possible to discern a direct link between the views of the Council of Trent and the consideration of pastoral ministry in the Second Vatican Council. Trent influenced Bishop Brian Charles Foley, the Bishop of Lancaster, in his two significant interventions at the recent Council. In the midst of a busy Council agenda, Bishop Foley insisted on the need for a specific document concerning presbyteral ministry. When the Council was preparing for the final promulgation of this text, the Bishop of Lancaster made a passionate appeal for an overtly pastoral understanding of the presbyteral office. His personal memoirs suggest the influence of the Tridentine debate *De*

23. Tr. McHugh J. and Callan C. *Catechism of the Council of Trent for Parish Priests* (New York: Joseph F. Wagner, 1923) p.4
24. Ibid. p.318
25. Ibid. p.318
26. Ibid. pp.330-331. Italics are mine.

Reformatione.[27] During the course of Trent's reflections, a Spanish bishop shared his own personal notebook of pastoral insights with Charles Borromeo. The saintly bishop was so impressed that he had the book printed and presented to the other bishops at Trent. At the heart of the matter was an insistence on the necessity for pastors to know their communities. Bishop Foley's second intervention at the Second Vatican Council took place on 26 October 1965. He complained about the Council's lack of reflection in the area of pastoral care. This, the bishop suggested, 'contrasts unfavourably with the Council of Trent which, in three long sessions (XX, XXI and XXIV), discussed this important matter and laid down certain precise and detailed rules for the priestly exercise of the care of souls. Because of lack of time neither the First nor the Second Vatican Council has treated of the priestly apostolate.'[28]

1.3 Developments after Trent

After the Council of Trent had completed and implemented its work, there was a historical period known as the Counter-Reformation. This was a time when many religious orders were founded and an age of intensive pastoral activity. There was certainly a focus on individualistic piety. However, this did not mean that pastoral care became entirely inward looking. An individual's contribution to the life of the divine Kingdom becomes more effective as the Gospel increases its reign in a disciple's life. This idea can be tested through reflection on the work of Robert Bellarmine.

Bellarmine was a formidable theologian of the Counter-Reformation period. He was a founding father of the *Collegio Romano*, which later became the Gregorian University. His theology was developed on a firm foundation of scriptural and patristic research. It was therefore most effective in an age of apologetical activity against heterodox opinions. Bellarmine published a work on the Church in 1586. This study, *On the Controversies of Christian Faith against the heretics of our time*, was essentially concerned with a refutation of Calvin's theories. This leading Protestant thinker taught the existence of two churches. He believed in the existence of a true community of the elect, which

27. Cf. Foley B. *Cura Animarum: A Voice for the Priesthood* in ed. Stacpoole A. *Vatican II by those who were there* (London: Geoffrey Chapman, 1986) p.256
28. Ibid. p.263

had been predestined to salvation. He also acknowledged the existence of a visible and external institution that contained others besides the elect. Bellarmine challenged this theory with the assertion that 'there is only one Church, not two. And this one true Church is the community of men brought together by profession of the true faith and communion in the same sacraments, and under the administration of recognized pastors and especially of the sole vicar of Christ on earth, the Roman pontiff.'[29] The heart of this definition is the understanding of the Church as a visible institutional society, with a sacramental and pastoral ministry. Bellarmine emphasizes the sacramental communion of the Church. Liturgical celebration is one of the primary means by which the Church receives the abiding presence of Christ. This idea is very much at the centre of Bellarmine's understanding of pastoral ministry. Sacramental character could not be reduced to a juridical concept. There was an overt pastoral component. Pastoral care could not be limited to a temporary function that did not reflect the abiding commitment of Christ to his communion of disciples. This would reduce ministry to the mechanistic and deny the fully human context in which pastoral ministry is exercised.

Bellarmine's post-Tridentine theological reflection found a natural home in the 'French School'. This important development looked to Pierre de Bérulle for its beginnings. Bérulle was the founder of the Congregation of the Oratory in France. He also promoted a renewal of biblical and patristic studies. In his view, the primary purposes of the presbyteral ministry were to follow Christ by a life of sincere worship and to enable others to share in this communion with the Trinity. Pastoral care, then, is to bring Christ to life in the lives of those served in ministry. Pastoral ministry is the practice of a theology of the incarnation. The pastoral minister participates in Christ's work of mediator between humanity and the Father. This understanding of ministry finds a comfortable haven in a sacramental economy. Furthermore, it is profoundly Catholic and implements the Tridentine vision of ministry.

One of the more important spiritual developments of the French School is concerned with devotion to the Sacred Heart of Jesus. This devotion promoted reflection on the humanity of Christ and the need

29. Cf. Hamer J. *The Church is a Communion* (London: Geoffrey Chapman, 1964) p.84

to focus on the human heart as the symbol of divine love and mercy. Therefore, it is difficult to accept fully the modern critical reappraisal of Bérulle and his tradition.[30] Bérulle's ideas, however, were not universally accepted even in his own time. The idea of total self-renunciation, that was involved in the French School idea of pastoral ministry, was opposed by the pragmatic Cardinal and Duke of Richelieu. He was a chief minister to King Louis XIII and lived a somewhat worldly life in the French Court. The academics of Louvain and Douai accused Bérulle of nascent Jansenism and Quietism. These reactions were understandable when Bérulle published his first work on self-abnegation in 1597. There is evidence of an undue focus on the fall of humanity from the blessing of original grace and the subsequent hopelessness of the human condition. Further study, however, produced a shift in emphasis and a more balanced approach. The development of devotion to the Sacred Heart, in particular, produced an essential focus on the divine love and mercy revealed in Jesus Christ.

This devotional approach contained an immense pastoral dimension. It is interesting to note that the French School has influenced the lives and ministry of many great figures in the generation after the Council of Trent. Vincent de Paul and Jean-Jacques Olier were both involved in the seminary formation demanded by Trent. The former also had a well-known ministry among those who suffered material deprivation and social marginalization. Francis de Sales and Jean-Marie Vianney had imbibed the ideas of Bérulle in a pastoral ministry of catechesis and spiritual direction.[31] Indeed, the tradition of the French School has important repercussions in the life of the Church today. The majority of bishops who were involved in the 1990 Synod on Priestly Formation were formed by the values of this tradition.[32] Finally, it can be asserted that the saintly inheritance of the French School provided the principal challenge to the powerful force of the Enlightenment.

1.4 The Enlightenment

The Enlightenment was a time of tremendous intellectual activity and, as we have already noted, provided the context for the development of pastoral theology. Catholic pastoral theology was naturally framed

30. Cf. Lane T. *A Priesthood in Tune* (Dublin: The Columba Press, 1993) pp.249-50
31. Francis de Sales was the Bishop of Geneva and Jean Vianney was the parish priest of Ars.
32. Cf. Lane T. (1993) op.cit. p.248

within a Tridentine understanding of pastoral ministry. However, it was a theological reflection that had to breathe within a very different kind of atmosphere. The Enlightenment was essentially a philosophical and political movement. It was an age that also witnessed the rise of the natural sciences and scientific method. One philosophical perspective suggests that the post-Enlightenment crisis could be described as a rejection of 'teleological form'.[33] Religion was subjected to the scrutiny of rationalism. Traditional theological source texts were expected to adopt the methodology of historical criticism. A presbyterian theologian suggests that these developments lead to a 'hermeneutics of destruction'.[34] David Bosch, the prominent Protestant missiologist, suggests that the Enlightenment affected Protestantism more than Catholicism. Catholicism, according to Bosch, did not make a formal response to the Enlightenment until the Second Vatican Council.[35] This response, when it came, was generally positive. The influence of the Enlightenment may be seen in the wide-ranging adoption of non-theological methodologies in the Council documents. However, the impact of the Enlightenment began to affect Catholic pastoral care practice at a much earlier stage, and there was a significant Catholic response to the Enlightenment at the First Vatican Council.

The Enlightenment project inevitably produced theological repercussions and a review of pastoral ministry. There were no positive appraisals of Catholic faith or pastoral practice by Enlightenment thinkers.[36] Indeed, the proponents of the Enlightenment appeared to reject any idea of the mediation of divine grace within an ecclesial and hierarchical ministry. This led to the uncritical acceptance and dominance of a radical anthropocentrism. There is, of course, a sensitive theological use of anthropocentrism in the work of twentieth century theologians such as Karl Rahner. However, the human being, in Rahner's understanding of the human person, is a transcendent being. This transcendence is particularly manifested in the capacity of the human person to hear the word of divine revelation and to respond to it. However, an uncritical intellectual anthropocentrism in the eighteenth century soon led to the development of an atheistic

33. Cf. Boyd I. *What are the clergy for?* in *Theology* May/June 1995, p.187
34. Cf. Farley E. *Theologia* (Philadelphia: Fortress Press, 1983) p.65
35. Cf. Bosch D. *Transforming Mission: Paradigm Shifts in Theology of Mission* (New York: Orbis Books, 1991) p.262
36. Cf. Lamb M. *Modernism and Americanism in Communio* vol. xxi no. 4, Winter 1994 p.636

secularism. This phenomenon has many negative consequences for contemporary mission and evangelization.

There were some positive effects of the Enlightenment. There was a gradual movement to widen the concept of pastoral care itself and to introduce the involvement of the laity. Furthermore, pastoral ministry became more accountable within society. The French concordat of 1801 is an example of one political act that influenced pastoral practice.[37] This enabled a new systematic approach to ecclesiastical appointments. Civil administration had assisted the implementation of a Tridentine desire to deal with unoccupied priests. However, there were some problems for an obdurate clergy. Parish priests, in particular, felt threatened by civil responsibilities and the apparent insecurity of their position. There was the inevitable civil temptation to make an assessment by administrative criteria rather than pastoral ability.

Catechesis, emphasized so much in the Council of Trent's decrees, was a particular problem area for the post-Enlightenment Church. In most of Europe catechetical instruction was transferred from a parish setting to the school classroom. This new environment was not always open to ecclesiastical control. Furthermore, there was always the possibility of new ideas being peddled, which were contrary to the Church's belief and practice. Catechetics could easily become unduly rational when it was offered outside of a community of faith. There was an attempt to balance this with the production of local catechisms. Joseph Deharbe, a Jesuit theologian, produced an especially dogmatic text in 1847. It was built upon firm apologetic principles and possessed a strident polemical foundation. It was revised after six years and used widely in England. In many respects, this aggressive catechetical response to the Enlightenment was a novelty within pastoral practice. It ran counter to the more sensitive pastoral approach of the French School. In this earlier tradition, catechetical instruction was a vital component of pastoral ministry. Nevertheless, catechetics had been lively, engaging, and attempted to invoke a total response of the whole person. Unfortunately, this was lost in the enthusiasm of many combatants. There is a paucity of pastoral theological reflection during the nineteenth century. In the post-industrial revolution society, pastoral theology was still involved with catechetical issues, but often

37. Cf. Aubert R. *The Continuation of Catholic Renewal in Europe* in ed. Jedin H. *History of the Church vol. viii The Church in the Age of Liberalism* (London: Burns & Oates, 1981) p.14

unable to recapture an earlier sensitivity and understanding of the human person.

Catechesis was the dominant theme of Thomas Powondra's *Systema theologiae pastoralis* published in 1818. This work began to develop the significant approach of Johann Michael Sailor. He was professor of pastoral theology at Dilingen and Landshut universities during the latter part of the eighteenth century. Sailor's schema of pastoral theology offers hope to a catechetical movement desperate for inspiration. There is a movement from consideration of the text to analysis of the event. The issues of divine saving action become important tools for understanding revelation. Anton Graf, in the Tübingen school, develops Sailor's approach even further. His systematic pastoral theology contained a particular focus on the work of the Holy Spirit. He also taught that the liturgy should be celebrated in the vernacular language and that the laity should receive communion from the chalice. These ideas were unacceptable at the time. Indeed, Graf left Tübingen in 1843 as a consequence of political pressure. A rich seam of pastoral theological reflection became a closed mine. The genuine heritage of Trent and the subsequent French School tradition became dormant. Unfortunately, positive efforts to revive this tradition foundered on the rock of clerical hostility. Vincent Palloti founded the *Society for the Catholic Apostolate* in 1835. Pius IX supported the initiative, but lay involvement in pastoral care was still generally treated with suspicion. This was, more or less, the sorry position of pastoral theology in the years approaching the First Vatican Council.

1.5 The First Vatican Council

The First Vatican Council is a significant event for contemporary pastoral theology. The Council was a reaction to the rationalism that had become generally acceptable since the advent of the Enlightenment. In many respects, this Council attempted a recovery of the right relationship between two kinds of revelation. The person of faith can receive revelation through the correct interpretation of the scriptures. The created world, understood with the use of reason, also reveals true knowledge of divine presence and action. There can never be a dichotomy between faith and reason. However, the Enlightenment had altered a fundamental Christian perspective and made all sources of revelation subservient to a reason without faith.

The First Vatican Council was not immediately concerned with pastoral ministry. Nevertheless, the world had certainly changed since the Council of Trent. The Enlightenment project had challenged the fundamental concept of belief. All theological disciplines were invited to confront the many developments since the work of Trent was concluded. In particular, there was a need to revisit the doctrine of revelation. By the time of the Second Vatican Council, the emerging and dominant ecclesiology proposed the pilgrim nature of the Church. The Church's self-understanding had not reached this point in the nineteenth century. The abandonment of the First Vatican Council, as a consequence of political and military pressures, is an important consideration. It is unfortunate that the post-conciliar period was filled with so much unfinished business. Hence, it seems that this Council's potential can only be fully understood through analysis of the preparatory documents or schemas. In the ecclesiology of the age, the Church was understood to be a 'perfect society'. This somewhat static notion of the Church was presented in the third chapter of the draft document entitled *Of the Supreme Pastor.* The same schema also contains an outlined understanding of ministry. There is 'a power that is divinely instituted which some have received in order to sanctify, teach and govern and which others have not received.'[38] Thus, there is an ecclesiological picture of an unequal and hierarchical society. It is also possible to recognize a firm assertion of the ontological understanding of sacramental character.

In the months leading up to the Council, there were two principal divisions within the Church. These groups were particularly concerned with the proposed conciliar debate on the papal office. The one side of the debate consisted of a liberal or Gallican faction. On the other side of the argument was the Ultramontane group. It is easy to caricature both these viewpoints and their journey through the Council. However, even at the time of the Council, there were balanced and positive assessments of the Council's work and of the factions involved. *The Year of Preparation for the Vatican Council* was published in 1869. The preface of this popular work was composed by Herbert Vaughan, who later became the Archbishop of Westminster and the founder of the Mill Hill Missionaries. In his introduction, Vaughan refers to the

38. Cf. Congar Y. *Moving Towards a Pilgrim Church* in ed. Stacpoole A.(1986) op.cit. p.133

'Babel of tongues and newspapers' in which the 'circumstances attendant upon the Convocation of the Vatican Council have been continually reported inaccurately.'[39] Perhaps even more important for our theme are his earlier words: 'The Church of God is a perfect kingdom, not *of* the world, but *in* it. It is a kingdom of souls, and has a divine mission to gather into itself the whole human race. It has a divine right to whatever is necessary for its perfect organization, and for the fulfilment of its divine mission.'[40] Statements such as these provide an understanding of the inter-face between doctrine and pastoral theology at the time of the First Vatican Council.

Pastoral theology is totally dependent upon a sound ecclesiology. The encyclical *On the Mystical Body of Christ* was not published until 1943. There is evidence that the foundations were laid more than seventy years previously. The concept of the Church as the 'mystical body' of Christ was contained in the first chapter of a draft dogmatic constitution *On the Church of Christ*, which was presented to the bishops of the First Vatican Council on 21 January 1870. A number of bishops, notably from French and Piedmontese dioceses, opposed this text with an expression of grave reservations. They believed that the language lacked clarity and that there was evidence of Jansenist theological tendencies. The chapter was discarded before it reached the general congregation of bishops. The idea of the Church as the mystical body of Christ did not find full recognition until Pius XII's encyclical in 1943.[41] The importance of this understanding of the Church is the attention it brings to the supernatural mystery of the Church, and therefore, to pastoral ministry within the communion of disciples. Unfortunately, an undue focus on external structures at the First Vatican Council disabled this important development.

Contemporary commentators often describe the nineteenth century Council as a victory for papalism and defeat for episcopal-conciliarism. The tension between the mystery of the Church and its institutional manifestation is inevitable. Nevertheless, the work of the First Vatican Council was incomplete. There is a need to avoid 'misapplied subtlety' in a consideration of the doctrinal development of primacy and

39. *The Year of Preparation for the Vatican Council* (London: Burns, Oates, and Co., 1869) p.ii
40. Ibid. p.i
41. This ecclesiological idea found magisterial acceptance before 1943 in Leo XIII's encyclicals *Satis Cognitum* (1896) and *Divinum Illud* (1897).

episcopate.[42] This is an area of contention. Some contemporary reflection on the work of the First Vatican Council is often inaccurate. The papal office, particularly papal judgement, cannot be isolated from the communion of the Church. Pastoral theology, in particular, had to wait until the bishops met again in Council before the implications of this communion were fully realized.

1.6 The English Scene

Nineteenth century theological debate and its influence on pastoral practice can be assessed by a brief reflection on one particular environment. Within the Catholic community, England manifested both liberal and ultramontane traditions in the years leading up to the First Vatican Council. The English tradition was generally moderate and well-balanced. Cuthbert Butler described his history of the nineteenth century Council as: 'The story told from inside in Bishop Ullathorne's letters'.[43] William Bernard Ullathorne was the first Bishop of Birmingham. He had been educated in accordance with the articles of the Gallican school. Later study encouraged him to adopt a position of 'sober Ultramontanism of the theological Bellarmine type.'[44] The bishop was certainly aware of the pastoral problems associated with any fanatical promotion of papal infallibility. He wrote to a fellow bishop on the eve of the Council of the need for a counter-balance, with the warning that 'if this is not done we shall see a wild enthusiasm, especially on the part of converts; and a disposition on the part of the clergy and even laity to lower the power of the episcopate; and a stronger centralization, leading ultimately to reaction; and a narrower door presented to those who are seeking the Church; and a fanatical extending of the papal prerogatives beyond the fact'.[45] This is indeed the view of a mind that is focused on pastoral care. Bishop Ullathorne's pastoral letter to the Diocese of Birmingham was written before his journey to Rome and expressed in a more cautious language. His judicious presentation of the Church's teaching expressed the matter in this way: 'The Church does not consist of body alone, or of head alone, but of head and body moving

42. Cf. Rahner K. and Ratzinger J. *The Episcopate and the Primacy* (Edinburgh: Nelson, 1962) pp.38-39
43. Butler C. *The Vatican Council vol.1* (London: Longmans, Green and Co., 1930) frontspiece
44. Ibid. p.143
45. Ibid. p.144

in joint action'.[46] There were stronger opinions and these were sometimes expressed more forcefully. Bishop James Chadwick of Hexham and Newcastle enjoyed a lively correspondence about the Council with Monsignor Robert Tate, the President of Ushaw at that time. Chadwick wrote to Tate about the infallibility debate on several occasions. This is one of his earlier offerings: 'There is no doubt, there is a dreadful opposition to its being defined, chiefly among the French, Germans & Hungarians. The French disgust me. It is plain Dupanloup & Maret do not believe in the "infallibility", & then their horrible french and gallican pride is up. Oh for another Waterloo.'[47] Theological debate, it would appear, is often framed against a historical and political background.

England had no pontifical universities for the academic pursuit of Catholic theology. Except for the short-lived Kensington University College, inaugurated by Cardinal Manning in 1873, the same situation remains one hundred years later. Nevertheless, there is evidence that pastoral ministry was taken seriously. Theological comment and reflection were conducted through the medium of periodical literature. There were also public lectures and published sermons. The Catholic Church in England was isolated from Europe in many respects. However, pastoral practice was certainly informed by the Tridentine tradition. The re-establishment of seminaries saw to that. Nicholas Wiseman, one-time rector of the English College in Rome, was a key figure in the intellectual development of pastoral life in this country. Wiseman was also the second rector of St Mary's College, Oscott. He sought a priesthood in which 'intellectual culture and very warm piety should be combined as much as possible in the highest degree'. He also looked for 'the active power of research, and a practice in laying hold of and destroying any new error.'[48] Wiseman delivered a series of lectures at St Mary's, Moorfields, during the Lent of 1836.[49] These texts present his fundamental understanding of pastoral ministry. Pastors are, above all, teachers of faith. They are appointed by the Lord as 'teachers

46. Ibid. p.145
47. Ed. Milburn D. *Impressions of an English Bishop at the First Vatican Council* in *The Wiseman Review* no. 493 Autumn 1963, p.223
48. Cf. Schiefen R. *Nicholas Wiseman and the Transformation of English Catholicism* (Shepherdstown: Patmos Press, 1984) pp.90-91
49. Wiseman N. *Lectures on the Principal Doctrines and Practices of the Catholic Church* (London: The Catholic Publishing and Bookselling Co., 1867)

to his people, shepherds to his flock'.[50] The language of these lectures is clearly influenced by the theology of Trent. Wiseman teaches that Christ has 'appointed ministers, and constituted a hierarchy, to whom was committed the care of his flock, with power and authority to instruct'.[51] Wiseman's Lenten lectures focus on the Petrine office and give scant consideration to the episcopal ministry at all.

Five years after this material had been published, and just after the First Vatican Council, Bishop Ullathorne preached at the consecration of two bishops. His understanding of the episcopal office is remarkable. He considers the nature of the bishop's office and his relationship to his diocese and the universal Church. The bishop is exalted by the Holy Spirit 'to the high priesthood, extending the sacramental power, consolidating the grace of government, conveying to the consecrated Prelates the plenitude of sacerdotal power, imprinting on their souls in light and unction that highest character and most indelible which constitutes the Bishop in the image and likeness of the one great High Priest'.[52] This is a clear example of the theological prelude to the Second Vatican Council's *Decree on the Pastoral Office of Bishops in the Church*. Twelve months later, the Bishop addressed the Fourth Provincial Synod of Westminster. This Synod examined the spiritual life of pastors. The Bishop of Birmingham immediately addressed the most important matter. He stated that 'the Sacred Scripture tells us that what God demands before all things of His priests is holiness.'[53] It is suggested that presbyteral ministers should pursue a three-fold sanctity. The first is 'detachment from the common life and pursuits of men, and dependence on God.'[54] Secondly, priests are to be 'devout in their oblation.'[55] Thirdly, they are to hold 'that imitative, that unitative degree of sanctity.'[56] This may disturb the faint-hearted reader in a more comfortable generation. Fortunately, there is evidence of a sensitive and understanding side to the good bishop. Bishop John Cuthbert Hedley, of Newport and

50. Ibid. vol.1 lecture iv, p.95
51. Ibid. vol.2 lecture x, p.7
52. Ullathorne W.B. *The Sermon delivered at the Consecration of the Bishops of Salford and Amycla* (London: Burns, Oates, & Co., 1872) p.4
53. Ullathorne W.B. *The Discourse delivered at the Opening Session of the Fourth Provincial Synod of Westminster* (London: Burns & Oates, 1873) p.6
54. Ibid. p.7
55. Ibid. p.8
56. Ibid. p.8

Menevia, preached at Ullathorne's funeral in 1889. He suggested that Ullathorne 'was not a man for many rules or many questions. If he could make a young heart realize its God – if he could touch a priest with the mission and message of his Lord – if he could get a labourer in the vineyard to listen to the love which speaks from the Cross – he was satisfied.'[57]

This was a time of much pastoral activity and institutional expansion in England. During Ullathorne's time as Bishop of Birmingham the number of priests rose from eighty-six to two hundred. The number of religious communities of women grew from seven to thirty-six. Over one hundred primary schools were founded. Sixty-seven new churches were built and forty-four new missions established.[58] Perusal of the bishop's pastoral letters, during nearly forty years in office, alludes to this activity. Bishop Ullathorne was constantly exhorting the faithful to be more generous in their financial support for all this activity. During the Jubilee Year of 1886, for example, a Lenten letter was published *On Giving Jubilee Alms to Mission Schools and Seminaries.* Bishop Ullathorne gave a testimony of his own ministry on the occasion of his retirement from office. He was grateful for the dedicated ministry of the clergy, the restoration of the Catholic hierarchy in 1850, with the subsequent establishment of canonical structures, the establishment of seminaries in accordance with the Tridentine decree, and last but not least, the sound financial situation of the Diocese.[59]

The Bishop of Newport published his own pastoral letters four years after he preached at Ullathorne's funeral. The ordained ministry is considered from the ontological perspective, and is understood to have 'certain prerogatives and powers.'[60] The primary purpose of this ministry is 'to teach the Holy Faith, to interpret it, and to guard it'.[61] Bishop Hedley also encourages the need to reflect on the work of evangelization. The whole Church, and not just the clergy, is to be involved in this important work. There is even a hint of collaborative ministry. The responsibility for mission 'no doubt affects the Clergy in

57. Hedley J. A Spiritual Man (London: Burns & Oates, 1889) p.23
58. Cf. Norman E. (1984) op.cit. p.202
59. Cf. *The Reply to the Address, presented by the Reverend Clergy to the Right Reverend Bishop Ullathorne, on his retirement from the Diocese of Birmingham.* Given at St Mary's College, Oscott, on 22 March 1988.
60. Hedley J. *A Bishop and his Flock* London: (Burns & Oates, 1903) p.132
61. Ibid. p.132

a different degree from the Laity, and in a different way. But it is a very grave mistake to suppose that we are not, every one of us, bound to labour, each in his own sphere, for the conversion of the non-Catholics who surround us on every side.'[62] Bishop Hedley's letters to his Diocese provide an interesting insight into English Catholic pastoral concerns at the end of the nineteenth century. They suggest a practice of pastoral care that is heavily dependent upon a Tridentine theology of the Church.

John Henry Newman established the Birmingham Oratory in February 1848. This was the same year that Ullathorne became the City's first Bishop. Newman's pastoral ministry was situated within a mission context of evangelization and the conversion of industrial communities. The papal brief of establishment in November 1847 particularly stated that the 'Oratory was to concern itself principally with the educated and upper classes.'[63] Unlike Faber's Oratory in London, the Birmingham Oratory soon developed a specific apostolate in education. However, this apostolate was not entirely restricted to the middle classes. After a sojourn at Maryvale, Newman moved to Alcester Street in 1849. Work began on the present site of the Edgbaston Oratory a little more than twelve months later. From the days of the Alcester Street foundation, the Oratory was involved in a thriving pastoral ministry with the poor. Archive evidence suggests that 'at midnight, the Oratory passage "smelt like one of the 'for gentlemen' on the railroad station".'[64] The catechetical work was important to the Oratorians within their general pastoral ministry. Newman, unlike Bishop Ullathorne, encouraged the participation of an informed laity. Newman thought that his bishop had a 'horror of laymen'.[65] This may not be entirely fair. Nevertheless, an example of Newman's pastoral theological skills may be found in the debate surrounding the infallibility issue.

Newman's opinions about the work of the First Vatican Council were entirely orthodox. Despite messages of sympathy and encouragement from various members of the Liberal group, he refused to endorse their position fully. However, he was worried about the

62. Ibid. p.224
63. Cf. Norman E. *The English Catholic Church in the Nineteenth Century* (Oxford: Clarendon Press, 1984) p.225
64. Cf. Gilley S. *Newman and his Age* (London: DLT, 1990) p.261
65. Cf. ibid. p.266

impact of the dogmatic definition of infallibility on the faith of some Catholics in England. Indeed, he expressed his concerns in a letter to Ullathorne at the Council with the poignant words, 'as for myself personally, please God, I do not expect any trial at all; but I cannot help suffering with the various souls which are suffering'.[66] This private letter was later made public and used in mischief against Newman. It is clear that Newman was engaged in a ministry of pastoral care that enabled his theological understanding to become balanced and sensitive.

Newman had been received into the Catholic Church by Dominic Barberi. This Italian Passionist missioner priest had a great desire to work in England from an early age. He never fully mastered the English language, and faced a real persecution from anti-Catholic elements. Nevertheless, his influence is worth recording. Nicholas Wiseman invited Father Barberi to St Mary's College, Oscott, as soon as he had been consecrated co-adjutor to Bishop Thomas Walsh in the Midland District. After some months at Oscott, Wiseman suggested Aston Hall, near Stone in Staffordshire, as a suitable place to found a Passionist Monastery. Dominic Barberi began his pastoral ministry with a fervour and zeal that was to take him well beyond Staffordshire. His style was reminiscent of the French School tradition. Catechetical sermons and instruction were accompanied by public devotions. Above all, there was the witness and example of a personal life of holiness. Dominic began a series of effective parish missions in 1843. These sermons contrasted with the more formal offerings of the local clergy. They have been described as 'plain, homely, affectionate and chatty'.[67] The simplicity and humility of this saintly pastor expressed everything that is good and effective in genuine pastoral ministry.

The influence of Cardinal Henry Edward Manning was crucial to the theological definitions of the First Vatican Council. Manning is an influential figure in the journey of pastoral theology towards the Second Vatican Council. As the Anglican Vicar of Lavington and Archdeacon of Chichester, Manning had been concerned with the poor.[68] Furthermore, he recognized that the whole Church should be

66. Cf. ibid. p.366

67. Cf. Wilson A. *Blessed Dominic Barberi C.P.* (London: Sands & Co., 1967) p.264

68. Cf. McClelland V.A. *Cardinal Manning His Public Life and Influence 1865-1892* (London: Oxford University Press, 1962) p.11

responsible for their pastoral care. He declared that 'the function of educating children does not belong to the sacred orders as such, but to all members of the Church, clerical and lay; that is to say, not to a portion of the Church, but to the whole body.'[69] This philosophy of pastoral action was developed even further when Manning became Archbishop of Westminster. This great pastor was ahead of his time in so many respects. Alan McClelland, former Head of the Centre for Educational Studies in the University of Hull, notes his admiration of General Booth and the Salvation Army, and the fact that his suffragen bishops did not share this enthusiasm.[70] His concern for social reform led to an interest in: the work conditions of agricultural labourers[71], the penal code and the plight of prisoners[72], the development of trade unions[73], and of course, his involvement in education.[74] McClelland writes with insight, of 'that overwhelming sympathy for the underdog, for the worthless, and for the ill-treated that he was wont to refer to as "practical Christianity".'[75] (Cardinals James Gibbons in the United States and William Walsh in Dublin also responded to similar concerns.) These pastoral concerns, together with a fundamental vision of society, were crowned in Leo XIII's encyclical letter *On the Condition of the Working Classes*, the first social encyclical in modern times.

Manning wrote two of the most significant English pastoral theological texts of the nineteenth century. He published two works on the priesthood: *The Eternal Priesthood* and *The Pastoral Office*. The first of these works is obviously dependent upon the scholastic view of priesthood in the theology of Thomas Aquinas. The ordained ministry is a participation in the priesthood of Christ. This means that 'the priesthood of Jesus Christ being the one, only, perpetual, and universal priesthood, all priests consecrated under the New law are made one with Him, and share in His own priesthood.'[76] Manning develops this with a term that is used in contemporary theological reflection on ministry: 'the word configuration expresses the conformity of the priest

69. Ibid. p.12
70. Cf. ibid. p.19
71. Cf. ibid. p.13
72. Cf. ibid. p.15 and p.131
73. Cf. ibid. p.135
74. Cf. ibid. p.27ff.
75. Ibid. pp.14-15
76. Manning H.E. *The Eternal Priesthood* (London: Burns & Oates, fifth edition) p.4

to the great High Priest.'[77] A review of contemporary material suggests that 'configuration' can be used instead of 'sacramental character'. However, Manning's reference to character is used in a typical Tridentine manner. He associates the term with the power to consecrate bread and wine and to absolve sinners. Manning investigates the relationship of the priest to others. One of the key themes in the Second Vatican Council's document on the presbyterate is concerned with the integration of life and mission in the priesthood. This is prefigured in the theological synthesis achieved by Manning in *The Eternal Priesthood*. The priest must be conformed to his Master.[78] This conformity can only be fully realized through sanctity of life. If 'priesthood itself is a source of sanctification to the priest'[79], the purpose of this sanctification is 'that the pastor's office is the highest discipline of charity'.[80] For the priest, charity is 'the urgent motive which constrains, sustains, and spends all his living powers.'[81] Pastoral charity, and every other aspect of presbyteral life, has a clearly defined purpose for Manning: 'This, then, is an axiom in the law and spirit of the sacerdotal life: that a priest is predestined for the greatest glory of God.'[82] In so many respects, these ideas prefigure the understanding of pastoral ministry in the texts of the Second Vatican Council. The chapter on *The Priest's Dangers* suggests that the difficulties of nineteenth century presbyteral life are still pertinent within ministry today: the problems of leaving the stability of seminary life; the difficulties associated with maintaining initial fervour; the dissipation that arises from a busy ministry; the opposite problem of an undemanding ministry; finally, the problem of lukewarm attitude and response. Manning believed that an idle priest 'is of all men most to be pitied. When his priesthood ceases to be sweet to him, it becomes first tasteless, and then bitter in the mouth.'[83] Manning's discussion of these matters is clearly rooted in the insights gained by episcopal oversight.

The Pastoral Office is particularly concerned with the office of bishop.[84] The initial discussion of episcopal jurisdiction is redolent of a

77. Ibid. p.7
78. Cf. ibid. p.37
79. Ibid. p.56
80. Ibid. p.59
81. Ibid. p.59
82. Ibid. p.68
83. Ibid. p.85
84. Manning H.E. *The Pastoral Office* (Printed for Private Use Only, 1883)

Tridentine theological vision. However, there is an important point in his summary of these jurisdictions: 'The Bishops are successors not of an Apostle one by one, but of the Apostles as a body; that is, the Episcopate succeeds the Apostolate as a whole to a whole.'[85] This statement indicates the germinating idea of episcopal collegiality. This is a hallmark of the Second Vatican Council's understanding of the bishop's office. Manning wrote in the aftermath of the First Vatican Council. The episcopate cannot exist apart from the petrine office: 'The Episcopate, which is one and indivisible, is such precisely by reason of the connection of the Bishops among themselves, and of their submission to one sole Bishop, who is universal and sovereign.'[86] As a leading member of the Ultramontane party at the First Vatican Council, Manning was aware of the Council's perspectives. The constitution that defined papal infallibility was the first dogmatic constitution. A second constitution schema had been prepared. This involved a necessary discussion of the episcopal office and an understanding of collegiality. The unfinished business of this Council is most unfortunate. Nevertheless, Manning suggests that 'rhetoricians and controversialists have delighted in saying that the Vatican Council extinguished the Episcopate, and made Bishops to be shadows and vicars of the Pope. There is no Council of the Church in which the power and jurisdiction of the Episcopate has been more explicitly declared, as we shall see in due time.'[87] After this point, there is hardly a reference in *The Pastoral Office* to the First Vatican Council. Perhaps the reader must look elsewhere for the meaning of Manning's words. Manning distinguishes three ages of Christian tradition as patristic, scholastic and the conciliar period. This may have been provocative prophecy. This great churchman knew that there must be another council to complete the work of the one he was personally involved in. We must now turn to a consideration of the Second Vatican Council and its pastoral theology.

85. Ibid. p.12
86. Ibid. p.27
87. Ibid. p.117

CHAPTER TWO

The Second Vatican Council

2.0 Introduction

This chapter is concerned with the theological reflection on pastoral ministry in the documents of the Second Vatican Council and certain post-conciliar sources. The context for a renewed understanding of pastoral care is the ecclesiological revision that took place during the course of this Council. This provided a theological environment for an emerging contemporary pastoral theology. It is necessary to affirm the idea of *development* here. The new ideas built upon the tradition of the past. One commentator has suggested that the Second Vatican Council was a 'radical break' with the previous tradition.[1] From a theological perspective this sociologist's view is untenable. Henri de Lubac was an influential theologian in the years leading up to the Second Vatican Council. His theological reflection attempted to bring the insights of the early Church Fathers into a dialogue with modern culture. He was particularly concerned with the ecclesiological implications of belief in the Trinity. This doctrinal reflection provided the development of his thoughts about communion and ecclesial community. This great contemporary theologian was filled with the realization of a need for renewal. Nevertheless, he was still able to affirm that the Church's structures 'are not 'ancient forms' which could be abandoned any more than the fundamental dogmas of our faith are out-of-date ideas in which a change of language would leave nothing subsisting.'[2] These present reflections are offered in this same spirit.

The texts of the Second Vatican Council offer the opportunity for a renewal of pastoral theological reflection. There is an element of compromise in the final formulation of the Council's documents. The results of this compromise may be discerned in contemporary pastoral care practice. There is a tension between the Tridentine understanding

1. Cf. Hornsby-Smith M. *Roman Catholics in England* (Cambridge: Cambridge University Press, 1987) p.2
2. Cf. de Lubac H. *The Motherhood of the Church* (San Francisco: Ignatius Press, 1982) pp.30-31

of ecclesial hierarchy and the emergence of a new ecclesiology of the pilgrim people of God. Our task is to examine the documents of the Second Vatican Council and suggest the principal theological themes which can be used to understand pastoral ministry in the life of the Church today. There is a clear focus on the episcopal ministry in these texts. The ministry of the bishop becomes the model for all pastoral care. Indeed, all pastoral ministry is understood in terms of its relationship to the episcopal ministry. An understanding of communion and relationship provides the foundation for a renewed understanding of pastoral ministry.

There have been many published assessments of the Second Vatican Council's achievements. Some of the best testimony may be found in the personal memoirs of those who took part in the work of the Council.[3] Political forces were evidently present from the beginning of the Council's history. These reflect the polemical interests that may be seen in earlier Church councils. At the beginning of the Council, in March 1962, Léon-Josef Suenens complained to John XXIII about the seventy-two schemata in preparation.[4] Suenens had been appointed Archbishop of Malines twelve months previously. He was well qualified to question the approach and methodology of those preparing for the Council's work, having been the Professor of Philosophy at the Malines Seminary and a vice-rector of the University of Louvain during the war years. Giovanni Battista Montini, Archbishop of Milan, raised similar concerns about the direction of the Council in October 1962.[5] (This was a particularly poignant intervention as Montini was elected Pope during the course of the Council.) The problems concerned the total absence of theological unity and an integrated vision in the preparation for the Council's work. The pre-conciliar enthusiasm amongst some theologians was imbued with a sense of anticipation. Some of these have suggested there was a deliberate attempt to wreck the Council's process.[6] The real problems, however, are concerned with methodology. The hallmarks of the scholastic methodology, so popular in the period between the First and Second Vatican Councils, are

3. E.g. ed. Stacpoole A. *Vatican II by those who were there* (London: Geoffrey Chapman, 1986)
4. Cf. Suenens L-J *A Plan for the whole Council* in ed. Stacpoole A. (1986) op.cit., p.89
5. Cf. ibid., p.91
6. Cf. Vorgrimler H. *Karl Rahner: The Theologian's Contribution* in ed. Stacpoole A. (1986) op.cit., p.34

fragmentation and a tendency to theological differentiation. The Second Vatican Council attempted to bring about a unity in the various theological disciplines and their doctrinal definitions. This great achievement of the Council is to be found in its Christological synthesis of doctrine in the mystery of Christ. Theological renewal was achieved through a retrieval of the biblical and classical patristic tradition. This process is clearly not evident in the initial preparatory documents of the Council. It can be argued that this integrity of method was, to some extent, due to the influence of Suenens and Montini. When the Council opened on 11 October 1962, Suenens had submitted a redefined plan to John XXIII. This plan was 'conceived in such a manner as to give the Council a pastoral, coherent overall direction'. It was to be both inward looking towards the life of the Church and focused outwards towards the world.[7] This plan for the Council appreciated the necessary continuity with the First Vatican Council. Nevertheless, there was also the perceived need for unambiguous renewal, in particular, the need to situate the life of the Church within an explicit orientation towards mission activity.

2.1 The Church

The bishops of the Second Vatican Council had a firm theological tradition at their disposal. However, their reflection on the Church was made complex by the inheritance of two distinct traditions that had evolved in the West and the East. The Latin tradition had always been universalist in its approach, whereas the Greek tradition tended to start with the empirical data of the local church. In a general sense, the West had always understood the situation of the Church in the world. Eastern ecclesiology had traditionally emphasized the more spiritual aspects of ecclesial life. The Second Vatican Council attempted a confluence of these diverse traditions. This is not always obvious. In particular, the Council's reflection on the local church is poor. Unfortunately, there was no adequate language to discuss this theme in a systematic manner. The Gospel, according to de Lubac, 'does not aim only at a new relation of individuals as such with the Father, outside of any social and institutional framework, but indeed at a "new covenant" whose consequence is the new people of God'.[8] The idea of the Church

7. Cf. Suenens L-J. *A Plan for the whole Council* in ed. Stacpoole A. (1986) op.cit., p.96
8. De Lubac (1982) op.cit., p.12

as the covenanted people of God provided the language for a renewal of ecclesiology and pastoral theology.

The first schema of the Council's document *On the Church* began with the unfinished business of the First Vatican Council in 1870. The first chapter of this schema noted the need to supplement a truncated perspective of the papacy with a fuller understanding of the episcopal office. Theologians recognized the need to understand this office within a definition of the Church as 'the community of the faithful in the Spirit of God, the body of Christ, the beginning of the Kingdom of God, the primal sacrament of God's eschatological salvation.'[9] The important point here is the movement away from a static idea of hierarchy towards a more dynamic vision of the Church as communion. This new direction did not find universal acceptance amongst the bishops in Council. However, the original schema, from the beginning, was considered grossly deficient by many of the Council Fathers. Bishop Emile-Joseph de Smedt, for example, accused the schema of triumphalism, clericalism and juridicism. It was strictly hierarchical, and de Smedt deplored the idea of the Church which suggested 'at the base the laity who count for nothing, at the summit the pope, who counts for everything.'[10] These objections may be summarily understood from within an eschatological perspective. Either the Church is a 'perfect society' and completely fulfilled in the here and now, or there is an evolutionary movement towards a future fulfilment as the communion of saints in Christ. The final *Dogmatic Constitution on the Church* thrusts towards the latter view. There is a definite movement from the juridical language of the draft document towards a more dynamic understanding of the Church within the context of an unfolding salvation history.

The eschatological nature of the Church is expressed in the first article of the final dogmatic constitution. The Church, 'in Christ, is in the nature of sacrament – a sign and instrument'[11] The 'condition of the modern world'[12] is declared to be the reason why the Church must develop 'her own nature and universal mission'.[13] This mission is essentially one of 'proclaiming and establishing among all peoples the

9. Cf. Rahner K. and Ratzinger J. *The Episcopate and the Primacy* (Edinburgh: Nelson, 1962) p.11
10. Cf. Holland T. *The Council Comes of Age* in ed. Stacpoole A. (1986) op.cit., p.61
11. *Lumen Gentium* (1964) art.1
12. Ibid. art.1
13. Ibid. art.1

kingdom of Christ and of God'.[14] The fundamental mission of the Church is given in 'the word, in the works and in the presence of Christ.'[15] The developing understanding of the Church's mission in this document provides an important unitative dimension to all pastoral ministry. The Council Fathers declared that the Church 'is driven by the Holy Spirit to do her part for the full realization of the plan of God, who has constituted Christ as the source of salvation for the whole world.'[16] This understanding of the Church enables a new theological understanding of the practice of pastoral ministry. The revised ecclesiology of the Dogmatic Constitution on the Church has patently altered the Church's understanding of ministry. The Council's document on the episcopal office builds upon the principles contained in the document on the Church. These are developed further in the document on the ministry and life of priests.[17]

2.2 The Ministry of Bishop

The episcopal office is central to an understanding of ministry within a Second Vatican Council ecclesiology. The local church may be considered as a 'sacrament' of the universal Church. This sacramentality is very much attached to the office of the bishop.[18] Unfortunately, the untimely interruption of the First Vatican Council had produced a mindset that challenged any revisitation of patristic themes. However, in this theological reflection on the sacramental nature of the episcopal office, the bishops of the Second Vatican Council were returning to early Christian sources. The theological understanding of the episcopal office is presented in the third chapter of the *Dogmatic Constitution on the Church*. This chapter is almost twice the length of any other in the document. Despite the reference at the beginning of article eighteen to a 'variety of offices'[19], these eleven articles are principally concerned with episcopal ministry. The most important teaching of the chapter is given in article nineteen. The bishops reflect on the fact that Christ constituted his apostles 'in the form of a college or permanent

14. Ibid. art.5
15. Ibid. art.5
16. Ibid. art.17
17. Cf. Bea A. *We who Serve* (London: Geoffrey Chapman, 1969) p.27
18. Cf. Nocent A. *The Local Church as Realization of the Church of Christ and Subject of the Eucharist* in ed. Alberigo G. (1987) op.cit., p.215
19. *Lumen Gentium* (1964) art.18

assembly'.[20] The Church is still defined as a 'hierarchically constituted society'.[21] However, there is a new emphasis on the collegial nature of the episcopal office, and thus, of all pastoral ministry, because 'this was its nature as instituted by Christ in the beginning'.[22] Some bishops suggested that the notion of episcopal collegiality challenged the doctrine of the papal primacy.[23] Fortunately, their view did not prevail. At the end of article twenty, in the document on the Church, there is the statement that 'the bishops have by divine institution taken the place of the apostles as pastors of the Church'.[24] The Church has always believed this doctrine. However, it was not fully developed by the Council of Trent. The Tridentine bishops were anxious to avoid any challenge to the papal prerogative.[25] The Second Vatican Council attempted to rediscover the basic unity of the Church as sacrament within the vision of an earlier patristic teaching.[26]

Pastoral ministry can only be understood within a context of service. This theme of servanthood is, in many respects, the key to understanding the 'sacred power' that unites all ministries in the Church. The *Dogmatic Constitution on the Church* states that the pastoral office, 'which the Lord committed to the pastors of his people, is, in the strict sense of the term, a service, which is called very expressively in sacred scripture a *diakonia* or ministry.'[27] The Council's documents contain almost two hundred references to service.[28] Furthermore, this service is understood within a Christological setting, because 'to serve means to co-operate with Christ in the divine design of salvation.'[29] The exercise of pastoral office as 'teachers of doctrine, ministers of sacred worship and holders of office in government'[30] is fundamentally an act of service that is ordered towards the completion of Christ's work in the fullness of time. These, then, are the principal

20. Ibid. art.19
21. Ibid. art.19
22. Cf. Ryan S. *The Hierarchical Structure of the Church* in ed. McNamara K. Vatican II: *The Constitution on the Church* (London: Geoffrey Chapman, 1968) p.166
23. Cf. Williams C. *The Church is hierarchical* in ed. Flannery A. *Vatican II on the Church* (Dublin: Scepter Books, 1966) p.48
24. *Lumen Gentium* (1964) art.20
25. Cf. Ryan S. in ed. McNamara K. (1968) op.cit., p.166
26. Cf. ibid. p.176
27. *Lumen Gentium* (1964) art.24
28. Cf. Bea A. (1969) op.cit., p.12
29. Ibid. p.20
30. *Lumen Gentium* (1964) art.20

themes of the dogmatic constitution that can be applied to our understanding of pastoral ministry.

It is important that the Second Vatican Council's *Decree on the Pastoral Office of the Bishops in the Church* is understood against the ecclesiological background of the dogmatic constitution we have already considered. There were originally two schemas: *On Bishops and Diocesan Government* and *On the Care of Souls.* The second schema was more promising from a pastoral theological perspective. Unfortunately, it was subsumed into the former schema, even though this text was criticized for its unequivocal administrative and juridical tone.[31] The third schema was given the title *On the Bishops' Pastoral Office in the Church*. It was placed before the Council bishops on 27 April 1964. It was still a controversial text. The preface and first two chapters failed to receive the necessary two-thirds majority vote. The rewritten text failed to address certain canonical issues concerning matters of jurisdiction, and it was not fully integrated into the final text. Analysis of the first two articles of this document suggest that the theological language of the introduction is more influenced by the pre-concilar doctrine of the encyclical *On the Mystical Body of Christ* than the *Dogmatic Constitution on the Church.* The second article of the document contains a discussion of the papal and episcopal offices without even an indirect reference to episcopal collegiality.

The substance of the document on the bishops' office is presented in the third article. The theme of episcopal collegiality is introduced with the statement that bishops are 'united in one college or body for the instruction and direction of the universal Church'.[32] This important theme for contemporary pastoral theology is discussed more fully in the first chapter of the document. The third article also introduces the substance of the second chapter. This concerns the role of the bishops in the local church. The bishops 'exercise this function individually as regards that portion of the Lord's flock which has been entrusted to each one of them, each bishop having responsibility for the particular church assigned to him.'[33] There is also a statement that introduces the idea of episcopal care for all the local churches: 'On occasion a number

31. Cf. Morsdorf K. *Decree on the Bishops' Pastoral Office in the Church* in ed. Vorgrimler H. *Commentary on the Documents of Vatican II vol.2* (London: Burns & Oates, 1968) p.165
32. *Christus Dominus* (1965) art.3
33. Ibid. art.3

of bishops will co-operate to provide for the common needs of their churches.'[34] The third chapter of the *Decree on the Pastoral Office of Bishops in the Church* provides a theological exposition of collegiality, together with its practical application in the foundation of episcopal conferences.

2.3 Collegiality

The theme of collegiality is one of the most important ideas of the Second Vatican Council. John Paul II declared, in his first address as the Bishop of Rome on 17 October 1978, that 'the concept of collegiality is the keystone of contemporary Catholic ecclesiology.'[35] This conviction was reaffirmed nearly twenty years later in the post-synodal apostolic exhortation following the extraordinary Synod of African bishops. This text states that 'the principle underlying the setting up of the Synod of Bishops is straightforward: the more the communion of the Bishops among themselves is strengthened, the more the communion of the Church as a whole is enriched.'[36] Collegiality refers particularly to the exercise of the episcopal office. However, even as the Council unfolded, the idea received an appreciative application to all pastoral care relationships within the Church. Collegiality represents a movement from a juridical concept of the Church, towards a vision of the Church as communion. Indeed, it is only possible to understand episcopal collegiality within the whole communion of disciples. Collegiality is situated within communion and is meant to serve the communion of the whole body.

It is necessary to affirm the perspective of development within continuity. The theme of collegiality in the Second Vatican Council completes the doctrinal work of the First Vatican Council. It is possible to discern the influence of the doctrine of collegiality in three areas of ecclesiology. The idea of collegiality has affected the Church's mission to local areas. There is an expression of this mission in the renewed exercise of the episcopal teaching office in episcopal conferences. Secondly, the doctrine of collegiality has influenced the expression of the papal office. This is particularly seen in the contribution of episcopal synods to consider areas of vital importance in the life of the

34. Ibid. art.3
35. Cf. O'Connell L. *Collegiality: theology and practice for the 80s* in *Theology Digest* vol.29 no.4 (Winter 1981), p.320
36. *Ecclesia in Africa* (1995) art.15

Church. Finally, there are significant implications of this doctrine for the development of ecumenical relationships. The communion of discipleship is strengthened and challenged by the theme of collegiality. There is a need for further progress and a wider reception of collegiality in the life of the Church. However, the work of theologians such as Yves Congar, before the Second Vatican Council, paved the way for a fuller understanding of the ecumenical implications of collegiality.

These implications of episcopal collegiality suggest that the doctrine may be approached from two perspectives. Theological reflection may begin with the idea of collegiality in the local church. The understanding of how it works in this context is then applied to the universal Church. However, the twenty-second article of the *Dogmatic Constitution on the Church* favours the alternative approach. This text situates the episcopal office within the broad context of the whole Church. The doctrine of universal collegiality is then applied to the particular context of a local church. The dogmatic constitution teaches that 'one is constituted a member of the episcopal body in virtue of the sacramental consecration and by the hierarchical communion with the head and members of the college.'[37] Nevertheless, the first approach still has a valid place. Ratzinger has noted that the word *ecclesia* usually referred to the local church in early Christianity.[38] The local church is a complete ecclesiological sacrament in itself, although the integrity of a particular community is determined by its unity with other churches. The real essence of catholicity is to be found in the *koinonia* or fellowship relationship amongst the bishops. This idea of fellowship associates collegiality to the New Testament office of the 'Twelve'. Their apostolic designation in the early church takes place after the Pentecost event. In this context, the 'Twelve' are an eschatological sign of the Kingdom of God and a significant symbol of the whole Christian community.[39] This theological reflection on collegiality represents more than an institutional structure. It is more than a 'collective act' on the part of the bishops working together, and speaking with one voice.[40]

37. *Lumen Gentium* (1964) art.22
38. Ratzinger J. *The Pastoral Implications of Episcopal Collegiality* in *Concilium* vol.1 no.1 Dogma (New Jersey: Paulist Press, 1965) p.22
39. Cf. ibid. p.20
40. Cf. de Lubac (1982) op.cit., 259

Collegiality, then, does not merely serve an administrative function. A recent papal text states that the Second Vatican Council 'rediscovered episcopal collegiality, that privileged expression of the pastoral service carried out by the Bishops in communion with the successor of Peter.'[41] The bishop is understood to be an ecclesial symbol of our heavenly Father. He unites the whole of the liturgical congregation in celebration of the work of our salvation. Collegiality is a consequence of faith in a triune God of faith and love. Local churches are united in a relationship which may be described as *perichoresis*, i.e., a communion of love and unity. The patristic term defines the loving unity between the Persons of the Blessed Trinity. It is applied to the communion of disciples in the sense that the constant vocation of the Church is an invitation to reflect the nature and action of the Trinity God. There are consequences of this teaching for pastoral care practice. They arise from a sense of common responsibility amongst the bishops, and a concern to address the needs of others involved in the relationship of fellowship. The bishop, in his office and person, is an expression of the communion shared by his local church with all the other churches. Articles six and seven of the *Decree on the Pastoral Office of Bishops in the Church* encourage a 'brotherly care' between bishops, and especially towards those in need. This reflection not only indicates the development of the inherited tradition, but also suggests its implications for contemporary pastoral care. These implications will be developed further in our definition of pastoral ministry.

2.4 The Diocesan Bishop

The bishop presides over a local church, 'in which the one, holy, catholic and apostolic Church of Christ is truly present and active.[42] Our discussion of collegiality suggests that there is an imperative for bishops to have a universal solicitude for all churches. However, analysis of articles eleven through to twenty-one of the *Decree on the Pastoral Office of Bishops in the Church* points to the diocese as the principal focus for the bishop's pastoral ministry. Bishops have the fundamental task to be 'witnesses of Christ'[43] who must 'proclaim the

41. *Tertio Millennio Adveniente* (1994) art.19
42. *Christus Dominus* (1965) art.11
43. Ibid. art.11

Gospel of Christ'.[44] This must be in a manner that makes full use of 'the various methods available nowadays for proclaiming Christian doctrine.'[45] As the bishops 'enjoy the fullness of the sacrament of orders'[46], the clergy of the diocese are 'dependent on them in the exercise of their power.'[47] There is a real authority here. However, the bishop exercises his ministry 'as one who serves'[48] and with the example of 'sanctity in charity, humility and simplicity of life.'[49] Indeed, the bishop must 'so unite and mould his flock into one family that all, conscious of their duties, may live and act in the communion of charity.'[50] To be an effective pastor of the faithful, the bishop 'should try to keep himself informed of their needs in the social circumstances in which they live.'[51]

The bishop's ministry is certainly not restricted solely to those who live within this communion of faith and charity. Pastoral action is directed towards all people, and in a particular way 'to those who have strayed in any way from the path of truth or who have no knowledge of the gospel of Christ and of his saving mercy'.[52] Pastoral ministry must recognize the relationship of the Church and society: 'Since it is the mission of the Church to maintain close relation with the society in which she lives the bishops should make it their special care to approach men and to initiate and promote dialogue with them.'[53] There are three ways in which this dialogue may prove fruitful. Doctrine may be presented 'so that it may be relevant to those difficulties and questions which men find especially worrying and intimidating.'[54] Secondly, Christian doctrine particularly promotes the value of 'the human person, in his liberty and bodily life'.[55] Thirdly, Christian principles can make an important contribution to certain contemporary concerns. In particular, episcopal ministry must be concerned with 'the possession, increase and just distribution of

44. Ibid. art.12
45. Ibid. art.13
46. Ibid. art.15
47. Ibid. art.15
48. Ibid. art.16
49. Ibid. art.15
50. Ibid. art.16
51. Ibid. art.16
52. Ibid. art.11
53. Ibid. art.13
54. Ibid. art.13
55. Ibid. art.12

material goods, concerning peace and war, and the fraternal coexistence of all peoples.'[56]

The documents of the Second Vatican Council distinguish between episcopal and presbyteral orders. The Council of Trent certainly upheld the difference between the presbyterate and the episcopate. Canons six and seven of the *Decree on the Sacrament of Orders*, promulgated on 15 July 1563, affirm the difference in 'power' between the two orders. However, Trent does not define the substantial nature of this difference. The First Vatican Council was unable to resolve this issue either. Joseph Kleutgen was an influential Jesuit theologian at this Council. He was involved in the preparation of many draft schemas for the Council's consideration. He certainly promoted the popular neo-scholasticism of this nineteenth century period. However, he ensured that the devotional elements of this movement were tempered with a rigorous intellectualism. One of his draft documents concerned the difference between episcopal and presbyteral orders. The text remained part of the unfinished business of this Council and was left for the bishops of the Second Vatican Council to complete. Kleutgen was not particularly concerned with the notion of episcopal jurisdiction. His neo-scholastic mindset may not have produced a very fruitful theological reflection. The matter could be approached from a very different perspective by the time of the Second Vatican Council. There was a focus on the historical data of the New Testament texts and patristic tradition at the recent Council. There was also an attempt to overcome the polemical concerns of Trent and respond more generously to the modern ecumenical movement.

2.5 The Ministry of Presbyter

Our brief overview of the historical prelude to the Second Vatican Council indicates the importance of pastoral ministry in the revised conciliar agenda. These concerns were, in effect, primarily directed towards the ministry of the episcopate. There was a draft schema *On the Care of Souls.* Unfortunately, the tone of this text was similar to the schema *On Bishops and Diocesan Government*, and was influenced more by juridical issues than pastoral concerns. There were draft schemas *On Clerics* and *On Priests*. These were also unsuitable for promulgation.

56. Ibid. art.12

The breakthrough came with a text that was presented before the Council on 12 November 1964. It was given the title *On the Ministry and Life of Priests*, and this was the schema that finally evolved into the *Decree on the Ministry and Life of Priests*. The journey to this point was certainly tortuous. There had been many calls for a theological reflection on the ministry of the presbyterate. However, the Commission on Doctrine rejected these because of the intense work taken up by the *Dogmatic Constitution on the Church*. Nevertheless, the work of the Council on the office of bishop naturally led to a focus on the nature of the presbyterate. It was during the debate on the document concerning the episcopal office that Bishop Foley of Lancaster made his important appeal for a more pastoral text on the presbyterate.

The most important feature of the November 1964 schema was its focus on presbyteral ministry rather than the life of the priest. This produced a document that reflected upon the virtues needed for a fruitful ministry rather than counsels directed towards personal sanctity. This focus was primarily due to the intervention of Bishop André Marie Charue of Namur. At the heart of Bishop Foley's intervention was the demand that priests should know their people. Unfortunately, the final document does not fully reflect the practical wisdom of this great pastor. However, the understanding of the priest from the perspective of pastoral care is an important development of the post-Tridentine tradition. This view of presbyteral ministry is confirmed by Balthasar when he states that 'the priesthood is primarily an ecclesial function, and objective ministry, and, on the basis of this ministry, subsequently a way of life.'[57] The thirtieth anniversary of the Council's document on presbyteral ministry was celebrated by an international symposium, organized by the Congregation for the Clergy in 1995. The final text speaks of the need to 'strike a balance between the interior life and pastoral activity, priests strive to make of the ministry itself a means of personal sanctification, making of their pastoral work a true prayer.'[58] There is clearly no dissonance intended between pastoral ministry and life. Tridentine theology had defined the essence of the ordained ministry within its relationship to the Eucharist. The

57. Balthasar H. *The Christian State of Life* (San Francisco: Ignatius Press, 1983) p.267

58. Congregation for the Clergy (1995) *International Symposium Celebrating the 30th anniversary of the promulgation of the Conciliar Decree Presbyterorum Ordinis* (Vatican City: Vatican City Press) p.16

Second Vatican Council document reflected upon the agenda for presbyteral ministry and did not fully commend Trent's model. The bishops at the Second Vatican Council also wanted to redefine the relationship between the presbyterate and the episcopal order. Furthermore, they were concerned to demonstrate the unity of pastoral and liturgical ministry. There is no foundation in this document for the creation of an unhealthy tension between the demands of pastoral care and sacramental ministry.

The document *On the Ministry and Life of Priests* outlines the priorities for the practice of pastoral ministry. These priorities are placed within a Christological theological context. Article twelve of the text begins with the crucial statement: 'By the sacrament of Order priests are configured to Christ the priest as servants of the Head, so that as co-workers with the episcopal order they may build up the Body of Christ, the Church.'[59] The word 'configured' is preferred to the word 'character'. Priests are called to exercise their pastoral ministry in union with Christ the High Priest. It is precisely through the practice of pastoral care that the priest grows in holiness and likeness to Christ. Priests are invited to enter into the pastoral renewal of ecclesial life, mission and dialogue with the world. They will strive for holiness, in order that they will be made 'daily more effective instruments for the service of all God's people.[60]

The affinity between a priest's life and his ministry is not fully harmonized in this document. One reason for this situation is an ambiguous understanding of the relationship between the sacramental ministry of the ordained and the common priesthood of all the baptized. The theological clarity needed here is absent in the second article of the text. Article three attempts to deal with this ambiguity by discussing the relationship between 'office' and 'ministry'. It states that 'the priests of the new testament are, it is true, by their vocation to ordination, set apart in some way in the midst of the People of God, but this is not in order that they should be separated from that people or from any man'.[61] Presbyteral ministers 'would be powerless to serve men if they remained aloof from their life and circumstances.'[62] There is

59. *Presbyterorum Ordinis* (1965) art.12
60. Ibid. art.12
61. Ibid. art.3
62. Ibid. art.3

the remnant, here, of an uneasy debate and lingering Reformation polemic between those who promote the common priesthood over ordained ministry, or vice versa. The Second Vatican Council document sought to provide a doctrinal basis for future discussion of this contentious issue. The text states that 'priests, in common with all who have been reborn in the font of baptism, are brothers among brothers as members of the same Body of Christ which all are commanded to build up.'[63] There is still a need to develop the Council's text and to clarify the role of ministerial priesthood within the priesthood of all believers.

The second article of the *Decree on the Ministry and Life of Priests* suggests other theological concerns requiring further reflection. The first issue involves the relationship of the ministerial priesthood to the priesthood of Christ. Jesus is constituted as the eschatological High Priest, precisely because of his redemptive sacrifice. The fundamental function of Christian priestly ministry, then, is to proclaim Christ's 'once-and-for-all-redemption'. This demands that the priest be configured to Christ in his ministry. It also suggests that the priest needs to discover communion with those saving events in Christ's life which brought about our redemption. The second theological issue concerns the re-establishment of the episcopal order as the plenitude of priesthood. This reaches beyond the medieval attempt to situate the fullness of priesthood in the presbyterate. Finally, there is the need to integrate liturgical and sacramental activity within a wider concept of ministry. The Council's document provides the vital hermeneutical tools for further investigation of these themes. The ministry of Jesus is understood within the context of an unfolding history of salvation that is not fully completed. This pastoral ministry is rooted in a paschal context, for 'all these activities, since they flow from the pasch of Christ, will find their consummation in the glorious coming of the same Lord, when he shall have delivered up the kingdom to God'.[64] It is still necessary to investigate further the biblical foundations for a pastoral ministry that is truly Christological. This investigation needs to reflect upon the enormous difference between the ministry of Jesus and the priesthood of his time, in particular, the manner in which Jesus was able to break through cultic barriers and bring salvation to those who were considered outcast.

63. Ibid. art.9
64. *Presbyterorum Ordinis* (1965) art.2

Article four of the document on the priesthood indicates the first role of presbyteral ministry. The primary task of priests concerns the ministry to proclaim the Gospel. They are called, 'as co-workers of the bishops to preach the Gospel of God'.[65] The purpose of preaching is the awakening and growth of faith in the unbeliever and the disciple alike: 'For by the saving Word of God faith is aroused in the heart of unbelievers and is nourished in the heart of believers.'[66] This article reflects a developed theology of preaching that is not contained in the *Decree on the Pastoral Office of the Bishops in the Church*. The teaching has influenced post-conciliar pastoral theological reflection. Daniel Goergen, an American theologian who has made the priesthood his special area of study, makes the assertion that 'all ordained ministry is an intensification, exemplification, sacramentalization of the ministry of the Word.'[67] The essential purpose of preaching is not given the complete treatment it deserves in some contemporary theological reflection. It will need to be evaluated within the context of liturgical celebration.[68] Participation in the priesthood of Christ is only made real in an environment of faith and service. This focus on faith enables a perspective in which presbyteral ministry and life are existentially conformed to Christ.

The second role of presbyteral ministry is concerned with sacramental and liturgical celebration. Article five of the document states that 'the purpose then for which priests are consecrated by God through the ministry of the bishop is that they should be made sharers in a special way in Christ's priesthood and, by carrying out sacred functions, act as his ministers who through his Spirit continually exercises his priestly function for our benefit in the liturgy.'[69] There is a relationship between personal consecration and communal celebration. There is also a relationship between sacramental ministry and the proclamation of the word. There are no grounds for dividing these two tasks or assuming the second is less important than the first. Robert Barron, a systematic theologian from Mundelein Seminary in Chicago, uses the device of mystagogy to bring these two aspects of ministry together. He suggests that 'the priest of Jesus Christ is, first and

65. *Presbyterorum Ordinis* (1965) art.4
66. Ibid. art.4
67. Ed. Goergen D. *Being a Priest Today* (Collegeville: The Liturgical Press, 1992) p.10
68. Cf. chapter five of this study.
69. *Presbyterorum Ordinis* (1965) art.5

foremost, a mystagogue, one who bears the Mystery and initiates others into it.'[70]

The next presbyteral role, considered in article six, is the pastoral share in the bishop's ministry of oversight. It is said of priests that 'in the name of the bishop they gather the family of God as a brotherhood endowed with the spirit of unity and lead it in Christ through the Spirit to God the Father.'[71] This Trinitarian context envelops all pastoral care and indicates the ultimate purpose of ministry. Furthermore, pastoral activity reaches its fulfilment in the eucharistic liturgy. All ministries find their home and determination in this paschal celebration. There is also an emphasis in this article on the Christological foundation of pastoral ministry. The bishops of the Second Vatican Council wanted to emphasize the theological dependency of presbyteral ministry on that of the bishops. However, there is a movement away from a 'filial' description of this relationship in the earlier documents of the Council, to a more 'fraternal' understanding of the relationship in the document on the presbyterate.[72] This relationship demands profound theological reflection, as the presbyter exercises a ministry, under the authority of the bishop, which is truly received from Christ the High Priest. The reason for building an ecclesial and eucharistic community is to promote missiological activity outside of the community. For this, disciples must be educated 'to reach Christian maturity.'[73] There is an inherent danger of the application of certain cultural standards of success and failure to the enterprise of ministry. This is clearly not the intention of the document: 'Although priests owe service to everybody, the poor and the weaker ones have been committed to their care in a special way. It was with these that the Lord himself associated, and the preaching of the Gospel to them is given as a sign of his messianic mission.'[74]

70. Barron R. *The Priest as Bearer of the Mystery* in *The Furrow* vol.46. no.4 April 1995, p.204
71. *Presbyterorum Ordinis* (1965) art.6
72. Cf. ibid. art.7
73. Ibid. art.6
74. Ibid. art.6

CHAPTER THREE

Post-Conciliar Developments

3.0 Introduction

The documents of the Second Vatican Council define the priesthood as a unity of nature and mission. These ontological and functional dimensions of the presbyterate need to be unconditionally interpreted within a theological framework. The fundamental theological integrity of this reflection needs to be emphasized at the beginning of this consideration of the post-conciliar documents. The presbyterate is similar to any other social institution in its presentation of phenomenological data for sociological analysis. However, the fundamental hermeneutical position of all the post-conciliar texts is their origin within a community of faith. This is easily forgotten in a culture dominated by secular perspectives.

A number of pastoral theological areas have received further reflection after the Second Vatican Council. These themes have been more fully developed by a process of synodal investigation.[1] This process of reflection has an important function in the life of the Church. The synods find their inspiration in the Second Vatican Council. They 'are part of the new evangelization: they were born of the Second Vatican Council's vision of the Church.'[2] The word 'synod' means, 'a journey made together', and is therefore an authentic symbol of contemporary ecclesiological models. These synods have tried to be an effective means of exercising the collegial ministry of the episcopate. Nevertheless, from an existential ecclesiological perspective, it is reasonable to question their general effectiveness. After a period of consultation throughout the universal Church, representatives of episcopal conferences gather together for a time of discernment and recommendation. The synod is then followed by the publication of a papal apostolic exhortation. So far, these have been 'devoted to the

1. The request for post-conciliar synods was actually made by Bishop Thomas Holland of Salford, on 16 October 1963. Cf. Holland T. *The Council Comes of Age* in ed. Stacpoole A. (1986) *Vatican II by those who were there* (London: Geoffrey Chapman, 1986) p.60
2. *Tertio Millennio Adveniente* (1994) art.21

mission of the laity, the formation of priests, catechesis, the family, the value of penance and reconciliation in the life of the Church and of humanity in general, as well as the forthcoming one to be devoted to the consecrated life.'[3] The synod process is meant to find its inspiration in the Second Vatican Council and its direction in the needs of the Church at the beginning of a new millennium.

In 1990, the bishops met in Rome for a Synod on the formation of priests in the modern world.[4] Extensive reference was made to the documents of the Second Vatican Council. The Synod became an opportunity to confirm conciliar pastoral theology, and to respond to any erroneous developments in the past thirty years. Two years later, the post-synodal apostolic exhortation *I will Give You Shepherds* was published, and became the most important document to deal with presbyteral ministry since the close of the Council.[5] During the course of the Synod, a number of bishops asked that the Congregation for the Clergy should prepare a practical exposition of presbyteral theological concerns. This document was published four years after the Synod. It is known as the *Directory on the Ministry and Life of Priests.* It has a clearly defined purpose, 'to respond to the principal questions of a doctrinal, disciplinary and pastoral nature, placed upon the priests by the demands of the new evangelization.'[6]

This investigation of post-conciliar pastoral theology will also make reference to other important texts. The universal Holy Thursday letters of John Paul II to priests throughout the world are particularly important sources. Each letter seeks to present an important aspect of contemporary presbyteral ministry. A number of curial texts, predominantly from the Congregation for Catholic Education, are also worthy of consideration. The *Charter for Priestly Formation*[7] is the most pertinent local document for this study. It has particular implications for the practice of pastoral ministry within England and Wales.

All these texts make extensive reference to the theological teaching of

3. *Tertio Millennio Adveniente* (1994) art.21

4. An earlier Synod in 1971 had dealt with: 'The Ministerial Priesthood' and 'Justice in the World'. Although, episcopal reflection on the priesthood was not as developed here as it was twenty years later.

5. This exhortation is usually known as *Pastores Dabo Vobis.*

6. Congregation for the Clergy *Directory on the Ministry and Life of Priests* (London: CTS Publications, 1994) Introduction

7. Approved by the Bishops' Conference of England and Wales at its Low Week meeting in 1990 and by Decree of the Congregation for Catholic Education, 8 January 1991.

the Second Vatican Council. They manifest dependency on each other and often use corresponding language to discuss the same ideas. Therefore, it is proposed that these documents should be dealt with in a thematic, rather than a chronological, manner. The theological material may be considered under the following aspects of presbyteral ministry and life: configuration to Christ, communion with others, and a socio-ecclesial critique of the 'signs of the times'.

3.1 Configuration to Christ

This theme finds expression in the Second Vatican Council's document on presbyteral ministry and life.[8] Configuration to Christ is presented in the post-conciliar documents as the primary aim and means of presbyteral pastoral ministry. This idea is founded upon a sacramental relationship, which configures presbyteral ministers 'to Christ the Head and Shepherd, the Servant and Spouse of the Church.'[9] This is achieved when those who are called to presbyteral ministry are helped 'to know and follow Jesus'.[10] The theme has a particular place in the definition of pastoral ministry in the final two chapters of this investigation. Balthasar defines pastoral ministry as a dynamic activity rather than a passive state. It is the 'act of entering into the Son of God, Christ Jesus'.[11] In the exhortation *I will Give You Shepherds*, configuration is presented as an unchanging feature of all priestly ministry. The priest 'of tomorrow, no less than the priest of today, must resemble Christ'[12] In a later section of the document, John Paul II suggests that 'reference to Christ is thus the absolutely necessary key for understanding the reality of priesthood.'[13]

Presbyteral identity is rooted in the messianic ministry of Christ within a discipleship that forms authentic knowledge and leads to an informed ministry.[14] This is clearly stated in the *Charter for Priestly Formation*: 'The mission of the Church is a continuation of the mission of Christ from the Father.'[15] The same document situates Christ's

8. Cf. *Presbyterorum Ordinis* (1965) article 12
9. *Pastores Dabo Vobis* (1994) art.3
10. Ibid. art.3
11. Balthasar H. *The Glory of the Lord vol. 1: Seeing the Form* (Edinburgh: T. & T. Clark, 1982) p.222
12. *Pastores Dabo Vobis* (1994) art.5 (quotation from Angelus address of 14 January 1990)
13. Ibid. art.12
14. Cf. ibid. art.11
15. Committee for Ministerial Formation *The Charter for Priestly Formation* (The Bishops' Conference of England and Wales, 1990) art.8

messianic ministry within the context of God's kingdom.[16] The evangelical terms of *exousia* and *dynamis* are often associated in New Testament language with the reign of God. However, these terms do not suggest a worldly notion of power or authority. We should never forget that the Kingdom of God is most clearly established and witnessed in the events of the paschal mystery. Participation in this mystery is where the disciple is most distinctly configured to Christ, as 'this fundamental attitude of service and sacrifice must be the model for all who follow Christ, and particularly for those who share his headship of the body which is his Church.'[17] Christian maturity is the personal development of configuration: 'Knowledge, indeed wisdom, is necessary to discover the mind of Christ and to understand how he would show God's love in particular circumstances'.[18] This knowledge is a fruit of faith, as the priest allows his life and ministry to be modelled on that of Christ Jesus. Godfried Danneels, the Archbishop of Malines and Brussels, believes that 'we cannot speak of the priest, nor understand him and make him understood, without placing ourselves directly and without any complication in the register of faith outside of which the priest has no meaning.'[19] This context of faith is totally necessary to understand the meaning of presbyteral ministry. Priests are 'called to prolong the presence of Christ, the One High Priest, embodying his way of life and making him visible in the midst of the flock entrusted to their care.'[20]

In a theological understanding of configuration, as it is developed in the post-conciliar documents, knowledge is authentic only when it produces the action of 'pastoral charity'.[21] This idea is also prefigured in the Second Vatican Council's document on the priesthood.[22] Various Christological models are used to describe this action of love in the ministry of Christ. He is the Shepherd who cares for the Father's flock that is entrusted to him. He is the Bridegroom who lays down his life for his Bride, the Church. This Church is his body, and he is its Head.[23]

16. Ibid. art.9
17. Committee for Ministerial Formation (1990) op.cit. art.27
18. Ibid. art.33
19. Danneels G. *The priest: Sign of the eternal in a culture of consumerism* in eds. McGregor B. and Norris T. *The Formation Journey of the Priest* (Blackrock: The Columba Press, 1994) p.29
20. *Pastores Dabo Vobis* (1992) art.15
21. Ibid. art.21
22. Cf. *Presbyterorum ordinis* (1965) art.14
23. Cf. ibid. art.22

All these different images are used to describe Christ's exercise of pastoral charity. They provide the context for understanding the same action in presbyteral ministry: 'The internal principle, the force which animates and guides the spiritual life of the priest inasmuch as he is configured to Christ the Head and Shepherd, is *pastoral charity*, as a participation in Jesus Christ's own pastoral charity'.[24] Configuration to Christ is the source of pastoral charity. This notion of pastoral charity produces a priestly identity in the life and ministry of the presbyter. The 'identity of the priest comes from the specific participation in the priesthood of Christ, in which the one ordained becomes, in the Church and for the Church, a real, living and faithful image of Christ the Priest'.[25] Through the mystery of Christ, the presbyter is 'inserted' into the Trinitarian mystery and the ecclesial community[26] Thus, a sure theological foundation is made for a priestly identity, which 'has its ultimate source in the charity of the Father.'[27]

In this way, the doctrine of configuration becomes an important safeguard in a pastoral theological consideration of presbyteral ministry. It 'is still necessary to affirm that the mentality and current practice in cultural and socio-political trends of our times cannot be transferred automatically to the Church. The Church, indeed, owes its existence and structure to the salvific plan of God.'[28] A complementary point is made later in the *Directory on the Ministry and Life of Priests*. This document suggests that 'rapid and widespread transformations and a secularized social fabric typical of the contemporary world are what make unavoidable the priest's duty of being adequately prepared, so that he does not lose his own identity and so that he might respond to the demands of the new evangelization.'[29] In this context, configuration provides an important pedagogical basis for presbyteral formation. Secularism is one of the most important 'signs of the times'. The effects of secularism provide the context for a renewed understanding of evangelization. This new understanding of evangelization demands a renewed theological reflection in the enterprise of presbyteral education.

24. Ibid. art.23
25. Congregation for the Clergy (1994) op.cit. p.8
26. Ibid. p.8
27. Ibid. p.9
28. Ibid. p.19
29. Ibid. p.75

Configuration to Christ achieves a renewed priestly identity. John Paul II emphasizes this theological teaching in the Holy Thursday letter to priests after the Synod on the formation of priests.[30] He refers to a 'new maturity'[31] in the interpretation of presbyteral identity and mission: 'This is an expression which indicates how necessary it is that Christ be the starting point for interpreting the reality of the priesthood.'[32] This traditional teaching of the Church is given new impetus and renewal in the work of the Second Vatican Council.[33] The concept of Christocentric configuration to the Father is also developed in the documents of the Council. This doctrine may be more firmly rooted in an ecclesiology that has rediscovered its basis in communion.

3.2 Communion

The theme of communion provides a fundamental hermeneutic for understanding post-conciliar ecclesiology. One commentator suggests that 'by taking this as a leitmotif, the council succeeded in uncovering one of the deepest questions of the time'.[34] This theme represents an important feature in any historical reflection on post-war social developments. Our age is determined by renewed attempts to build human community. The notion of communion, in the theological development of the Second Vatican Council, is a reflection of this desire for genuine community. Indeed, conciliar ecclesiology does not consider ecclesial structures as ultimate in themselves, but as a means to communion. According to Guy-Paul Noujeim, the Maronite Patriarchal Vicar of Sarba-Kesrouan in the Lebanon, the *Catechism of the Catholic Church* understands authentic faith knowledge to be 'the communion of all people with the Father through the Son in the Spirit, rather than a mere accumulation of statements and definitions about the articles of faith.'[35]

The concept of the Church as a communion of disciples is essential for an authentic understanding of the presbyterate. The idea of communion, that 'appears with a certain prominence in the texts of the

30. Cf. John Paul II *Letter of the Holy Father Pope John Paul II to priests for Holy Thursday* (Vatican City: Libreria Editrice Vaticana, 1991)
31. Ibid. p.6
32. Ibid. p.6
33. Ibid. p.8
34. Kasper W. *Theology and Church* (London: SCM, 1989) pp.149-150
35. Noujeim G-P. *Eastern tradition reflected in new catechism's spirituality* in *L'Osservatore Romano* 24 March 1993, p.10

Second Vatican Council, is very suitable for expressing the core of the mystery of the Church, and can certainly be a key for the renewal of Catholic ecclesiology.'[36] It is necessary to recognize the dynamic of theological retrieval at work in this post-conciliar ecclesiology. In the last chapter, the doctrinal potential of collegiality was recognized in the pastoral theological development of an ecclesiology of communion. This was a return to biblical and patristic theological models. Kevin McDonald, an ecumenist and a moral theologian, has reflected on a patristic ecclesiology of communion. He concludes: 'Communion, therefore, is what we are created for; it is the goal of our redemption; it is salvation itself.'[37] Peter Drilling, a teacher of systematic theology at Christ the King Seminary in New York, agrees with this sentiment. He suggests that 'the goal of being human is to achieve communion and conversation with God.'[38] This suggests the central place of this theme within the wider Christian tradition.

John Paul II states that 'the ecclesiology of communion becomes decisive for understanding the identity of the priest, his essential dignity, and his vocation and mission among the People of God and in the world.'[39] This was affirmed at the episcopal synod of 1971. The bishops declared that 'priests will adhere more faithfully to their mission the more they know and show themselves to be faithful to ecclesial communion.'[40] They also stated that 'it is necessary to keep always in mind the special character of the Church's communion in order that personal freedom, in accordance with the recognized duties and charisms of each person, and the unity of life and activity of the People of God may be fittingly combined.'[41] Personal freedom should always be considered within a context of communion ordered towards the unity of the Church. The future John Paul II observed that 'it is this kind of unity that is obtained between diverse members by a communication that tends always to be more profound and abundant.

36. Congregation for the Doctrine of the Faith *Letter to the Bishops of the Catholic Church on some aspects of the Church understood as Communion* (London: Incorporated Catholic Truth Society, 1992) p.3

37. McDonald K. *Communion and Friendship: A Framework for Ecumenical dialogue in Ethics* (Rome: Pontifical University of St. Thomas, 1989) p.29

38. Drilling P. *Trinity and Ministry* (Minneapolis: Fortress Press, 1991) p.25

39. *Pastores Dabo Vobis* (1992) art.12

40. *The Ministerial Priesthood in the Synod of Bishops, 1971.* In National Conference of Catholic Bishops *Norms for Priestly Formation vol.1* (Washington: United States Catholic Conference, 1993) p.309

41. Ibid. p.311

Consequently, plurality, even diversity itself, is to be understood in relation to communion, with the tendency towards unity.'[42]

The Christological context is not negotiable in a theology of communion. This is because the mystery of the Church is essentially related to the mystery of Jesus Christ. As Jesus is sent by the Father, and can do nothing apart from him[43], neither can the presbyter exercise his mission outside of his unity with the Trinity. The priest must be in communion with Jesus in order to assume Christ's mission: 'In the Church and on behalf of the Church, priests are a sacramental representation of Jesus Christ'.[44] Ecclesial mission is succinctly defined in the *Charter for Priestly Formation*: 'Its saving purpose is to bring all people into the communion (*koinonia*) of the loving unity enjoyed within the Trinity.'[45] Indeed, all creation is sustained in communion by a God who exists in a state of 'being in communion'.[46] This theological perspective is a necessary corrective in an understanding of ministry that is still dominated by scholasticism. An Orthodox theologian points to the Christomonistic dangers here, with the 'great difficulties in relating the Church's ministry to that of Christ. Finally, and because of all this, ministry and ordination are not basically approached from the angle of the concrete ecclesial community but of the individual person (his 'ontology' or his 'function').'[47] There are signs of a movement away from this individualism in post-conciliar theological reflection. Drilling, for example, offers this insight: 'ministry's goal is to foster community in the image and likeness of the triune God in the church and in the wider society.'[48]

Accordingly, the basis for an ecclesiological sense of communion is firmly rooted in the relationship between Christ and the Church. The Church's entire pastoral ministry 'intrinsically needs communion with Christ, the Head of his Body.'[49] The specific communion of the presbyteral minister with the Trinity is poignantly addressed as a

42. Cf. de Lubac H. *The Motherhood of the Church* (San Francisco: Ignatius Press, 1982) p.223
43. Cf. John 20:21 and John 15:5
44. *Pastores Dabo Vobis* (1992) art.15
45. Committee for Ministerial Formation (1990) op.cit. art.8
46. Cf. Gaillardetz R. *In Service of Communion: A Trinitarian Foundation for Christian Ministry* in *Worship* vol.67 no.5 September 1993, p.421
47. Zizioulas J. *Being as Communion* (London: DLT, 1985) p.209. John Zizioulas has episcopal pastoral responsibility in Scotland.
48. Drilling P. (1991) op.cit. p.34
49. Congregation for the Clergy (1994) op.cit. p.7

'relationship in an intimate and personal manner, in a dialogue of adoration and of love with the three divine Persons, conscious that he has received the gift for the service of all.'[50] And in a statement of summary significance, 'the communion of the priest is fulfilled above all with the Father, the ultimate origin of all his power; with the Son, in whose redemptive mission he participates; with the Holy Spirit, who gives him the power for living and fulfilling that pastoral charity which qualifies him in a priestly way.'[51] This communion is not gained through human effort: 'It is essential to the Christian understanding of *communion* that it be recognized above all as a gift from God, as a fruit of God's initiative carried out in the paschal mystery.'[52] In an ecclesiology that is open to the Holy Spirit, 'the Church is never an absolute *fait accompli*, an institution. It is always an eschatological reality, a people-in-communion . . . on its pilgrim way to God who is Trinity.'[53]

Everything that is proposed of this Trinito-Christocentric communion is applied to presbyteral relationships with others within the Church: 'The priest's communion-relation with the Church in its aspect of mystery and ecclesial community comes from this fundamental union-communion with Christ and the Trinity.'[54] The Bishops' Conference of England and Wales stated that 'Christ came on earth as one who serves and the early Church was a community of mutual service, intent on spreading the kingdom of God throughout the world.'[55] The distinction between the priesthood of all believers and the ministerial priesthood can only be clearly seen and understood within a context of communion: 'This view of the ministerial priesthood as ordered to the service of the common priesthood of all the baptized is essential in a Church which understands itself as "communion". The early Church's emphasis on its character as a community of love and service is expressed in the notion of "communion".'[56] Any reflection on the post-synodal apostolic exhortation must affirm the communion between the priest and the Church. The presbyteral minister can only be defined and fully understood as a being in relationship.

---

50. Ibid. p.10
51. Ibid. p.22.
52. Congregation for the Doctrine of the Faith (1992) op.cit. p.4
53. Lawler M. and Shanahan T. *The Church is a Graced Communion* in op.cit. p.489
54. Ibid. p.23
55. Committee for Ministerial Formation (1990) op.cit. art.23
56. Ibid. art.30

The ordained ministry is said to have a radical 'communitarian form'[57] and can only be exercised within this framework. Communion is more than a vital means of promoting presbyteral ministry. Indeed, we might claim that the sacramental fraternity of communion defines the ontological root of the presbyteral ministry. It is a communion, not only with the bishop and presbyterate, but also with all the laity. This is because the presbyteral minister's 'role and task within the Church do not replace but promote the baptismal priesthood of the entire people of God, leading it to its full ecclesial realisation . . . Priests are there to serve the faith, hope and charity of the laity.'[58] The priest must live amongst those he is sent to serve in a spirit of radical community. Christ is sent by the Father and presbyteral ministry takes place within a pastoral character of readiness for mission: 'In the exercise of their ministry and the witness of their lives, priests have the duty to form the community entrusted to them as a truly missionary community.'[59] No authentic evangelization can take place outside of 'unity in the communion'.[60]

Communion is not only an expression of 'love for the Lord'[61] which then creates an 'unconditional love for all Christians'.[62] It enables the priest to be a true *pontifex* or 'bridge builder'. In intimate terms, the priest is said to be 'the bridge between man and God, making himself a brother of men who wants to be their pastor, father and master.'[63] The heart of community is a mutual giving and receiving which enables a truly loving solicitude to establish itself. There is also a relationship of communion 'between these and all who, having passed from this world in the grace of the Lord, belong to the heavenly Church . . . This means, among other things, that there is a *mutual relationship* between the pilgrim Church on earth and the heavenly Church in the historico-redemptive mission.'[64]

This loving solicitude becomes a mandate for a universal charity. It is not the intention of the post-conciliar documents to restrict this communion to a narrow framework. The presbyter acts 'in communion

57. Cf. *Pastores Dabo Vobis* (1992) art.17
58. Ibid. art.17
59. Ibid. art.32
60. Congregation for the Clergy (1994) op.cit. p.25
61. Ibid. p.30
62. Ibid. p.30
63. Ibid. p.31
64. Congregation for the Doctrine of the Faith (1992) op.cit. p.7

with the Bishop, with Peter and under Peter... In this way priests, like the Apostles, act as ambassadors of Christ.'[65] The missionary and pastoral mandate is to the whole world. This means that Christian ministry must find new opportunities in a multi-faith society. There is a particular application of communion to the Church's missionary mandate. This is witnessed when there is an 'effective and affective communion, in order to carry out the ever more urgent "new evangelization".'[66] A true understanding of ecclesial communion is an indispensable requirement for genuine evangelization towards non-believers. Marie-Dominique Chenu taught theology in the Dominican House of Studies at Le Saulchoir. He was a particularly influential theologian in the years before the Second Vatican Council. Chenu has grasped the breadth of communion demanded by a post-conciliar ecclesiology. In the Council's texts 'man is not presented primarily in his psychological and moral individuality, but in his congenital commitment to the whole universe, whose energies he is gradually discovering and exploiting.'[67] The post-conciliar texts confirm this essential understanding and promote the importance of authentic communion to the exercise of pastoral care.

3.3 The 'Signs of the Times'

The concept of the 'signs of the times' is not new. This idea has an ancient theological heritage that reaches back to the original proclamation of the Gospel.[68] It is an eschatological theme and is rooted in a scriptural understanding of time as *kairos*. Salvation unfolds 'from age to age'[69] within a dynamic understanding of history. Time has an intrinsic potency that enables its openness to grace and its fulfilment. The 'signs of the times' speak of divine action and human response. The opposite is also true. Time invites a decision that may involve human rejection of revelation in history. This rejection may also be characterized by certain 'signs of the times'.

Historical circumstances necessarily affect presbyteral ministry and

65. *Pastores Dabo Vobis* (1992) art.16
66. John Paul II *Letter of the Holy Father Pope John Paul II to priests for Holy Thursday 1993* (Vatican City: Liberia Editrice Vaticana, 1993) p.6
67. Chenu M-D. *A Council for all Peoples* in ed. Stacpoole A. *Vatican II by those who were there* (London: Geoffrey Chapman, 1986) p.21
68. Cf. Mark 13
69. Cf. Eucharistic Prayer III. Congregation for Divine Worship *The Roman Missal* (Alcester: Goodliffe Neale, 1975) p.498

life. The Council Fathers proclaimed that 'the joy and hope, the grief and anguish of the men of our time'[70] must become the concerns of the ecclesial community of disciples. This reality is firmly acknowledged and explored in the post-conciliar documents which have been considered in this present study. The *Directory on the Ministry and Life of Priests* suggests that 'in the current era of the life of the Church and society, priests are called to live their ministry with depth, anticipating the ever more profound, numerous and sensitive demands not only of a pastoral nature, but also social and cultural, which they must face.'[71] One post-conciliar document begins with the important idea that 'deep cultural and theological changes are among the most conspicuous signs of our time.'[72]

It is important to apply a theological hermeneutic to the theme of the 'signs of the times'. This theological interpretation is indispensable in a changed social situation: 'In such circumstances sound theological doctrine constitutes an indispensable prerequisite both for correctly interpreting the signs of the times and for facing new situations, avoiding on the one hand stagnation and on the other dubious adventures and experiments.'[73] John Paul II names this theological reflection as 'Gospel Discernment'.[74] It is important to emphasize the ambivalent and contradictory nature of social reflection in a pastoral theological context. This is because the contemporary situation contains a 'mixture of difficulties and potentialities, negative elements and reasons for hope, obstacles and alternatives, as in the field mentioned in the Gospel where good seed and weeds are both sown'.[75] The 1971 synod statement has this reflection: 'We should all scrutinize the signs of the times in this age of renewal and interpret them in the light of the Gospel in order that we may work together in distinguishing between spirits, to see if they come from God'.[76]

The Gospel provides the basis for interpreting the historical situation in a community of faith: 'This interpretation is a work which is done in

70. *Gaudium et Spes* (1965) art.1
71. Congregation for the Clergy (1994) op.cit. p.35
72. Congregation for Catholic Education (1976) *The Theological Formation of Future Priests* in National Conference of Catholic Bishops (1993) op.cit. p.63
73. Ibid. p.64
74. *Pastores Dabo Vobis* (1992) art.10
75. Ibid. art.10
76. *The Ministerial Priesthood* (1971) in National Conference of Catholic Bishops (1993) op.cit. vol.1, p.295

the light and strength provided by the true and living Gospel, which is Jesus Christ, and in virtue of the gift of the Holy Spirit.'[77] Gospel discernment does not lead to the indifferent presentation of facts. Rather, it is an understanding of historical events that is freely open to responsibility and decision. This discernment is exercised within a context of trust in the love of Christ as the 'Lord and Master, the Key, the Centre and the Purpose of the whole of man's history.'[78]

Pastoral theology provides a specific role for presbyteral ministers in this discernment. Priests receive the duty 'to interpret these "signs" in the light of faith and subject them to prudent judgment.'[79] It is worth highlighting the two concerns of the *Directory on the Ministry and Life of Priests*. There is the complex phenomenon of the new religious movements, which are often called sects or cults.[80] Pastoral theology recognizes the diverse and complex reasons for their popularity. The *Directory on the Ministry and Life of Priests* also stresses the anonymity of many individuals within contemporary society. It is suggested that one reason for the popularity of these new movements is found in their ability to offer a solution to social isolation. The response to this social phenomenon should be a radical interpretation of ecclesial communion. No one should be treated with indifference: 'This is a responsibility which indeed falls on all the faithful, but in a special way on the priest, who is the man who brings about communion.'[81] Secondly, the document focuses on the manner in which ministry is diminished through a lack of renewal in the spiritual life. This issue is concerned with configuration to Christ. A secular society creates personal burdens for the presbyter: 'Pastoral ministry is a fascinating undertaking, yet arduous, open to misunderstanding and marginalization, and, especially today, to fatigue, challenge, isolation and, at times, solitude.'[82] John Paul II reminds those who are called to share in Christ's priestly ministry, that they are to enter 'in a special way into Christ's paschal mystery'.[83] The Sacred Congregation for Catholic Education believes that 'the very faith of the priests of tomorrow will

77. *Pastores Dabo Vobis* (1992) art.10
78. Ibid. art.10
79. Congregation for the Clergy (1994) op.cit. p.35
80. Cf. ibid. p.37
81. Ibid. p.37
82. Ibid. p.38
83. John Paul II *Letter of the Holy Father Pope John Paul II to priests for Holy Thursday* (Vatican City: Libreria Editrice Vaticana, 1991) p.4

be exposed to greater dangers than before.'[84] These concerns are rooted in a need for the development of authentic communion and configuration to Christ in presbyteral life and ministry. There is a significant relationship between the three themes of this chapter.

Closer attention to the doctrines of configuration to Christ and communion may alleviate some of the crises of presbyteral life and ministry. Three particular problem areas are highlighted in an American document about contemporary existential ecclesiology.[85] There is an issue concerning the relevance of presbyteral ministry. This is supposed to be caused by 'the sudden review of doctrine and discipline occasioned by the Council. This may have left some priests, who are teachers and shepherds of their communities, somehow less secure in their message and with themselves.'[86] Secondly, the document is concerned with 'the 'bitter loneliness,' and even of the 'seeming sterility of the past labours' which priests may sometimes experience.'[87] Finally, there is concern with a problem called presbyteral 'apartness'. The bishops believe that this problem 'may obscure the reality and function of the priesthood' and 'arises from a current temptation of priest and people alike to underestimate the consecration of Holy Orders.'[88] The problem occurs when this consecrated apartness is not fully appreciated.

There are a number of 'signs of the times' which have an enormous impact on the faith life of an ecclesial community. These also affect the practice and reception of presbyteral ministry. A list of hopeful 'signs of the times' is presented in the exhortation *I will Give You Shepherds* and other documents. 'Despite many contradictions, society is increasingly witnessing a powerful thirst for justice and peace'[89] This is often received within ecclesial communities as a need for repentance 'of the acquiescence given, especially in certain centuries, to intolerance and even the use of violence in the service of truth.'[90] There is 'a more lively sense that humanity must care for creation and respect nature, a more open search for truth'.[91] This is developed further in a document from

84. Sacred Congregation for Catholic Education (1976) *The Theological Formation of Future Priests* in National Conference of Catholic Bishops (1993) op.cit. p.64
85. Cf. US Catholic Conference *The Church in Our Day* (London: Catholic Truth Society, 1968)
86. Ibid. p.44
87. Ibid. p.46
88. Ibid. p.48
89. *Pastores Dabo Vobis* (1992) art.6
90. *Tertio Millennio Adveniente* (1994) art.35
91. *Pastores Dabo Vobis* (1992) art.6

the Congregation for Education. The text affirms that 'theology has a "political" function that is original and unique, because it throws light on problems and directs action in man's various occupations, according to the indications and precepts of God's word.'[92]

John Paul II refers to 'a greater effort to safeguard human dignity, a growing commitment in many sectors of the world population to a more specific international solidarity and a new ordering of the world in freedom and justice'.[93] This theme is now presented in the context of the beginning of a new Millennium: 'On the threshold of the new Millennium Christians need to place themselves humbly before the Lord and examine themselves on the responsibility which they too have for the evils of our day. The present age in fact, together with much light, also presents not a few shadows.'[94] There is also the suggestion that 'we are witnessing an extraordinary global acceleration of that quest for freedom which is one of the great dynamics of human history.'[95] Another positive sign is suggested in the context of science: 'Parallel to the continued development of the potential offered by science and technology and the exchange of information and interaction of cultures, there is a new call for ethics, that is, a quest for meaning'.[96] It is worth noting that all these 'signs' transcend political systems, and are beyond a particularly religious culture. Their contribution to the renewal of pastoral ministry is noted and celebrated.

Specific religious signs of optimism are also mentioned. There are new possibilities of evangelization as a consequence of more openness to religious values. There is an increased awareness of the Scriptures. There are signs which suggest the growth of new local churches and the fidelity of other churches in the face of persecution.[97] The *Charter for Priestly Formation* presents a number of further hopeful signs. There is the increased involvement of the lay faithful in the Church's life. There is the development of women's role in ministry. There are fragile signs of an ecumenical dialogue which is leading to increased

---

92. Congregation for Catholic Education (1976) *The Theological Formation of Future Priests* in National Conference of Catholic Bishops (1993) op.cit. p.69
93. *Pastores Dabo Vobis* (1992) art.6
94. *Tertio Millennio Adveniente* (1994) art.36
95. John Paul II *Address to the Fiftieth General Assembly of the United Nations Organization* New York, 5 October, 1995
96. *Pastores Dabo Vobis* (1992) art.6
97. Ibid. art.6

collaboration.[98] The work for unity amongst Christians was recognized in this context in the Council's document on Ecumenism: 'The sacred Council exhorts, therefore, all the Catholic faithful to recognize the signs of the times and to take an active and intelligent part in the work of ecumenism.'[99]

A number of negative 'signs' are mentioned too. On the local level we witness a growing social deprivation[100], with racial prejudice and increased discrimination. There is an economic and environmental decline which affects the elderly and family structures.[101] These local concerns also find expression in the universal documents. There is also the perception of a rationalism that renders human reason insensitive to encounter with revelation. This is seen as a fundamental problem in contemporary pastoral theological documents. Society is said to be 'secular and often indifferent to religious problems and no longer in sympathy with either the faith or the teaching of the Church.'[102] There is a reported development of an individualistic subjectivity that affects the quality of human relationships. There is the growth of consumerism and materialism. These are accompanied by a hostile secular outlook: 'How can we remain silent, for example, about the religious indifference which causes many people today to live as if God did not exist, or to be content with a vague religiosity, incapable of coming to grips with the question of truth and the requirement of consistency?'[103]

There is the growing phenomenon of family break-up and a distortion of the true meaning of sexuality. This is mentioned particularly in the eighteenth article of the *Charter for Priestly Formation.* There is also evidence that 'the fundamental dimension of human existence constituted by the family is under serious threat from various quarters in contemporary society.'[104] There is an increasingly

98. Committee for Ministerial Formation (1990) op.cit. arts.11-15
99. *Unitatis Redintegratio* (1964), art.4
100. Cf. Commissions Justice et Paix d'Europe (1994) *Social Justice for all* and Committee for the World of Work (1995) *A New Community of Work*. Both these documents focus on the need to interpret unemployment and other social phenomena in the light of the Gospel and magisterial teaching.
101. *Pastores Dabo Vobis* (1992) arts.16-17
102. Sacred Congregation for Catholic Education (1976) *The Theological Formation of Future Priests* in National Conference of Catholic Bishops (1993) op.cit. p.65
103. *Tertio Millennio Adveniente* (1994) art.36
104. John Paul II *Letter of the Holy Father Pope John Paul II to priests for Holy Thursday* (Vatican City: Libreria Editrice Vaticana, 1994) p.11

common philosophical environment of a distorted sense of freedom.[105] Human beings are treated as objects to be exploited. This is very much concerned with the immediacy of sensual familiarity. Many people are living in the present, without responsible reference to the past or the future. There is also a demand for gratification and a truly anaesthetised involvement with life.

There are also corresponding problems in the area of religious values. Some of these are rooted within the life of the Church itself. They threaten to seriously undermine the effectivity of pastoral care practice. A particular mention is made of 'the lack of due knowledge of the faith among many believers; a catechesis which has little practical effect, stifled as it is by the mass media whose messages are more widespread and persuasive'.[106] Theological pluralism is considered to be a serious threat to the unity of faith. This unity is indispensable for Christian maturity. Relativism is an unfortunate product of multi-cultural and multi-religious societies, and contributes towards a general subjectivism in matters of faith. There have always been partial and conditional ways of belonging to the Church, and in this present age, an unprecedented acceptance of this challenge to communion.[107]

The bishops of the Second Vatican Council had noted and reflected on some of these 'signs of the times'. It was stated that this generation is 'troubled and perplexed by questions about current trends in the world'.[108] Discussion of the *Pastoral Constitution on the Church in the Modern World* belongs more particularly to the next chapter. Here, it is presented as an important foundation for understanding the 'signs of the times' in this present age. This document states that 'at all times the Church carries the responsibility of reading the signs of the time and of interpreting them in the light of the Gospel, if it is to carry out its task.'[109] This responsibility is advanced beyond recognition and interpretation: 'It is as if theologians must write a new chapter in theological and pastoral epistemology, beginning – methodologically – with the facts and questions of the present day, rather than the ideas and problems of the past.'[110]

105. *Pastores Dabo Vobis* (1992) art.7
106. Ibid. art.7
107. Ibid. art.7
108. *Gaudium et Spes* (1965) art.3
109. Ibid. art.4
110. Congregation for Catholic Education (1976) *The Theological Formation of Future Priests* in National Conference of Catholic Bishops (1993) op.cit. p.76

Certainly, reflection on the 'signs of the times' has many implications for the exercise of pastoral ministry. Nevertheless, there is a need for careful and sensitive analysis of the data.[111] The ambiguity of some of these 'signs', indicates a more fundamental hermeneutical dynamic. Their ambivalence creates problems of methodology which must be dealt with effectively if pastoral theological reflection is to be genuine. Ralph Martin is a lay evangelist who belongs to a charismatic covenant community. He focuses on the acquisition of knowledge as the root of this ambiguity: 'There has been a veritable accelerating explosion of knowledge and technology. It has become commonplace to hear that the overwhelming majority of human knowledge from the beginning of time has been amassed in this century.'[112] He then suggests that 'this very acceleration is itself one of the signs of the times that we need to see as significant.'[113]

The importance of these 'signs of the times' cannot be exaggerated. First of all, they suggest the context in which ecclesial communion must express itself. Secondly, they have a most profound influence upon the attempt to exercise a pastoral ministry that is configured to Christ the High Priest. In many respects, these 'signs' provide a socio-cultural interface with existential ecclesiology. They accommodate the environment in which the mystery of salvation must come to birth in our own time. Their paradox may only be fully appreciated at the end of this investigation. Even the negative 'signs of the times' cannot overwhelm the essential mystery of faith. A later exploration of this mystery implicates the paschal mystery as the Christological paradigm for all pastoral ministry. And on a vast contemporary social canvas, the pastoral mystagogue has a unique opportunity to paint the necessary themes of life-giving redemption.

3.4 Formation for Pastoral Ministry

We have examined recent documents under the themes of configuration to Christ, communion and the 'signs of the times'. There are obvious pedagogical implications in their application to formation for pastoral ministry. Some of these findings have been gathered

---

111. The next chapter of this study deals with the disillusionment experienced in certain circles after the period of post-conciliar renewal.
112. Martin R. *The Catholic Church at the End of An Age* (San Francisco: Ignatius Press, 1994) p.15
113. Ibid. p.15

together in a document that seeks to promote good educational practice.[114] Pastoral studies have much to learn from an integrated reflection on these three theological themes. Above all, there is a need to grow in the practical exercise of a pastoral charity, which is considered to be the fruit of an appropriated theological reflection. This is a particularly pertinent point to make within a wider educational context. The American bishops noted that 'in the 1960s, there was a parallel movement affecting the educational methodology employed in the area of religious education. Religious educators discovered that content was being learned but not appropriated by their students.'[115]

Both the exhortation *I will Give You Shepherds* and *The Charter for Priestly Formation* examine the complex condition of the world today. Their analysis illustrates the 'need to promote a more dynamic and active pedagogy, open to the realities of life and attentive to the process of personal growth, which is ever more differentiated and complex'.[116] There is an implicit reference to the need for Gospel Discernment in a text relating to the function of seminary educators. This must be applied to the particular contemporary pedagogical methodologies which may be used in formation: 'The use of managerial skills, social analysis, and a client-centred approach by pastoral field educators has resulted in pastoral departments rooted in the social sciences rather than in the science of theology.'[117]

It is necessary to exercise a critical appraisal of all formation areas, and particularly pastoral studies. The *Directives* document makes this important point about certain current educational positions: 'These are valid to the extent that they express a pedagogical position rooted in evangelical values and in the ecclesial orientation appropriate to candidates for the priesthood, but they are less fruitful, and even at times a source of disorientation when they do not fully satisfy this condition because of unilateral and questionable methods and contents.'[118] The negative 'signs of the times' have impinged on

---

114. Congregation for Catholic Education *Directives Concerning the Preparation of Seminary Educators* (Rome: Vatican Press, 1993)
115. Bishops' Committee on Priestly Formation *Pastoral Formation and Pastoral Field Education in the Catholic Seminary* (Washington: National Conference of Catholic Bishops, 1985) p.5
116. Congregation for Catholic Education (1993) op.cit. p.6
117. Bishops' Comittee on Priestly Formation (1985) op.cit. p.4
118. Congregation for Catholic Education (1993) op.cit. p.7

pedagogical technique and content in many ways. There is a secularist mentality which does not accept revelation as the basic foundation for theological reflection. Theology must have contact with other scientific disciplines. Although, it must always be remembered 'the two fields of theology and the natural sciences must be kept very distinct, each respecting the autonomy of the other. In fact, they have different ends.'[119]

The social sciences have many interpretations of 'relationship'. However, relationships are not primarily means of personal self-fulfilment in a pastoral theological framework. Rather, relationships must be considered within an understanding of ecclesial communion. Pastoral relationships are ordered towards the care of others and a thirst for their salvation. In this sense, the Johannine paradigm of Christ's encounter with the Samaritan woman at the well of Sychar[120] is a perfect example of thirsting for another's salvation. This is ministry within a framework of pastoral charity. This does not deny the important complementary relationship of theology and the social sciences. However, this relationship needs to be understood within a correct perspective. There is an episcopal acceptance of social scientific pedagogy in the exercise of pastoral ministry.[121]

The doctrine of configuration to Christ confirms the need for all ministerial formation to be rooted in the spirit of the Gospel. The seed which is sown in the field of faith, will bear the fruit of fidelity to the deposit of faith in the Gospel and the Tradition. Furthermore, it will lead to the witness of pastoral charity. In the words of the *Directives*: 'The purpose and goal of formation in the seminary can be understood only in the light of faith.'[122] This important foundation and environment of faith is given even more prominence in the apostolic constitution *Fidei Depositum*:[123] 'The principal task entrusted to the Council by John XXIII was to guard and present better the precious deposit of Christian doctrine in order to make it more accessible to the Christian faithful and to all people of good will.'[124]

119. Congregation for Catholic Education (1976) *The Theological Formation of Future Priests* in National Conference of Catholic Bishops (1993) op.cit. p.75
120. Cf. John 4
121. Bishops' Committee on Priestly Formation (1985) op.cit. p.8
122. Congregation for Education (1993) op.cit. p.13
123. This document, of 11 October 1992, introduces the recently published *Catechism of the Catholic Church*.
124. *Catechism of the Catholic Church* (London: Geoffrey Chapman, 1994) p.2

If the presbyterate is to be exercised within a communion of faith, then there are certain pedagogical implications. Above all, there is the necessity to live and minister within a collaborative framework. Fragmentation and theological pluralism are obvious dangers to authentic ecclesial collaboration. This must be acknowledged from an educational perspective, as 'theological disciplines are now open to new problems, new philosophies, and new contributions of science. In consequence of this, religious questions are becoming ever more complex and subject to different interpretations.'[125] The fundamental problem here is the need for a specific pastoral theological methodology. This issue will be tackled in the final chapters of this present study.

125. Congregation for Catholic Education (1976) *The Theological Formation of Future Priests* in National Conference of Catholic Bishops (1993) op.cit. p.66

CHAPTER FOUR

The Parish and Pastoral Theology

4.0 Introduction

The institution of the parish provides a particularly important environment for pastoral theological concern. The parish also offers a specific focal point for the scrutiny of presbyteral ministry. This chapter will begin with an investigation of relevant canonical definitions. It continues with an investigation of the theme in the ecclesiological documents of the Second Vatican Council, especially the *Pastoral Constitution on the Church in the Modern World*.[1] This will provide an ecclesiological foundation for understanding the parish in contemporary pastoral theology. The bishops of the Second Vatican Council sought to develop (rather than to change) the content of Catholic faith. There was an attempt to find a new way of presenting doctrine within a new socio-cultural context. It is necessary to offer a pastoral sociological critique of the parish as a community. This will enable the creation of a theological symbol in order to discuss contemporary pastoral theological themes. The next three chapters may also be understood within the context of the parish. Chapter five is concerned with the investigation of the liturgical and sacramental ministry of the parish. The sixth chapter will focus on mission and evangelization, and the seventh chapter will examine the 'priesthood of the faithful' and the lay apostolate.

The word *parish* has an ancient lineage. It is derived from the Greek word that meant 'to dwell by, beside or near, or technically to be an alien.' The word is used sixty times in the Septuagint to translate the Hebrew term with the same meaning. One contemporary pastor prefers the more dynamic idea of sojourner: 'It means a people visiting a land or travelling through'.[2] The historical development of the parish institution is not an important concern for this study. However, it is worth noting that the early Christian period involved a variety of

1. Promulgated by the bishops of the Second Vatican Council, on 7 December 1965.
2. Bausch W. *The Christian Parish* (Mystic: Twenty-Third Publications, 1980) p.69

community structures which suited particular sociological contexts. According to one opinion: 'It would appear that the original Christian parish (cf. 1 Peter 2:11; cf. 1:17) was an effort to meet the needs of those who were "strangers and aliens" (Eph. 2:19)'.[3] Certainly, these observations help pastoral theological reflection to maintain a vibrant and visionary model of parish. A contemporary sociological perspective suggests that 'the concept of the parochial unit in ecclesiastical structure and organization would appear to have arisen as a result of the need for delegation of administrative authority and determination of jurisdiction and responsibility which followed the rapid spread of Christianity and the geographical extension of the Church.'[4]

Dependence upon circumstance is a recognized feature of the history of the parish as an institution. Indeed, the earlier and medieval development of the parish reflected the structures of civil society as much as Christian theology. It is not until the Tridentine reforms of the sixteenth century that the parish is fully established as a canonical unit with legal rights and responsibilities. And even then, the institution of the parish was considerably in tune with social patterns until the end of the sixteenth century. The Council of Trent aimed at giving pastoral care a juridical foundation. It is necessary to examine the parish as a legal framework for the exercise of pastoral ministry.

4.1 A Canonical Concept

The Code of Canon Law[5] has this definition: 'A parish is a certain community of Christ's faithful stably established within a particular Church, whose pastoral care, under the authority of the diocesan Bishop, is entrusted to a parish priest as its proper pastor.'[6] Informed by a conciliar understanding, the canonical definition is a useful starting point for our investigation. The themes of the previous two chapters are immediately obvious. There are the notions of ecclesiological communion, a local diocesan church, episcopal oversight, and a presbyteral office that shares in the bishop's ministry. Ecclesial legislation develops the theme more fully. In another canon, the 'proper pastor' of a parish is the parish priest. It is said of him: 'He

3. Lane T. *A Priesthood in Tune* (Dublin: The Columba Press, 1993) p.275
4. Ward C. *Priests and People* (Liverpool: Liverpool University Press, 1965) p.30
5. Promulgated on 25 January 1983, in fulfilment of John XXIII's announcement in 1959 of the Ecumenical Council and revision of the Code of 1917.
6. Code of Canon Law, canon 515

exercises the pastoral care of the community entrusted to him under the authority of the diocesan Bishop, whose ministry of Christ he is called to share'. The Code contains an understanding of pastoral ministry that is totally imbued with the theological teaching of the Second Vatican Council. The parish priest exercises an office, 'so that for this community he may carry out the offices of teaching, sanctifying and ruling with the cooperation of other priests or deacons and with the assistance of lay members of Christ's faithful, in accordance with the law.'[7]

These two canons provide an important pastoral theological understanding of the nature and mission of a parish. Through institutional structures, a community is able to maintain, celebrate and communicate its fundamental values. If ecclesial life is to produce the 'pastoral care' mentioned in both these canons, then recognizable structures must be present. Clearly, the Church's law is based upon an ecclesial model of service and pastoral charity. The Second Vatican Council's understanding of communion is an essential element of this model too, and is central to a properly understood legal concept of the parish as community. The focus on parish as a particular communion of disciples is important. The Gospel can be effectively communicated and lived only in a tangible communion. This may not be the communion offered within the structures of a parish.[8] However, it is true that most Catholic Christians receive their understanding of the Church within a context of parish life. It is within this community, that they are initiated into the Church's life and celebrate the liturgical presentation of Christ's saving presence. Full participation in ecclesial life, and the framework for sharing faith with others, necessarily finds concrete expression in a particular communion of disciples.

Canon 518 provides a geographical basis for the parish institution: 'As a general rule, a parish is to be territorial, that is, it is to embrace all Christ's faithful of a given territory'.[9] In an earlier age, the 'territory' was determined by its financial ability to support clergy and the church building.[10] This economic factor in the formulation of law is an underlying source of concern about the viability of traditional parish

7. Ibid. canon 519
8. This communion may be found in a chaplaincy situation or even within one of the ecclesial movements so prevalent in the Church today.
9. Code of Canon Law, canon 518
10. Cf. Winter M. *Mission or Maintenance* (London: DLT, 1973) p.5

structures. If the parish becomes too large, some would argue, there are serious doubts about its ability to deliver a sense of community and a successful pastoral ministry. Nevertheless, the legal concept of parish is able to flourish, even in a larger structure, if the principles of legitimate diversity, subsidiarity and shared responsibility for ministry, are applied in a creative manner.

4.2 The Parish Within Pastoral Theology

The next task is to explore the theme of parish within an ecclesio-theological context. Article eleven of the *Pastoral Constitution on the Church in the Modern World*, defines the fundamental purpose of this document: 'The people of God believes that it is led by the Spirit of the Lord who fills the whole world. Moved by that faith it tries to discern in the events, the needs, and the longings which it shares with other men of our time, what may be genuine signs of the presence or of the purpose of God.'[11] This is the first time that a Council has defined the mystery and self-understanding of the Church in terms of its relationship with society. Thus, the parish communion of faith is rooted in the society in which it finds itself. Unfortunately, this point is often discussed within a solely sociological perspective. The theological element is largely ignored or undeveloped. However, the *Dogmatic Constitution on the Church* makes an important point about Christ's ministry, which may be applied to the Christian community: 'This kingdom shone out before men in the world, in the works and in the presence of Christ.'[12] In terms of the parish, this suggests an interface between the presence and the activity of the parish and the society in which this community is placed.

The communion of disciples is called to be an influence within society. It is said of the Church: 'In language intelligible to every generation, she should be able to answer the ever recurring questions which men ask about the meaning of this present life and of the life to come'.[13] The influence of society upon the Church is often unacknowledged in ecclesiological reflection before the Second Vatican Council. The Council's *Pastoral Constitution on the Church in the Modern World* invites us 'to speak of a real social and cultural

11. *Gaudium et Spes* (1965) art.11
12. *Lumen Gentium* (1964) art.5
13. *Gaudium et Spes* (1965) art.4

transformation whose repercussions are felt too on the religious level.'[14] Hence, there is the need for a sincere dialogue between Church and society. The bishops in Council declared that 'ours is a new age of history with critical and swift upheavals spreading gradually to all corners of the earth.'[15] Any pastoral theological consideration of the parish must recognize the transient nature of cultural and social values. Furthermore, cultural ideological pluralism creates an instability of faith. It reduces the belief structures of parish life and threatens to overwhelm authentic ecclesiological models. 'The accelerated pace of history'[16], means that society has moved beyond its description, even at the time of the Second Vatican Council. For example, the pastoral constitution makes reference to the 'traditional institutions, laws and modes of thought and emotion' that are not in 'harmony with today's world.'[17] This is increasingly so. John Foster was an American pastor in Maryland. Just before the publication of the pastoral constitution, he wrote: 'To understand and to be understood by the society which it seeks to animate is a task which the modern parish finds increasingly more difficult.'[18] Thirty years later, the truth of this statement is even more immediate.

Despite the reality of social changes, the pastoral constitution is able to state that 'the Church likewise believes that the key, the centre and the purpose of the whole of man's history is to be found in its Lord and Master. She also maintains that beneath all that changes there is much that is unchanging, much that has its ultimate foundation in Christ, who is the same yesterday, and today, and forever.'[19] This theme is common to all the developing schemas which eventually produced this document. It is a Christian anthropological assertion that all human beings are made in the divine image, and that Christ has dominion over all creation. This dominion is part of a salvific plan and should lead to a sincere hope within the ecclesial community. For God has 'constituted Christ as the source of salvation for the whole world.'[20]

The concept of communion is intrinsic to this theological understanding: 'For by his innermost nature man is a social being; and

14. Ibid. art.4
15. Ibid. art.4
16. Ibid. art.5
17. Ibid. art.7
18. Foster J. *Requiem for a Parish* (Westminster: The Newman Press, 1962) pp.29-30
19. *Gaudium et Spes* (1965) art.10
20. *Lumen Gentium* (1964) art.17

if he does not enter into relations with others he can neither live nor develop his gifts.'[21] This theme, which has already been discussed, is presented here as a hermeneutic of Christian anthropology. Disciples of Christ are truly a pilgrim people, who 'united in Christ and guided by the Holy Spirit, press onwards towards the kingdom of the Father'.[22] Communion with the Trinity provides the fundamental interpretation of parish life and mission. Only from within this communion, can parish members discern their ecclesiological mission to be 'bearers of a message of salvation intended for all men.'[23] This is because there is true social communion with all who share creation in God's image and likeness. Furthermore, this is the context for the Second Vatican Council's understanding of atheism in contemporary society: 'The dignity of man rests above all on the fact that he is called to communion with God.'[24] Reflection on this truth leads to the pastoral constitution's understanding of atheism, as 'one of the most serious problems of our time.'[25] It is proposed to investigate the themes of faith and believing, as contemporary cultural phenomena, in chapter six of this study. Nevertheless, the issue needs some analysis here if the parish is to be an ecclesial communion of faith in dialogue with the rest of society.

The pastoral constitution has the following critique of the causes of atheism. First of all, there is a 'critical reaction' against religious belief.[26] Believers themselves can be responsible for this, when they are inadequately catechized, false in their presentation of divine truths, and failing in witness to the Gospel.[27] Individual disciples may contribute towards another reason for atheism and indifference in our society: 'Modern civilization itself, though not of its very nature but because it is too engrossed in the concerns of this world, can often make it harder to approach God.'[28] Furthermore: 'The sense of power which modern technical progress begets in man encourages this outlook.'[29] Finally, political autonomy can seek an atheistic social emancipation: 'It holds

21. *Gaudium et Spes* (1965) art.12
22. Ibid. art.1
23. Ibid. art.1
24. Ibid. art.19
25. Ibid. art.19
26. Ibid. art.19
27. Cf. ibid. art.19
28. Ibid. art.19
29. Ibid. art.20

that religion, of its very nature, thwarts such emancipation by raising man's hopes in a future life, thus both deceiving him and discouraging him from working for a better form of life on earth.'[30]

Within the Christian anthropology that underpins this pastoral constitution, there is a clear concern for social development and the right use of technological advance. There is also the conviction that an authentic Christian catechesis will lead to a wider acceptance of Gospel values. Observance of social obligations are central elements of Christian life: 'Then, under the necessary help of divine grace, there will arise a generation of new men, the molders of a new humanity.'[31] Consideration of this issue is central to understanding the parish's mission. It is important to consider the role of the parish community within a contemporary context, especially as the cultural context for sociological understanding sometimes suggests a violent break with tradition. The parish is an ecclesial communion, which is said to be a 'brotherly communion', in existence to 'render mutual service in the measure of the different gifts bestowed on each.'[32] When this is fully understood and appropriated, the parish is seen by those who belong to it to have an evangelizing purpose in every aspect of social life.[33] The Church is gifted, but must also observe Christ's 'precepts of charity, humility and self-denial', in order to be 'on earth, the seed and the beginning of that kingdom.'[34] Within the parish communion, there is 'a diversity of members and functions.'[35] Often, this diversity of charisms is seen in terms of the internal welfare of the parish structure. Nevertheless, there is an imperative to widen this perspective. Within a theological vision that recognizes the need to minister in a context of solidarity with all of society, pastoral ministry is offered to the whole world 'as the theatre of human history'.[36]

4.3 After the Council's Work of Renewal

The documents of the Second Vatican Council necessarily influence a theological understanding of the parish. The consequence of the

30. Ibid. art.20
31. Ibid. art.30
32. Ibid. art.32
33. Hence the need for the study of lay ministry in the seventh chapter of this present work.
34. *Lumen Gentium* (1964) art.5
35. Ibid. art.7
36. *Gaudium et Spes* (1965) art.2

Council's implicit pastoral theological reflection is a revised agenda for all ecclesial institutions. In many respects there is no such thing as a theology of the parish. There is, of course, a theology of the Church. This ecclesiological reflection on a divinely appointed institution contains human and social elements that are subject to change from age to age. Hence, there is a need for a pastoral sociological element in this study. One contemporary writer has this definition of parish: 'a community of people – including, of course, at least one who is a priest – in a particular locality who find Jesus to be a light, a guide, a power, a strength, an inspiration, who associate with one another in an organized way, and who avail of all means which help them to come to know him more deeply, and to follow him more closely.'[37] There is an obvious Christological focus in this definition, which has appropriated conciliar teaching, and transcends the canonical definition. A parish is about the people who belong to it rather than the structures which might preoccupy so much of their energies. This does not mean that structural elements have no place. However, any structures and activities within the parish communion are there to lead us to Jesus and to understand the meaning of his Gospel.

There is a need to examine the aftermath of the Council, and how conciliar theology changed an understanding of the parish. It is possible to discern three phases of development after the Council.[38] First of all, there was an initial exuberant openness to conciliar teaching. Often, this teaching was reinterpreted and developed in ways that might be described as misrepresentation. Next, there was a time of disappointment. Some expectations remained unfulfilled.[39] This led to a number of crises. There was a dramatic decline in vocations to presbyteral ministry and religious life, with many leaving active ministry. There was a marked decline in church attendance and a widespread breakdown of penitential practice, particularly in the celebration of the Sacrament of Penance. During this time, a number of studies expressed disappointment in the perceived lack of progress in

37. Lyons E. *Partnership in Parish* (Blackrock: The Columba Press, 1987) p.10

38. Cf. Kasper W. *Theology and Church* (London: SCM, 1989) p.166 ff. Ratzinger has a similar three-phase analysis in Ratzinger J. *Principles of Catholic Theology* (San Francisco: Ignatius Press, 1987) p.382ff. His final diagnosis is slightly different to Kasper's. The real problem is the receptivity of conciliar teaching: 'The task is not, therefore, to suppress the Council but to rediscover the real Council and to deepen its true intention in the light of present experience.' (Ratzinger J. (1987) op.cit. p.391)

39. Cf. Kasper W. (1989) op.cit. p.167

a certain direction. Unfortunately, these works contained a number of misrepresentations too. The diagnosis and prescription of these publications is often drastic. Their tone is negative. Examples of such works are Winter's *Mission or Maintenance* and Archer's *The Two Catholic Churches.*

Michael Winter taught in two English seminaries and was involved in a wide range of pastoral ministries. He presents his basic thesis in the introduction to his book: 'If we analyse the demands of the situation, and then examine how the Catholic mission is responding to these exigencies, the disparity between expectation and fulfilment is catastrophic.'[40] Unfortunately, Winter's style is often too sensational. Historically, his reflection is too near the period of post-conciliar renewal, and so there may be unrealistic expectations. Theologically, it has failed to take full account of the social context which underpins the work of the *Pastoral Constitution on the Church in the Modern World.* Winter acknowledges 'the sociological fact that we in England are working in an irreligious environment.'[41] His response to this situation is the establishment of structureless communities, that have thrown off the shackles of medievalism, and 'invite the free assent of faith'.[42] The objectives of these new communities are 'achieving satisfactory worship, witness, apostolate, and charity'.[43] However, it is difficult to appreciate how these might be sincerely achieved in a structureless environment.

This author proposes that 'the parish is of an unworkable size.'[44] In particular, it is too large to enter into effective evangelization, and 'authentic mission (to convert non-believers) will not start again until the parish structure has been superseded by something more dynamic.'[45] Pastoral theological reflection is seen within a narrow context, in 'a world in which the priest or the nun or the committed lay person is hardly ever met.'[46] To the present writer, these sentiments have failed to appropriate the renewed ecclesiological perspective of the Second Vatican Council. Pastoral ministry is confined to the sanctuary, in a way that fails to take account of the dialogue between Christian

40. Winter M. (1973) op.cit. p.1
41. Ibid. p.6
42. Ibid. p.6
43. Ibid. p.37
44. Ibid. p.38
45. Ibid. p.40
46. Ibid. p.40

faith and society. In the words of another commentator, 'in many ways, the mission which a modern industrialized city parish carries out today, is far more perplexing than that of penal times.'[47] If this is true, then parish size is not the real issue. Winter concludes that 'the parish as we know it now is an obstacle to the kind of mission which the Church must exercise in the post-Christian pluralistic societies of the English-speaking nations.'[48] Even within smaller communities, it is possible to witness immaturity of faith, oppressive leadership structures, and an ecclesiological confusion that leads to a contraction of authentic ministry.

Antony Archer was a Dominican friar and a parish priest in Leicester. He also offers a negative critique of post-conciliar changes. There is little in his study that is positive or hopeful. Once again, the fundamental thesis is presented in the Introduction: 'The title is intended to suggest one constant strand in this development: the way the Catholic Church has tended to favour the religion appropriate to the powerful, one kind of church over another.'[49] The evidence for this view is not presented very clearly. It is said of the Second Vatican Council that 'it did not intend to depart from the framework of the ultramontane church'.[50] This is difficult to accept in the context of the ecclesiological renewal presented in the conciliar texts, and reflected upon in the previous chapter of this study. Indeed, the Council was theologically prepared in a number of areas: biblical, liturgical, catechetical and ecumenical. Despite the healthy debate of all opinions, analysis of voting patterns at the Council suggests that the final documents were accepted by most of the bishops.

Archer's book is an assertion that changes inaugurated by the Second Vatican Council led to an alienation of the working classes. At the same time, the author laments the adoption of so-called middle class values. Nevertheless, Archer writes of the working classes that 'in a practical sense these communities had been bound together primarily by the shared values and experiences of working-class life rather than on any specific activity of the church.'[51] It would appear, then, that the anti-institutional polemic of this work is misplaced. There is nothing in our

47. Foster J. (1962) op.cit. p.29
48. Winter M. (1973) op.cit. p.66
49. Archer A. *The Two Catholic Churches* (London: SCM Press, 1986) p.vii
50. Ibid. p.126
51. Ibid. p.128

discussion of conciliar teaching which suggests 'the Council's move towards an intellectual élite'.[52] The disillusionment of this book is based on a parody of conciliar doctrine. For example, 'a theology of a personal encounter with Jesus, for which the model seemed not unlike meeting someone in the street, was derived from the Council's teaching.'[53]

The real issue is the manner in which proposed conciliar doctrine is received in the parish. There is a problem, but it is also possible to suggest a solution. There is a need to recognize the principles which underlie the teaching of the Second Vatican Council.[54] The Council's work is a renewal, based on a new appreciation of primary theological sources. In particular, the Council found new life in biblical and patristic studies. This renewal was not a repudiation of recent tradition, especially the theological developments of the First Vatican Council. Given this theological basis, it is then possible to offer this interpretation of the Council's work. The documents of the Second Vatican Council are meant to be inspired by the pastoral concerns which face the communion of disciples in their lives today.[55] This is seen above all, in the pastoral theological reflections of the *Pastoral Constitution on the Church in the Modern World*. There is a need for time to appropriate a renewal of enormous proportions. This renewal not only concerns the content of the Council's documents, but the manner in which it is being proclaimed.

4.4 A Pastoral Sociological Perspective

The views of writers such as Winter and Archer need to be tested in a sociological analysis of the parish. Blochlinger makes the important suggestion that, until the time of the Second Vatican Council, there had been no thorough pastoral sociological analysis of parish structures.[56] The few studies that have been made in pastoral sociology suggest that the parish community reflects the identity of a wider social community.[57] From a sociological position, social condition

52. Ibid. p.252
53. Ibid. p.253
54. Cf. Kasper W. (1989) op.cit. p.169
55. Cf. ibid., p.171
56. Cf. Blochlinger A. *The Modern Parish Community* (London: Geoffrey Chapman 1965 p.173. As recently as 1984, Hornsby-Smith makes the same assertion: 'A full analysis of the changing parish remains to be written.' Cf. Hornsby-Smith M. *Priests, People and Parishes in Change: Reflections of a Sociologist* in *New Blackfriars* vol.65 no 766 April 1984, p.166)
57. Cf. ibid. p.221

and cultural norms are important perspectives for understanding parish life.

There has been some work in this area. Analysis of Ward's sociological study of a Liverpool parish, about the time of the Second Vatican Council, yields some interesting conclusions. Regular pastoral visitation on the part of the parish clergy is cited as the principal reason for this statement: 'The personal relationship which existed between the priests of the parish and the parishioners was the most important single factor in the social structure of the parish.'[58] Clearly, there is not a dominant ecclesiology of communion: 'The ideal of the territorial parish as the Church in microcosm appeared to be accepted in the abstract by almost all the parishioners, but to have a rather limited impact on the patterns of interaction and behaviour of most of them.' Later, there is a most important observation: 'Loyalty, however, was, so to speak, directed upwards towards the institution itself and not so much in a horizontal direction towards the individuals of whom the parish was composed.'[59] John Hickey wrote about urban Catholicism from within both historical and sociological agendas.[60] Detailed examination of the Church in Cardiff since 1829 suggests a close-knit and independent Catholic community 'with its own institutions, and the Roman Catholic priesthood provided a regular supply of ready-made and acceptable leaders.'[61] Since the end of the Second World War, the process of social integration has gathered pace: 'As an external factor making for isolation, religious hostility to Catholics has declined considerably in importance.'[62] Hickey believes there are a number of reasons for this: a growing indifference towards all religion, the long-established presence of a Catholic hierarchy by the end of the war, social and economic upward mobility, the national bonding brought about by war, and inter-marriage.[63]

The parish is the local actualization of the Church. If this is a theological issue, then it is legitimate to question the role of behavioural sociology in the analysis of parish and ministry. Francis Houtart and Jean Remy are two sociologists who are aware of the

58. Ward C. (1965) op.cit. p.115
59. Ibid. p.115
60. Hickey J. *Urban Catholics* (London: Geoffrey Chapman Ltd., 1967)
61. Ibid. p.157
62. Ibid. p.159
63. Ibid. pp.159-169

problems. However, they declare that 'a given sociological investigation may help to verify a hypothesis that would assist the systematic analysis of de-Christianizing factors in the modern world.'[64] Sociological analysis of the parish and its structures may help to focus on the appropriate questions: 'The result of the sociological diagnosis must be translated into terms of pastoral work, and this may well change the light in which the clergy first saw their problem.'[65] There is the opportunity to create informed opinion and develop the parish as an ecclesial community, as sociological research investigates concrete situations. It is appropriate to highlight the Curia's official recognition of the value of sociological analysis and its place in dialogue with secular authorities. For example, we read in a document concerning the pastoral care of migrants: 'The phenomenon is so widespread, complex and important that it has become a characteristic of our time, demanding of scholars, sociologists, educators and public authorities deeper insight and organized participation and collaboration.'[66]

In England, the work of Michael Hornsby-Smith is the best known study of sociological data concerning the Catholic Church. He writes: 'For Catholics, the teaching of the Second Vatican Council has had a profound influence in changing the dominant emphases and orientations which make up the normatively prescribed belief and value system.'[67] He describes the aftermath of post-conciliar renewal as 'a transitional period, perhaps an adolescent period'.[68] The National Pastoral Congress of 1980 is his chosen date for 'a new open, pluralist, participative, "explorer" model of the Church.'[69] Reflection upon a number of research surveys suggests that there is a 'new' post-conciliar Church: 'In sum, it has been possible to demonstrate wide variations in beliefs and practices among English Catholics.'[70] In other words, there is an empirical reflection of the pluralism and insecurities discerned in

64. Houtart F. and Remy J. *A Survey of Sociology as Applied to Pastoral Work* in *Concilium* vol.3 no.1 *The Pastoral Mission of the Church* (New Jersey: Paulist Press, 1965) p.91
65. Ibid. p.92
66. *Pastoral Care of People on the Move in the Formation of Future Priests* in National Conference of Catholic Bishops (1994) *Norms for Priestly Formation vol.II* Washington: United States Catholic Conference, p.41
67. Hornsby-Smith M. *Roman Catholics in England* (Cambridge: Cambridge university Press, 1987) p.6
68. Ibid. p.22
69. Ibid. p.22
70. Ibid. p.65

the theological analysis of the *Pastoral Constitution on the Church in the Modern World.*

What are the sociological factors which influence the parish? Hornsby-Smith concludes: 'Our data suggest that the effects of social mobility on religious practice and belief are generally slight and not so significant as had originally been anticipated.'[71] This appears to contradict Archer's thesis that the Church has become more bourgeois. And if the Catholic sub-culture of earlier decades has largely disappeared, there are sociological reasons for this phenomenon: 'In the four decades since the Second World War English Catholics have very largely converged both structurally and culturally to the norms of the wider society.'[72] There is an important interaction here between sociological analysis and pastoral theology. Hornsby-Smith argues: 'The current state of paradigmatic change is characterized by both conflict and consensus, continuity and change, and by general processes of accommodation and adaptation on the part of both priests and lay people.'[73] He refers to the work of Winter when he writes about the 'problem of the "greedy" parish which consumes all the available time and energies of its active members'[74], and leaves no resource for mission. Interestingly, mission is understood to be 'the pursuit of social justice through struggles in the wider society to transform unsatisfactory social structures.'[75] To the present writer, this is perhaps an indication of Hornsby-Smith's own agenda, rather than a presentation of the complete nature of ecclesial mission. Hence, there is the need for a fuller investigation of the Church's mission in the sixth chapter of this study, in order to understand pastoral ministry more completely.

On balance, the sociological work of Hornsby-Smith and his research colleagues is considered here to provide an important contribution to an understanding of the contemporary parish. Despite the fact that he must give 'some credence to an interpretation of steady institutional decline'[76], his work leads him to suggest that when 'wider perspective is taken it can reasonably be claimed that there are signs of

71. Ibid. p.88
72. Ibid. p.211
73. Hornsby-Smith M. *The Changing Parish* (London: Routledge, 1989) p.44
74. Ibid. p.89
75. Ibid. p.89
76. Ibid. p.207

new life in the Catholic parishes.'[77] The parish is still the most prominent ecclesial institution for Catholics: 'It is the locus of almost all their community-like endeavours: the gathering place for regular worship, the induction of its new members and frequently for the confirmation of their faith, for much of the social interaction between fellow Catholics, and the source of almost all post-school religious experiences, teaching and moral guidance.'[78] It is 'the major social institution for most Catholics.'[79] And despite the critical voices about parish size and institutions, 'it remains the main focus of contact and often religious identity for the majority of those who retain their Catholic allegiance.'[80]

4.5 Towards a New Understanding of Parish

Pastoral theology must focus on the institution of the parish, because this is still the place where most individuals and groups relate to the local church. Foster recounts the following imaginary conversation: '"I've got the best lot of parishioners you could ask for," one parish priest will say. One might retort: "What have you got them for?" A parish may be a "plum", but plums live a much different kind of existence from salt.'[81] This section is an analysis of contemporary parish renewal, in order that we may discern how parish communities can become 'salt of the earth' and 'light of the world'.[82] The Second Vatican Council was the catalyst for enthusiastic renewal. The years after the Council also precipitated a number of disappointments and crises. Now, it is possible to suggest a movement beyond the acrimonious reviews of certain writers such as Winter and Archer. Hornsby-Smith's post-National Congressional 'new model' has, in many respects, also been superseded.[83] This does not necessarily mean a total revision of the notion of the parish as institution. Before the Second Vatican Council, there were attempts at renewal of pastoral practice in France. This ferment provided a clear impetus to ecclesiological revision during the course of the Council. The ministry of the Abbé Michonneau in

77. Ibid. p.208
78. Ibid. p.5
79. Ibid. p.199
80. Ibid. p.199
81. Foster J. (1962) op.cit. p.7
82. Matt. 5:13-14
83. A fuller account of the National Pastoral Congress is given below.

Paris suggested a parish-based pastoral renewal before the Council began its work. Michonneau was the parish priest in the Parish of *Sacré Coeur de Colombes* in Paris. His insights are gained from an extensive reflection on his pastoral ministry. This work is presented as an example of a growing French intuition of an ecclesiology of communion. In 1934 Congar had produced a challenging essay on the Church's pastoral mission within contemporary society.[84] This was an attempt to apply honesty to the situation. It also illustrates the historical context for Michonneau's reflections.

Ten years before John XXIII announced the inauguration of the Second Vatican Council, the English edition of Michonneau's *Revolution in a City Parish* was published. This is an account of pastoral ministry in a large Parisian suburb.[85] Contemporary pastors and pastoral theologians may find the author's language somewhat aggressive. For example, those who are not fully committed to Christianity are simply called 'pagans'.[86] Active members of the parish are called 'militants'.[87] In answer to the question: 'Do you think that we should do away with Latin and Gregorian chant?' Michonneau responds: 'Never! Latin must remain the liturgical language.'[88] Nevertheless, it is necessary to engage with the dominant pastoral reflections of this work, rather than the occasional myopic observations of the author. Such an engagement suggests that Michonneau's practice of pastoral care demonstrates a theological vision of the parish that is fully realized and endorsed in the ecclesiology of the Second Vatican Council.

First of all, there is an honest recognition of the parochial existential cultural situation. Michonneau writes of many parishioners that 'their mentality is pagan and completely foreign to the Christian spirit, indifferent to our creed and careless of the demands of our moral code.'[89] Theological appropriation does not take place outside this context. Later, he contends: 'In our days religion has vanished from the hearts of our people; they consider it as something outworn, dead.'[90]

84. Cf. Nichols A. *Yves Congar* (London: Geoffrey Chapman, 1989) p.9
85. Michonneau G. *Revolution in a City Parish* (London: Blackfriars, 1949)
86. Eg. ibid. p.1
87. Eg. ibid. p.90
88. Ibid. p.41
89. Ibid. p.1
90. Ibid. p.5

The parish must recognize the true nature of this cultural environment, and have a clear missionary plan. Michonneau establishes the character of a parish within a theology of communion. Thus, 'the parish must cease to be a mere parish milieu; it must become again a community.'[91] Within this ecclesiological understanding, 'everyone must take an active part in the work'.[92] One decade later, the Council affirmed the pastoral theological implications of Michonneau's parish involvement: 'our apostolate must aim, not at organizing those who already are practising Catholics and who go to Mass and the Sacraments, but rather, to penetrate the different milieus with the spirit of Christianity, so that the need for a Christian life will drive them to Christ, who is communicated to us by the Church and the Sacraments.'[93]

This Christocentric focus for pastoral ministry is developed in an understanding of parish liturgical celebration. For 'the parish is a community, and its prayer must be communal.'[94] The liturgy is not a panacea for 'any and every pastoral problem.'[95] Rather, there is a need for evangelization first: 'We do insist, however, that it is foolish to hope to attract them without a long preparation, without a change in their present mentality.'[96] This leads Michonneau to an important conclusion: 'We insist on the necessity of creating and developing a catechumen-directed liturgy which will not supplant our traditional liturgy, but yet which will be useful in evangelizing a people who are woefully ignorant and who learn more from participation than from listening.'[97] Michonneau suggests that if his parish had worked towards the 'establishment of a catechumenate, we certainly should plan it for an age group older than our present catechism class age. Since we mean the training of the catechumenate to result in a life-dedication to the cause of Christ, it is absurd to ask such an outlook from ten- or twelve-year-olds.'[98]

Inevitably, there are consequences for presbyteral ministry: 'A modern priest, more than ever before, should be free to exercise his priesthood to the utmost, and not be bound down to merely temporal

91. Ibid. p.16
92. Ibid. p.16
93. Ibid. p.7
94. Ibid. p.29
95. Ibid. p.46
96. Ibid. p.6
97. Ibid. p.36
98. Ibid. p.114

and material tasks.'[99] Michonneau's understanding is consonant with the Council's *Decree on the Ministry and Life of Priests*. He believes 'that the apostolate demands an interior life capable of developing a priestly spirituality, properly so called.'[100] This is followed by a most important conclusion 'that the apostolate itself is our proper means of sanctification.'[101] He is certain that 'those who agree that the apostolate demands deep spirituality should also see that the apostolate itself can promote and sustain the spiritual life.'[102] These themes are taken up anew, and developed further, in a later publication, *The Missionary Spirit in Parish Life*. In this work, Michonneau declares his theological vision of the presbyterate. He believes 'the priesthood is not something personal to each one of us, but is inconceivable except as a participation in the priesthood of the bishop.' And, 'the 'presbyterium' was originally a team participating in the priesthood of the bishop and giving expression to it by its activity.'[103] This study clearly positions presbyteral life and ministry at the centre of parochial mission. However, even Michonneau's insight does not achieve the developing theological vision of the Second Vatican Council.

Michonneau's portrayals of cultural and ecclesiological data have developed further in two dramatic ways. Analysis of European society suggests that it has become even more resistant to the Gospel during the past fifty years. Secondly, if *The Missionary Spirit in Parish Life* were written today, it would have to take account of the maturation of lay ministry since the Council. This does not denigrate Michonneau's prophetic contribution. Rather, it establishes a context for a current application of pastoral theological principles. Now is the time for earnest reflection on pastoral care and action. This is not 'impatient and hectic activism'[104], but rather a theological contextualisation of 'all the human presuppositions for faith, and the ways of arriving at faith'.[105] In the face of modern atheism and indifference, this will be the fundamental task of every ecclesial communion, and an important focus for the preaching ministry. It is essential to recall at this point, the

99. Ibid. p.73
100. Ibid. p.150
101. Ibid. p.151
102. Ibid. p.154
103. Michonneau G. *The Missionary Spirit in Parish Life* (Cork: Mercier Press, 1952) p.173
104. Kasper W. (1989) op.cit. p.176
105. Ibid. p.176

new agenda for presbyteral ministry outlined in the *Decree on the Ministry and Life of Priests.* The ministry of preaching, which awakens faith and brings it to maturity, is the first priority of the pastoral ministry.[106]

Foster states that 'the contemporary mission of the Church, we are told is, in essence, to form man in his wholeness. The challenge which the Church faces and must accept is one which makes the highest demands on her mystery.'[107] In the documents of the Second Vatican Council, there is a direct correlativity between systematic doctrine and pastoral action. The challenge for contemporary ecclesial communities such as the parish, is to appropriate doctrine in a manner that informs structures, processes and programmes. A parish pastor might feel his task to be keeping alive the rumour that God is still active. This study presents the thesis that this work would be even more effective if the Second Vatican Council's theological understanding provided some resolute management of the endeavour.

Blochlinger's view (dependent upon Rahner) is that 'the parish is not, as has for so long mistakenly been held, a part of the Church; rather, in it the whole Church of Christ works in a limited space.'[108] Existential ecclesiological principles may be applied to the parish, particularly as 'there are no specific statements applying exclusively to the parish'.[109] There may be many differences between one parish community and another. However, a practical and experiential pluralism must be firmly grounded in an informed pastoral theology. And even if this is still unfolding in the post-conciliar period, the shared feature of every parish is its foundation in an ecclesiology of communion. Throughout this chapter, the theme of community has been a prominent, even if sometimes silent feature of theological reflection.

The canonical aspects of the parish can easily reduce this institution to an administrative concept. The parish (and any other ecclesial community) is best understood as a communion of disciples who seek to express the life of the Gospel. Jean Vanier, the founder of l'Arche communities for the mentally handicapped and their helpers, has many

106. Cf. the discussion of this subject in chapter two.
107. Foster J. (1962) op.cit. p.39
108. Blochlinger A. (1965) op.cit. p.viii
109. Ibid. p.150

years of involvement in community. He has written out of a penetrating reflection upon his encounter with community. Through this process he has revised his paradigmatic work *Community and Growth.* The Introduction to a recent edition declares that 'the question for every person and community is how to remain rooted in the soil of one's faith and one's identity, in one's own community, and at the same time to grow and give life to others, and to receive life from them.'[110] The word 'community' is applied here to a very specific notion. Nevertheless, these concepts may be applied to other communion structures including the parish. As Vanier proclaims, 'the message of Jesus invites his disciples to love one another and to live community in a special way.'[111] Belonging to a community of authentic faith means an experience of: openness to vision, the mission of a loving concern for others, communion with others through symbol and celebration, and healing that leads to growth.[112] Vanier makes an important point for ecclesial communities such as the parish: 'A community is not simply a group of people who live together and love each other. It is a place of resurrection, a current of life: one heart, one soul, one spirit. It is people, very different one from another, who love each other and who are all reaching towards the same hope and celebrating the same love.'[113] Here is a positive and hopeful definition, reminiscent of the theology of the Second Vatican Council, and born out of an authentic pastoral ministry.

The ecclesiological doctrine of communion was expressed in the National Pastoral Congress, which took place in Liverpool in 1980. After an extensive period of consultation, over two thousand delegates gathered together 'to explore the implications for the Catholic Church in our country of the renewal introduced by Vatican II.'[114] Some of the recommendations are particularly pertinent to this study. The Pastoral Congress acknowledged that the Council's work still needed to be received in many ecclesial communities. With regard to the parish, the group on the local church stated: 'In order to become a loving, caring, worshipping community, we recommend that parishes should become a communion of Christian communities incorporating small

110. Vanier J. *Community and Growth* (London: DLT, 1989) pp.6-7
111. Ibid. p.11
112. Cf. ibid. pp.18-31
113. Ibid. pp. 57-58
114. O'Shea J. et. al. *Parish Project* (London: Harper Collins Religious, 1992) p.83

neighbourhood, area and special interest groups, including all the lapsed and practising.'[115] On the other hand, it was decided the parish was too small for some initiatives, and that these should be developed within a deanery group of communities.[116] Discussion papers circulated before the Congress, led to a new awareness of the deanery and an emphasis on the community dimension of all structures.[117] The Congress sector on 'the People of God' reported: 'We unanimously affirm that each individual is called by Christ to life in community by his baptism'.[118]

If the parish community is to implement the conciliar spirit, then 'there is a need for the parish to promote itself to its own parishioners and to people outside.'[119] Particular reference was made to ecumenical relationships and activity, solicitude to the Third World and Church in need, and pastoral councils which promote co-responsibility.[120] To a parish community, the Congress offered 'signposts' and directions. This was not a statement of what the pilgrim people already is, but rather of what this people may become.

It is still too early to provide a full assessment of these National Congressional 'signposts'. However, Desmond Ryan's *The Catholic Parish* is a recent attempt to draft a contemporary examination of the parish from a sociological perspective. Ryan is a sociologist from the University of Edinburgh. The fieldwork originated in a need to establish the reasons for falling mass attendance figures in the Archdiocese of Birmingham.[121] The research was broadened with the realization that this problem could not be addressed in an isolated context. Ryan suggests his work is a study of 'the local experience of the Church in the modern world.'[122] After analysis of various aspects of parish life, Ryan determines that 'a thriving parish has a lot going on. It stretches across the landscape of life with activities here, activities there, a horizon dotted with opportunities for fulfilment and service, a

115. Official report of the National Pastoral Congress *Liverpool 1980* (Slough: St Paul Publications, 1981) p.116

116. Eg. right ordering and mission of the local church, media matters, financial matters, sacramental preparation and adult formation. cf. ibid. pp.116-117.

117. Cf. ibid. p.54

118. Ibid. p.130

119. Ibid. p.131

120. Ibid. pp.131-133

121. Cf. Ryan D. *The Catholic Parish* (London: Sheed & Ward, 1996) p.xiii

122. Ibid. p.xiv

community with space for the variety of gifts to be exercised.'[123] This indicates an interesting convergence of sociological observation and theological critique. It leads Ryan to conclude that 'religious energy' ultimately seeks 'communal expression'.[124] The relationship between priest and people is an essential component of this parish community development.[125] There is an accent on the fruitful results of lay involvement and the animating role of presbyteral ministry.[126] The essential focus on the eucharistic liturgy is also acknowledged, 'where the mass ritual once took priority over, even substituted for, the parish community – a fact unequivocally attested to by its liturgy – now the mass *expresses* the parish.'[127] Nevertheless, the potential of this theme is not fully developed. It is clear from the sections on liturgy and sacraments that many respondents did not fully understand the essential nature of the Second Vatican Council's liturgical renewal. In Ryan's own notes, the Rite of Christian Initiation of Adults is understood to be a catechetical exercise more than a liturgical celebration.[128] A true understanding of post-conciliar liturgical reform is essential for an authentic contemporary fertile pastoral theology.

In the post-synodal apostolic exhortation, *On the Church in Africa and its Evangelizing Mission towards the Year 2000*, John Paul II lists the parish as the primary structure of evangelization, for it is the ordinary environment for missionary apostolate and liturgy: 'In it they can express and practise there the initiatives which faith and Christian charity bring to the attention of the community of believers. The parish is the place which manifests the communion of various groups and movements, which find in it spiritual sustenance and material support.'[129] In conclusion, it can be asserted that the parish community will remain an important focus for contemporary pastoral theology. It is the place, above all others, where ecclesial ministry and pastoral care are commonly exercised. It is the ecclesial community where most disciples of Jesus celebrate the Church's liturgy.

123. Ibid. p.185
124. Ibid. p.185
125. Cf. ibid. p.199
126. Cf. ibid. p.150
127. Ibid. p. 44
128. Cf. ibid. p.254. The RCIA is placed by Ryan in the section on adult religious education, cf. ibid. pp.93-96
129. *Ecclesia in Africa* (1995) art.100

CHAPTER FIVE

Liturgical Celebration

5.0 Introduction

This chapter is an investigation of the liturgical renewal which has taken place since the Second Vatican Council. This is an indispensable element of any contemporary pastoral theological reflection. This theme is central to understanding the parish as an ecclesial communion. The analysis of liturgical celebration also deepens an awareness of presbyteral ministry: 'The purpose then for which priests are consecrated by God through the ministry of the bishop is that they should be made sharers in a special way in Christ's priesthood and, by carrying out sacred functions, act as his ministers who through his Spirit continually exercise his priestly function for our benefit in the liturgy.'[1] The first part of this chapter is an investigation of the reasons for liturgical change and development. This will provide the basis for an inquiry into the nature of liturgy. The third part of the chapter will be an investigation into the Rite of Christian Initiation of Adults[2] and the particular theological contribution this has made to contemporary pastoral ministry.

5.1 Contemporary Liturgical Renewal

The Fathers of the Second Vatican Council promulgated the *Constitution on the Sacred Liturgy* on 4 December 1963. The date is significant. Annibale Bugnini[3] notes that the date is exactly four centuries after the bishops at the Council of Trent gave the task of liturgical reform to the Holy See.[4] The Tridentine reforms were essential at the time of the Reformation, primarily because of the role

1. *Presbyterorum ordinis* (1965) art.5
2. Usually known by the abbreviation RCIA
3. Bugnini was secretary of the Commission for liturgical reform in 1948. He held a number of similar positions until he completed his term as secretary of the Congregation for Divine Worship in 1975.
4. Cf. Bugnini A. *The Reform of the Liturgy 1948-1975* (Collegeville: The Liturgical Press, 1990) p.37

of liturgy as a proclamation of doctrinal orthodoxy in a period of ambivalent heterodoxy. Liturgical celebration was an important consideration at Trent, because sacramental celebration is the concrete expression of the Father's saving plan in a Church founded by the Word of God made flesh. Four hundred years later, there was a perceived need for a further liturgical renewal. There was a movement for liturgical renewal in seventeenth century France. This was soon taken up in German-speaking regions during the next century. In 1956, the Congregation of Rites[5] sponsored a Pastoral-Liturgical Congress in Assisi. During this meeting, it was recognized that the movement for liturgical reform had reached worldwide proportions. Josef Jungmann insists that this liturgical movement was essentially a pastoral development in the context of renewal. This was an understandable viewpoint as Jungmann taught liturgical theology at Innsbruck and has been concerned with the implications of liturgical celebration within pastoral ministry.

The schema on liturgy was the first agenda item to be examined by the Fathers of the Second Vatican Council. Bugnini noted the reason for this. His history of the Council mentions the seven drafts of the original schemata. The first four drafts were doctrinal documents and were unacceptable to the Council Fathers. However, the decision to investigate the liturgy first was not simply a choice for the easier option. This document assumed the mantle of conciliar renewal in a way that immediately grabbed the imagination of the Catholic psyche. The Tridentine reform was not rooted in pastoral concern, but rather, in the need to deal with apologetics and right order in faith and practice.

The fundamental reasons for liturgical change and renewal are pastoral in character. The Council Fathers set out 'to adapt more closely to the needs of our age those institutions which are subject to change'.[6] Some elements of the liturgy are unchangeable because they are divinely instituted. However, there are also 'elements subject to change. These latter not only may be changed but ought to be changed with the passage of time, if they have suffered from the intrusion of anything out of harmony with the inner nature of the liturgy or have become less suitable.'[7] The nature of liturgical celebration reflects the

5. Precursor of the Congregation for Divine Worship.
6. *Sacrosanctum Concilium* (1963) art.1
7. Ibid. art.21

nature of theological development. Pastoral theological reflection suggests the need to withstand any attempt to carve expression and ritual in tablets of stone. The Council's liturgical constitution affirms the idea of change: 'Even in the liturgy the Church does not wish to impose a rigid uniformity in matters which do not involve the faith or the good of the whole community.'[8] This liturgical renewal must be accomplished with regard to the tradition: 'Parts which with the passage of time came to be duplicated, or were added with little advantage, are to be omitted. Other parts which suffered loss through accidents of history are to be restored to the vigour they had in the days of the holy Fathers, as may seem useful or necessary.'[9]

These reasons for change do not provide the fundamental purpose of liturgical renewal. Jungmann declares that 'it is above all in the liturgy that the mystery of Christ and the true picture of the Church ensuing from it must encounter the faithful and become for them the life-giving reality.'[10] Liturgy also has an ecclesiological foundation. It is 'through the liturgy, especially, that the faithful are enabled to express in their lives and manifest to others the mystery of Christ and the real nature of the true Church.'[11] As the Council promoted an ecclesiological revision, it was necessary to develop a corresponding liturgical awareness. This was furthered by an ecclesial imagery which is sacramental rather than juridical. Liturgical celebration is an expression of the whole community. It can never be considered an individual's prerogative.

Liturgical renewal was seen by the Council Fathers to be a divine work. It is 'a sign of the providential dispositions of God in our time, and as a movement of the Holy Spirit in his Church.'[12] Liturgy 'consists in the full, active participation of all God's holy people in the same liturgical celebrations' and is 'the principal manifestation of the Church'.[13] Thus, the pastoral theological context of the liturgy is assured. The celebration of the Eucharist, in particular, creates and sustains ecclesial communion. This liturgical celebration of the events

8. Ibid. art.37
9. Ibid. art.50
10. Jungmann J. *Constitution on the Sacred Liturgy* in Vorgrimler H. *Commentary on the Documents of Vatican II vol.1* (London: Burns & Oates, 1967) p.9
11. *Lumen Gentium* (1963) art.2. Cf. too, Vagagini C. *Fundamental ideas of the Constitution* in ed. Baraúna W. (1966) op.cit. p.98
12. *Sacrosanctum Concilium* (1963) art.43
13. Ibid. art.41

of our salvation defines the nature of the Church as the vehicle of divine saving action.

5.2 The Nature of Liturgy

It is essential to understand the nature of liturgy in order to appreciate the pastoral function of liturgy within an ecclesial community. The constitution declares that 'no other action of the Church can equal its efficacy by the same title and to the same degree.'[14] Liturgy is 'the summit toward which the activity of the Church is directed; it is also the fount from which all her power flows.'[15] This echoes the statement in the *Dogmatic Constitution on the Church*, that the Eucharist is the 'source and summit of the Christian life'.[16] James Crichton has reflected upon various aspects of liturgical celebration, within the context of an extensive pastoral ministry. He is convinced that 'the purpose of the Constitution is not just to change rites and texts. Its chief aim is to promote a truly pastoral action, of which the summit and source is the liturgy.'[17] This is why the same author believes that pastors 'should relate their entire pastoral ministry ever more closely to the liturgy.'[18] The discernment of a pastoral dynamic to the liturgical reform of the Second Vatican Council is an indispensable principle for understanding the nature of liturgical celebration. The liturgy is the fruit of evangelization. Before people can 'come to the liturgy they must be called to faith and to conversion.'[19] This faith is celebrated in liturgical activity, especially the Eucharist, so that: 'The renewal in the Eucharist of the covenant between the Lord and man draws the faithful and sets them aflame with Christ's insistent love.'[20] Liturgy is truly the summit towards which ecclesial mission is directed.

This pastoral analysis of the constitution has still not reached the heart of liturgical activity. Liturgy has a central place in the life of the community of disciples. It is necessary to establish the efficacy of

---

14. Ibid. art.7
15. Ibid. art. 10
16. *Lumen Gentium* (1964) art.11
17. Crichton J.D. *Changes in the Liturgy* (London: Geoffrey Chapman, 1965) p.10
18. Ibid. p.3. The same sentiment is expressed elsewhere: 'No other ecclesial action, therefore, is as efficacious as the celebration of the liturgy. The latter is the culmination toward which all evangelizing and pastoral activity are aimed; at the same time it is the source of the supernatural life that nourishes the Church's being and activity.' Bugnini A. (1990) op.cit. p.40
19. *Sacrosanctum Concilium* (1963) art.9
20. Ibid. art.10

liturgical celebration. This will indicate the fundamental nature of liturgical celebration in the Council's document. The basis of the Second Vatican Council's teaching about liturgy lies in an understanding of the paschal mystery.[21] The dying and rising of Christ is not only the foundation of the kerygmatic proclamation in the apostolic ministry. Liturgy is an embodiment of this kerygma so that the work of salvation is made present in the life of the community. Its 'festal character' defines liturgical celebration.[22] Liturgical celebration reminds us that the paschal mystery can only be understood within the 'festal quality' of a communal event.[23]

This consideration of liturgy as the celebration of the paschal mystery determines the true nature of liturgy in the *Constitution on the Sacred Liturgy*.[24] Christian faith that is firmly rooted in the paschal mystery indicates a need to be precise about the meaning of faith. It is also necessary to indicate the intrinsic relationship between faith and the saving events of Christ's dying and rising. Here, a distinction might be drawn between the Church's profession of faith in the Creed, or the *fides quae creditur* and the process of 'believing' in the life of an individual or the community, that is the *fides qua creditur*.[25] This distinction provides the context for understanding the relationship between faith and the paschal mystery. The final act of God's self-revelation is, in Johannine language, an hour of glory. This hour is a Trinitarian action in a soteriological revelatory adventure. This in turn forms the content of objective faith in the believing Church. The community of disciples are those who have come to know the reality of these saving events, and are empowered to live out the dynamism of this saving action in their lives.

Revelation cannot simply be reduced to a series of propositions. It is the unfolding demonstration of God's love in divine action. This is clearly a divine initiative. It is the means by which the community of

21. Cf. Bouyer L. (1965) op.cit. p.12. Also, Jungmann J. *Constitution on the Sacred Liturgy* in ed. Vorgrimler H. (1967) op.cit. p.11. The Paschal Mystery is first discussed in art.5 of the constitution, and then in arts. 6, 61, 106, 107, 109.
22. Cf. Ratzinger J. *Feast of Faith* (San Francisco: Ignatius Press, 1986) p. 62
23. Cf. ibid. p.62
24. Cf. also, *Lumen Gentium* (1964): 'As often as the sacrifice of the cross by which "Christ our Pasch is sacrificed" (1Cor.5:7) is celebrated on the altar, the work of our redemption is carried out.' (art.3); 'Through baptism we are formed in the likeness of Christ: "For in one Spirit we were all baptized into one body" (1Cor.12:13). In this sacred rite fellowship in Christ's death and resurrection is symbolized and is brought about' (art.7)
25. Cf. de Lubac H. *The Christian Faith* (San Francisco: Ignatius Press, 1986) ch.4

faith can claim knowledge of God. Therefore, the norm of liturgical celebration is always divine invitation rather than human need.[26] The Lord reveals his fidelity to the spoken creative word in a series of covenants. This divine fidelity is accomplished by saving acts.[27] The response of the community of faith to this salvation is to enter into liturgical celebration. The event of the Exodus journey is the primary paradigm of how faith is moulded by saving act and its festal celebration. The antithesis also holds true. The people are lost and exposed to death when the community fails to remember the events of divine salvation.[28] Hence, there is the need to focus on the Lord's saving activity in revelation, in order to understand the content of faith and an appropriate response.

In the Christian community, faith is recognition that God has created and called a new people into existence. Through the covenant event of Christ's death and resurrection, he becomes the Head of this renewed people. This is an important statement, for the Church exists through divine action: a people created out of love and called into an experience of salvation through the revelation of Christ.[29] Henri de Lubac discusses this issue further. The Church 'can be considered either as calling all men to herself in order to gather them together in view of their salvation or as being this very gathering of those who have become "believers", the faithful.'[30] The act of belief, then, is a proclamation of what the Christian community has come to experience through the saving works of God. Louis Bouyer understands liturgy to be the embodiment of faith realities. Liturgy serves this divine work of calling a people into being, because 'it makes of all her members those worshippers in Spirit and in truth that the Father was seeking.'[31]

Revelation of the paschal mystery is a work of the Holy Spirit. The response of the community of disciples is faith in the soteriological events of this revelation. However, there is a further element which needs consideration. This might be described as a renewed life-experience, when the believer begins to reflect the revelation received. The Eucharist is a proclamation that the life of sin is dead, and that

26. Cf. Ramshaw E. *Ritual and Pastoral Care* (Philadelphia: Fortress Press, 1987) p.16
27. E.g. 'I cried out to the Lord, and he answered in my distress' (Ps. 4:1)
28. E.g. Deut. 1:26 ff.
29. Cf. Ex. 3:14; John 1:1-18; Heb. 1:1-3; Eph. 1:1-23
30. De Lubac H. (1986) op.cit. p.172
31. Bouyer L. (1965) op.cit. p.7

there is new life given in the dying and rising of Christ. The fundamental assertion of this truth is also found in the sacraments of inititiation. Most ecclesial communities might recognize signs of this new life in their midst. There are also many contradictions of this new life, and examples of the old life of sin. Despite these contrary realities, liturgical celebration is not a false statement. It is the communal proclamation of an eschatological reality, to be truthfully found in the adventure of life as well as revelation and faith. From a subjective perspective, faith is seen as the personal appropriation and celebration of God's love and salvation.

Subjective faith can all too often be viewed from the darkness of human trials, rather than the light of divine revelation. This is another reason for the declaration that liturgy is to be a celebration of the paschal mystery. Liturgy is a celebration of those events, which not only achieve redemption, but give: 'perfect glory to God.'[32] Bouyer rightly states the intention of liturgy as 'our subjective response to God's great gift of grace.'[33] The paschal mystery is itself a liturgical act, in which all liturgy finds its meaning and understanding. This is seen above all, in the Eucharistic *anamnesis*, or act of remembering, of those saving events of Christ's 'blessed passion, resurrection from the dead, and glorious ascension.'[34] The Eucharistic celebration is not a passive memorial of these events. It is a dynamic entrance into the saving realities which are being celebrated. Liturgical action is an eschatological event which looks forward to the day when life-experience will reflect revelation and faith. Jungmann confirms this when he writes of the Council's understanding of the paschal mystery. Liturgical celebration is 'a remembrance of God's redeeming acts of salvation, the presence of salvation and the promise of the consummating future.'[35]

The heart of all this is believing faith in the abiding presence of the Trinity in the Church's liturgy. A theological understanding of *anamnesis* is a powerful vehicle for understanding this presence. The constitution reflects this theology within the context of the paschal mystery: 'To accomplish so great a work Christ is always present in his

32. *Sacrosanctum Concilium* (1963) art.5
33. Bouyer L. (1965) op.cit. p.7
34. Ibid. art.5
35. Jungmann J. *Constitution on the Sacred Liturgy* in ed. Vorgrimler H. (1967) op.cit. p.12

Church, especially in her liturgical celebrations. He is present in the Sacrifice of the Mass not only in the person of his minister, "the same now offering, through the ministry of priests, who formerly offered himself on the cross," but especially in the eucharistic species.'[36] The Eucharist makes the paschal mystery most present to the community of disciples. However, the whole sacramental economy is very much rooted in the events of this Mystery. Faith, in both objective and subjective senses, finds its meaning, purpose and expression in celebration of the paschal mystery.

There are certain consequences of a renewed understanding of the nature of liturgy. Cipriano Vagagini is a Benedictine monk and used to be a Professor of Liturgy at the Roman University of Sant' Anselmo. He appreciates that 'the reform is a result of an increased appreciation for and participation in the liturgy of the Church.'[37] If liturgical celebration of the paschal mystery is a fundamental expression of Christian faith, then involvement is a key issue. If the liturgy is to be lived in the adventure of Christian life, then all must participate in its celebration. Active participation is the directive principle in the Council's work of liturgical renewal.[38] This is a constant theme in contemporary liturgical reflection. Post-conciliar reforms have sought full liturgical participation in the whole eucharistic assembly.[39] Joseph Gelineau is a French liturgist who, like Crichton, has spent many years in pastoral ministry. He believes the post-conciliar liturgical reform to be 'the precursors of much deeper changes in the conduct of Christian assemblies.'[40] These changes suggest the need to focus on conversion, rather than ritual, in a contemporary understanding of liturgical participation.[41]

There are also reasons for this involvement within a revised ecclesiological perspective: 'This union between liturgy and ecclesiology is the direct result of that very sacral, sacramental image of the Church, an image outside of the prevailing juridical tradition, an

---

36. *Sacrosanctum Concilium* (1963) art.7

37. Vagagini C. *Fundamental ideas of the Constitution* in ed. Baraúna W. (1966) op.cit. p.96

38. Cf. Baraúna W. *Active participation, the inspiring and directive principle of the Constitution* in ed. Baraúna W. (1966) op.cit. p.132. Although the movement for active participation was authoritatively endorsed by Pius X in 1903 (cf. Crichton J.D. *Worshipping with Awe and Reverence* in *Priests and People* vol.9 no.12 December 1995)

39. Cf. Piil M. *The local Church as the subject of the action of the Eucharist* in eds. Finn P. and Schellman J. *Shaping English Liturgy* (Washington: The Pastoral Press, 1990) p.174

40. Gelineau J. *The Liturgy Today and Tomorrow* (London: DLT, 1978) p.9

41. Cf. Kavanagh A. *What is participation? – or, participation revisited* in *Doctrine and Life* vol.23 July 1973, p.349

image which has helped so much to discover a more profound understanding of the liturgy.'[42] Unfortunately, this sacramental model of the Church has not always produced authentic liturgical renewal. Chris Walsh observes that a wide gap 'has opened up between description and reality, between ideology and fact.'[43] This reflection is offered after a lengthy period as a teacher of liturgy at Ushaw College. In April 1964, Cardinal Julian Doepfner, the Archbishop of Munich, delivered a sermon about the authentic nature of liturgical renewal. He declared that authentic renewal 'is to realize the power of unifying love in the liturgy, which must be activated in the community and borne out by its members into the world.' The consequences of authentic liturgy extend beyond the worshipping community: 'Otherwise the liturgy is deprived of its essential fruit and no matter how well carried out, will be but "echoing brass, or the clash of cymbals" (I Cor. 13:1), whereas in reality, it is the consecration of the people of God for their mission in the service of their brothers.'[44]

Liturgical renewal is not primarily concerned with revisionary reform. It finds meaning in a total appropriation of the paschal mystery in the lives of all believers. When renewal is a 'reality in the lived experience of the people'[45], then it has fulfilled its true purpose. The real situation is sometimes very different. The lay faithful are often inactive in the liturgical celebration and their passive involvement has little effect on their lives outside the celebration.[46] Brian Wicker was involved in the world of literature as well as theology. He argued for an authentic notion of renewal, in a study published in the same year as the conciliar text on the Church's liturgy. Wicker understood the essential nature of liturgical renewal, by requiring that the whole community of the faithful understand itself within a liturgical tradition perspective. Only then, will this community 'begin to acknowledge its apostolic task of bearing the burden of salvation history for its own epoch, and so presenting to the world the fundamental message of the Gospel.'[47]

In reflective mood, Walsh believes that 'liturgy has been divorced

42. Vagagini C. *Fundamental ideas of the Constitution* in ed. Baraúna W. (1966) op.cit. p.100
43. Walsh C. *Task Unfinished* in ed. Crichton J.D. et.al. *English Catholic Worship* (London: Geoffrey Chapman, 1979) p.139
44. Doepfner J. *The Liturgy and the World* in *Doctrine and Life* vol.14 December 1964, p.599
45. Walsh C. *Task Unfinished* in ed. Crichton J.D. et.al. (1979) op.cit. p.140
46. Cf. Maldonado L. *Liturgy as Communal Enterprise* in ed. Alberigo G. et.al. *The Reception of Vatican II* (Tunbridge Wells: Burns & Oates, 1987) p.312
47. Wicker B. *Culture and Liturgy* (London: Sheed & Ward, 1963) p.187

from service, from witness, from its entire context.'[48] This sentiment is reflected in the words of other liturgists: 'Being rich in rites does not necessarily mean being rich in grace.'[49] And again: 'The liturgy has to enter into their lives and their manner of living, and as long as it remains a reality divorced from their lives and all that they experience in living, it will not become the centre of their lives.'[50] Only when the nature of liturgical celebration is truly understood, can this integrity be found. Thomas Dubay, an American fundamental theologian and retreat director, writes of 'the undue emphasis many people place on the merely human aspects of worship, that is, on the feelings of welcome, warmth, closeness and cordiality, or on the tendency to make a liturgical function something of a theatrical performance rather than a prayerful worship.'[51]

The homily is an important element of liturgical celebration. The homily is 'to be highly esteemed as part of the liturgy itself.'[52] However, the homily is a contentious area of liturgical practice. Crichton has harsh words to say about homilies and homilists: 'Sometimes the sermon is degraded by the triviality of its content and of its treatment. Rarely is it seen to be a part of the liturgy... and in this country it has usually been regarded as "instruction", that is, the unreflecting repetition of the contents of an out-of-date catechism, or a series of moralistic exhortations to get people to do things that the preacher often does not do himself.'[53] One source of this concern may be a misunderstanding of the nature of the homily. It is necessary to focus on the constitution's definition: 'By means of the homily the mysteries of the faith and the guiding principles of the Christian life are expounded from the sacred text during the course of the liturgical year.'[54] The preacher is a 'herald'[55] of the mystery of Christ revealed in the unfolding drama of salvation history.[56] Walter Burghardt is an

48. Walsh C. *Task Unfinished* in ed. Crichton J.D. et.al. (1979) op.cit. p.144
49. Gelineau J. (1978) op.cit. p.23
50. Borello A. *The contextualization of liturgy and especially liturgical texts* in eds. Finn P. and Schellman J. (1990) op.cit. p.301
51. Dubay T. *Faith and Certitude* (San Francisco: Ignatius Press, 1985) p.21
52. *Sacrosanctum Concilium* (1963) art.52
53. Crichton J.D. *The Nature of the Liturgical Homily* in ed. Milner P. *The Ministry of the Word* (London: Burns & Oates, 1967) pp.27-28
54. *Sacrosanctum Concilium* (1963) art.52
55. The New Testament Greek verb associated with the act of preaching is *keryssein*. This is derived from the noun *keryx* meaning 'herald'.

American theologian and expert in the area of pastoral homiletics. He believes that an imaginative homily makes 'God's wonderful works come alive, immerses in the mystery, evokes a religious response.'[57] The appropriate response to this proclamation is a changed life.

The homily is an embodiment of the liturgical nature. It belongs within a community of disciples which is gathered together in liturgical celebration. The scriptures are proclaimed to this community and 'they become the living word of God precisely in the process of proclamation when they become "event", a divine happening, an intervention of God himself in the liturgical assembly.'[58] Owen Edwards is a Benedictine liturgist. He believes that 'congregations, then, are to be *moved* and they are to be moved to *act.* Beliefs that do not have behavioural implications and impetus are not significantly different from unbelief.'[59] The homily is truly part of a liturgical celebration that is the fruit of evangelization and moves the community to mission. It stands at the centre of this movement, without being too firmly identified with the elements of mission. Striving towards a liturgical definition, Burghardt's understanding transcends a purely catechetical notion: 'preaching is prayer, a homily is liturgical prayer, a paean of praise for God's wonderful works among His people, an inspired word that helps others to see Jesus with their own eyes, hear him with their own ears'.[60] Preaching demands a naming of grace that is then proclaimed. This forms the fundamental spirituality of the presbyteral minister.[61] The *General Introduction of the Roman Missal* brings these elements together, in the dialectic focus on revelation and daily life: 'The homilist should keep in mind the mystery that is being celebrated and the needs of the particular community.'[62]

5.3 The Rite of Christian Initiation of Adults

Article sixty-four of the *Constitution on the Sacred Liturgy* is arguably the most radical development of the whole document: 'The

56. Cf. Edwards O. *Elements of Homiletic* (Collegeville: Pueblo Publishing Co., 1982) p.15
57. Cf. Burghardt W. *Preaching: The Art and the Craft* (New York: Paulist Press, 1987) p.23
58. Crichton J.D. *The Nature of the Liturgical Homily* in ed. Milner P. (1967) op.cit., p.29
59. Edwards O. (1987) op.cit. p.12
60. Burghardt W. (1987) op.cit. pp.36-37
61. Cf. Cozzens D. *The Spirituality of the Diocesan Priest* in ed. Goergen D. *Being a Priest Today* (Collegeville: The Liturgical Press, 1992) p.67
62. Congregation for Divine Worship *The Roman Missal* (Alcester: C. Goodliffe Neale Ltd., 1975) p.xxiv

catechumenate for adults, comprising several distinct steps, is to be restored and brought into use at the discretion of the local ordinary. By this means the time of the catechumenate, which is intended as a period of suitable instruction, may be sanctified by sacred rites to be celebrated at successive intervals of time.'[63] This was not the first attempt to restore the ancient catechumenate. The potential of the patristic catechumenate was explored in the preparation of the post-Tridentine *Roman Ritual*.[64] After twenty-five years study of the patristic model, the preparatory commission suggested a revived catechumenate of liturgical rites. Unfortunately, this work was not accepted in the definitive *Roman Ritual* of 1614.[65] Thomas of Jesus was a Carmelite friar in the seventeenth century. He published a number of missiological studies and was clearly influenced by the work of the earlier commission. There is some evidence that a liturgically constituted catechumenate existed as late as 1866 in the Chinese mission of Setschunan.[66]

Jungmann has little to report on the constitution's article sixty-four in his history of the Second Vatican Council's development.[67] He does mention the need for episcopal approval before the adult catechumenate can be used. He also remarks on the 'observation of individual Fathers that the article could be dispensed with'.[68] Fortunately, the majority of the bishops did not accept this. In the years since the Council, the re-introduction of the catechumenate has proved one of the most instrumental focuses for the themes we have investigated in this study of the liturgical aspect of pastoral theology.

In September 1964, the Consilium[69] began work on the RCIA[70] Bugnini reports a discussion which centred on details rather than structure. This relatively unknown liturgical phenomenon had originated in the context of the younger local churches. It was not part of ecclesial life outside of a missionary situation.[71] There were two

63. *Sacrosanctum Concilium* (1963) art.64
64. Cf. Fischer B. *The Rite of Christian Initiation of Adults: Rediscovery and New Beginnings* in *Worship* vol.64 no.2 March 1990, p.99
65. Cf. ibid. p.100
66. Cf. ibid. p.101
67. Cf. Jungmann *Constitution on the Sacred Liturgy* in ed. Vorgrimler H. (1967) op.cit. pp.49-50
68. Ibid. p.49
69. The body entrusted with implementation of the conciliar liturgical reforms.
70. Cf. Bugnini A. (1990) op.cit. p.584
71. Cf. ibid. p.584

fundamental concerns: that the whole idea was an unnecessary anachronism, and that this form of sacramental initiation involved extending the Sacrament of Confirmation to the presbyteral ministry.[72] These concerns were still present when the first text was published in 1972. The past twenty years has witnessed the amelioration of the Consilium's concerns and the maturity of this revised liturgy. Analysis of contemporary social culture has even confirmed the need for rites of scrutiny and exorcism. The development of sacramental theology has restored the intrinsic unity between the sacraments of initiation. The RCIA is born out of a conciliar understanding of sacramental liturgy: 'The Council emphasized the pre-eminence of the proclamation of the Gospel, which should lead through faith to the fulness of the celebration of the sacraments.'[73] This leads to a further consideration: 'Many priests not suffering from a personal identity crisis ask themselves another question: What methods should be used so that sacramental practice may be an expression of faith really affecting the whole of personal and social life, in order that Christian worship should not be wrongly reduced to a mere external ritualism?'[74]

The RCIA is a liturgical text, although, it suggests a broader notion of liturgical rite.[75] This liturgical celebration contains catechetical models of evangelization and catechesis. It strives to involve the whole person. It is celebrated in the ritual of a worshipping assembly. The pastoral dynamic of liturgical celebration is seen most clearly in the restored catechumenate. The Congregation for Divine Worship defines these liturgical events as a process of four 'periods' divided by three 'steps'.[76] These liturgical rites seek the promotion of the divine gift of new life. They also assist the growth of a mature faith. The whole rite is perceived in terms of 'formation' rather than 'instruction'. One criticism of the revised catechumenate concerns its length. However, Michael Mulvihill suggests that the catechumenate 'is meant to be adequate in both length and depth so as to bring about the transformation of persons for and in Catholic ecclesial

72. Cf. ibid. p.586
73. *The Ministerial Priesthood* (1971) in National Conference of Catholic Bishops (1973) *Norms for Priestly Formation vol.1*, p.296
74. Ibid. p.296
75. Cf. Kemp R. *A Journey in Faith* (New York: Sadlier, 1979) p.6
76. Cf. Congregation for Divine Worship (1972) *Rite of Christian Initiation of Adults* London: Geoffrey Chapman, p.4

life.'[77] Mulvihill offers the perspective of a missionary to this debate.[78] He understands that the development and maturity of faith demands a process in time.[79]

This liturgical celebration begins when 'the beginnings of the spiritual life and the fundamentals of Christian teaching have taken root in the candidates.'[80] The purpose of the catechumenate is not only concerned with the teaching of doctrine. It is also meant to lead the catechumens 'to a profound sense of the mystery of salvation in which they desire to participate.'[81] The final period of this formation begins after the sacraments of initiation are celebrated. This is a 'time for deepening the Christian experience, for spiritual growth, and for entering more fully into the life and unity of the community.'[82] This period was called the Mystagogia in the patristic catechumenate. The Rite of Christian Initiation of Adults is a liturgical celebration that can be understood only within a post-conciliar pastoral theological reflection. The Church is constituted as a community of disciples, that exists in unity of life and mission as it shares in the priestly, prophetic and kingly office of Christ.[83] This model of the Church as community of disciples is both a statement of what the Church is, and a profession of faith in what the Church seeks to become. In this respect, the Rite of Christian Initiation of Adults invites the Church to reflect upon the nature of renewal and reform.[84] The pastoral process of this liturgical rite suggests a potential life-changing dynamic.[85] The catechumenate enables us to renew our understanding of sacramental initiation and pastoral ministry.[86] Mulvihill is convinced that 'the entire event of initiation is not about catechumens or the elect alone, but concerns the whole Christian community.'[87]

---

77. Mulvihill M. *The Liturgy of Christian Initiation* in *Liturgy* vol.17 no.1 October-November 1992, p.7
78. Mulvihill teaches liturgy at the Mill Hill Missionary Institute.
79. Cf. also Stack G. *An Outline Catechumenate* in *Liturgy* vol.3 no.2 December 1978-January 1979, p.56
80. Congregation for Divine Worship (1972) op.cit. p.17
81. Ibid. p.37
82. Ibid. p.5
83. Cf. *Lumen Gentium* (1964) art.31
84. Cf. Mick L. RCIA, *Renewing the Church as an Initiating Assembly* (Collegeville: The Liturgical Press, 1989) p.10
85. Cf. Brennan P. *Power In Rite* (Mill Hill: T.Shand Publications, 1986) Introduction
86. Cf. Caroluzza T. *What kind of Pastor does the Catechumenate want* in ed. Wilde J. *Parish Catechumenate: Pastors, Presiders, Preachers* (Chicago: Liturgy Training Publications, 1988) p.10
87. Mulvihill M. *The Liturgy of Christian Initiation* in op.cit. p.5

The Rite of Christian Initiation of Adults is a series of liturgical events that promote a certain ecclesiological definition: 'How a group initiates new members is a clear reflection of how the group understands its purpose and identity.'[88] There is no ambiguity about this identity. The revised catechumenate invites candidates to membership of the ecclesial community and 'a life of service to the world in imitation of their Lord.'[89] The basis of this universal ministry in the Church is found in the *Dogmatic Constitution on the Church*: 'Therefore all in the Church, whether they belong to the hierarchy or are cared for by it, are called to holiness'.[90] This is clearly the purpose of the 'liminal or threshold state' which is a necessary part of any initiation process.[91] Initiation is focused on a community called to holiness. Hence, the fundamental hermeneutic of this ecclesiological model is conversion. The whole community is called to enter into liturgical celebration through conversion. This is an invitation to a radical discipleship. This theme is at the heart of a conciliar ecclesiology. The Second Vatican Council taught that the Lord 'willed to make men holy and save them, not as individuals without any bond or link between them, but rather to make them into a people who might acknowledge him and serve him in holiness.'[92] This holiness is accomplished by conversion and celebrated in liturgical rites within the ecclesial community.

The call to authentic conversion of life is personal but not individualistic. It certainly involves a turning away from sin and a believing in the Good News: 'The RCIA calls us to confront the reality of sin with a robust honesty. We are sinners and we live in a sinful culture.'[93] Nevertheless, the liturgies associated with the elect suggest that this too is an ecclesial event. This practical expression of the paschal mystery is experienced within community. This demands a rigorous attention to the quality of liturgical celebration. Gilbert Ostdiek teaches liturgy at the Catholic Theological Union in Chicago. He is convinced that 'attitudes, values, and ways of acting are subtly nurtured through the liturgy.'[94] This reflects a conciliar understanding

88. Mick L. (1989) op.cit. p.26
89. Ibid. p.31
90. *Lumen Gentium* (1964) art.39
91. Cf. Mick L. (1989) op.cit. p.34
92. *Lumen Gentium* (1964) art.9
93. Mick L. (1989) op.cit. p.73
94. Ostdiek G. *Catechesis for Liturgy* (Washington D.C.: The Pastoral Press, 1986) p.9

of the nature of liturgy. The Church meets with the salvific ministry of Christ in liturgical celebration. Liturgical celebration enables the worshipping community to meet with the Saviour. This encounter enables the community to reflect on the reality of sin and failure. The candidates for initiation 'must have the intention of achieving an intimate knowledge of Christ and his Church, and they are expected particularly to progress in genuine self-knowledge through serious examination of their lives and true repentance.'[95] The rites of exorcism are not only concerned with deliverance. The candidates 'receive new strength in the midst of their spiritual journey and they open their hearts to receive the gifts of the Saviour.'[96] There is a growing testimony to the efficacy of these liturgical exorcisms. Many parish communities have witnessed the tangible presence of the Lord in their liturgical celebrations.

It is clear that the Rite of Christian Initiation of Adults has many implications for post-conciliar pastoral theology. A liturgy that is centred on community involvement demands a renewed pastoral leadership. Thomas Caroluzza has been involved in the catechumenate for many years. He has reflected on the pastoral ministerial needs of the RCIA in the context of a post-conciliar ecclesiology. Caroluzza is convinced that the catechumenate's 'way of reshaping the church will endure and stand the test of time. The catechumenate fosters the gradual unfolding of the mystery of the church lived today, handed on for tomorrow.'[97] The catechumenate is now mandatory in canon law. An adult 'who intends to receive baptism is to be admitted to the catechumenate and, as far as possible, brought through the various stages to sacramental inititiation'.[98]

The catechumenate demands a number of ministries if it is to be effectively implemented. This implies that there is now a canonical foundation for collaborative ministry within a parish context. The revised catechumenate is said to have an 'imaginative impact upon pastoral activities of all kinds.'[99] This suggests that the RCIA can provide a paradigm for post-conciliar pastoral care. The community is

95. Congregation for Divine Worship (1972) op.cit. p.70
96. Ibid. p.70
97. Caroluzza T. *What kind of Pastor does the Catechumenate want?* in ed. Wilde J. (1987) op.cit. p.6
98. Code of Canon Law (1983) canon 851
99. Imbelli R. and Groome T. *Signposts towards a Pastoral Theology* in *Theological Studies* vol.53 no.1 March 1992, p.135

'the matrix from which all pastoral care emerges.'[100] The introductory notes to the various periods and steps of the RCIA provide a theological understanding of the collaborative involvement that is needed in the pastoral exercise of this liturgical rite. The catechumenate is not solely the prerogative of the ordained ministry. Indeed, there are distinct pastoral ministries to be fulfilled by those who are not ordained. Within the community there are particular offices of catechist and sponsor, which call for deeper and committed involvement to ministry. Furthermore, the whole local church is called to ministry and a share in the pastoral care of the catechumens: 'It is desirable that the entire Christian community or some part of it take an active part in the celebration.'[101]

This creates a new climate for presbyteral ministry. The priest is seen in the rite to be a builder of community, and one who must call forth the gifts available within the parish. Robert Hovda, editor of the journal *Living Worship*, believes that 'presiding in liturgy does not exhaust the pastoral role but, rather, it is its climax.'[102] This office of the presbyterate is given much prominence within a context of pastoral ministry. There 'is no single office of servanthood within that community more important as a potential enabler and sustainer of renewal.'[103] It is precisely within the context of the liturgical celebration, that the ministry of presbyterate is given fresh impetus within the community context.

How can the whole community be involved in the catechumenate? All who are gathered together for this liturgy must be personally responsive to the Eucharistic dynamic of gathering, listening and responding. This reflects the Council Father's concern that all should participate in the liturgical celebration. Collaborative co-responsibility is the pastoral response to liturgical participation. Estanislaw Karlic, Archbishop of Paran· in Argentina, believes that 'the paschal mystery made present by the liturgy has the dynamism of the love of God, who has as his aim the salvation of every moment of human life.'[104] All who

100. Duggan R. *Pastoral Care from a Roman Catholic Perspective* in *Concilium* no.5 *Catholic Identity* (London: SCM Press, 1994) p.102
101. Congregation for Divine Worship (1972) op.cit. p.18
102. Hovda R. *What kind of Presider does the Catechumenate want?* in ed. Wilde J. (1987) op.cit. p.20
103. Hovda R. *Strong, Loving and Wise* (Collegeville: The Liturgical Press, 1976) p.vii
104. Karlic E. *Catechism beautifully illustrates the nature of liturgical action* in *L'Osservatore Romano* 28 April 1993, p.9

participate in liturgical action are invited to allow the celebration to suggest forms of pastoral ministry to them. There must be an active response to the liturgical celebration before it can be considered complete.

Focus on the ministries contained in the catechumenate provides an important context for understanding pastoral ministry. This ministry is often understood in terms of power and jurisdiction in a canonical system. Theoretically, this might be divorced from a pastoral context altogether. The RCIA provides an understanding of ecclesial ministry that finds expression only within a community of faith. This reduces the possibility of regarding ministry as a personal possession. The catechumenate enables pastoral ministry to be concerned with mission. Pastoral ministry can be understood only as collegial, co-operative and co-responsible, in an ecclesiology of communion. Hence, there must be a willingness to recognize specific ministries which arise out of the community's need. This is not a denial of the rights of competent authorities to regulate ministry for the good of the whole Church. Pastoral care is 'ultimately about a conversion of heart and mind to Jesus Christ, a conversion that results in a life more committed to God's work and the Church's mission.'[105] This study suggests that the introduction of the RCIA has enhanced these features of pastoral ministry.

It is important to evaluate the theological and liturgical forms of the catechumenate in the context of its development since the Second Vatican Council. The Rite of Christian Initiation of Adults has not always been understood within its liturgical context. There is even the possibility that it may not survive many more years.[106] The liturgical rite has often been distorted and reduced to a catechetical programme. Jorge Estévez, the Bishop of Valparaiso in Chile, suggests that 'we cannot forget that the creed develops around the baptismal liturgy and still has an important place in it today.'[107] Ratzinger develops this point further. He declares that 'the Church's creed has been developed, above all, from the existential context of the catechumenate, and it was in this context that it was promulgated.'[108] This theme is developed even

---

105. Duggan R. *Pastoral Care from a Roman Catholic Perspective* in *Concilium* no.5 *Catholic Identity* (London: SCM Press, 1994) p.104
106. Cf. McHugh T. *The Rite of Christian Initiation of Adults Twenty years on* in ed. Murphy J. *New Beginnings in Ministry* (Blackrock: The Columba Press, 1992) p.89
107. Estévez J. *Catechism highlights centrality of sacraments in Christian life* in op.cit. p.9
108. Ratzinger J. *Principles of Catholic Theology* (San Francisco: Ignatius Press, 1987) p.26

further, with the assertion that 'Christian doctrine arose initially in the context of the catechumenate; only from there can it be renewed . . . the development of a contemporary form of catechumenate is one of the pressing tasks confronting the Church and theology today.'[109] Pastoral practice often suppresses the liturgical dimension of the Rite of Christian Initiation of Adults. The liturgical context is often ignored or drastically reduced. Liturgy can involve the whole community and highlights the fundamental aspect of celebration. There is a lack of authentic catechumenal liturgical processes and an undue promotion of catechetical structures. This can often reduce the meaning of initiation.[110]

This point needs further development. The problem is not a design fault of the Rite of Christian Initiation of Adults. Rather, it is the attempt to use the catechumenate within an ecclesiological model that does not reflect a conciliar theology. Furthermore, the rite cannot succeed if sacramental significance is not unified within a living Christian process.[111] The only authentic understanding of Christian life is provided by involvement in the paschal mystery through conversion. This conversion journey is both personal and communal in a post-conciliar ecclesiology. If a parish community has not been brought to this ecclesiological understanding, then it is not possible to bring others to truly participate in this journey. There is a significant theological move from a pre-conciliar subjective devotionalism towards a contemporary sacramental life that is orientated in the liturgical community. Unfortunately, this understanding of liturgical celebration belongs to theological theory rather than pastoral practice. The problems of the catechumenate are symptomatic of all post-conciliar liturgical renewal. The RCIA is totally dependent upon a received ecclesiology of communion. This demands an analysis of the evangelization which brings about this communion in ecclesial life. The next part of our investigation is concerned with the pastoral theological nature of ecclesial mission.

---

109. Ibid. p.27

110. Cf. Kavanagh A. *What is participation? – or, participation revisited* in op.cit. p.350

111. Cf. Fink P. *The Church as Sacrament and the Sacramental Life of the Church* in ed. Richard L. et.al. *Vatican II The Unfinished Agenda* (New York: Paulist Press, 1987) p.80

CHAPTER SIX

Ecclesial Mission

6.0 Introduction

An investigation of contemporary pastoral theology must involve an examination of mission and evangelization. It is important to be unambiguous about the purpose and extent of this analysis. Before the Second Vatican Council, it was understood that evangelization was concerned with the initial proclamation of the Gospel and the establishment of ecclesial structures where they did not previously exist. Increasingly, there is recognition that mission and evangelization are essential, even in societies where the Church is already established. Since the meeting of CELAM[1] in 1983, this mission has been particularly named as the 'new evangelization'. Hence, this chapter is an extrapolation of conciliar teaching about missionary activity, and its application to parish activity in a local ecclesial community. This chapter is not particularly concerned with a theological consideration of missiology in itself. Rather, it suggests that an authentic understanding of ecclesiology is essentially missionary.

There were two distinct missiological systems before the Second Vatican Council. One system proposed a Christocentric model. This proclaimed a theology of personal evangelization, leading to individual conversion and faith. Another position suggested a more ecclesial-centred model. This emphasized the establishment of hierarchical structures within indigenous ecclesial communities. Conciliar and post-conciliar theological development proposed a synthesis of these two approaches. The means of this marriage is an ever-deepening understanding of evangelization. Paul VI suggests that evangelization includes a personal application and an 'adherence to a programme of life' and 'a new manner of being'. It also has an ecclesial dimension and 'reveals itself concretely by a visible entry into a community of believers.'[2]

1. Meaning, the *General Conference of the Latin American Episcopate.*
2. *Evangelii Nuntiandi* (1975) art.23

6.1 The Nature and Purpose of Mission

The bishops at the Second Vatican Council stated that 'the Church is driven by the Holy Spirit to do her part for the full realization of the plan of God, who has constituted Christ as the source of salvation for the whole world.'[3] The same sentiment is expressed elsewhere. The Council's reflection on social communication contains the assertion that 'the Catholic Church was founded by Christ our Lord to bring salvation to all men.'[4] These declarations not only proclaim the missionary nature of the Church, they also announce the purpose of mission in the historical fulfilment of a divine plan of salvation. Mission is important because it provides a direction to history and gives a purpose to human advancement. Some contemporary missiologists would not support this clear understanding of ecclesial mission. David Bosch, for example, believes that 'mission remains undefinable'.[5] Mission, within a Catholic theological perspective, becomes one of the principal foundation stones of a Christian anthropology. Balthasar believes that mission defines the vocation to be human. It is 'not something general and impersonal like a ready-made coat; it has been designed specifically for him and given into his possession as the most personal of all gifts. By it he becomes, in the fullest sense of the word, a person.'[6]

The Second Vatican Council has investigated 'the Church's pastoral work of salvation'[7] more than any previous council. There are clear missiological implications in the *Dogmatic Constitution on the Church* and the *Pastoral Constitution on the Church in the Modern World*. The specific text concerned with the Church's missionary activity is the *Decree on the Church's Missionary Activity*.[8] The curial department of Propaganda Fide began work on a missionary activity schema some two years before the first session of the Council. Despite the wealth of expertise in the commission preparing this document, it failed to present contemporary missiological evidence in an accurate manner.

3. *Lumen Gentium* (1964) art.17
4. *Inter Mirifica* (1963) art.3
5. Bosch D. *Transforming Mission* (New York: Orbis Books, 1991) p.9
6. Balthasar H. *The Christian State of Life* (San Francisco: Ignatius Press, 1983) p.74
7. Brechter S. *Decree on the Church's Missionary Activity* in ed. Vorgrimler H. (1969) *Commentary on the Documents of Vatican II vol.4* (London: Burns & Oates) p.87
8. Indeed, in the opening sentence of this document there is a deliberate attempt to associate the Decree with *Lumen Gentium*. Most documents of the Second Vatican Council have implications for an understanding of ecclesial mission.

Furthermore, it had not recognized the enormous theological shift that was taking place elsewhere, particularly within ecclesiology. Robert Schreiter teaches doctrinal theology at the Catholic Theological Union in Chicago. He discerns three features of the final approved document which distinguished it from the earlier text. First of all, the document recognizes the origin of mission within the life of the Trinity. Secondly, the text acknowledged the Council's ecclesiological revision. And thirdly, there is a renewed appreciation of other religions.[9]

The missionary decree is meant to be contemporary. It addresses 'the present state of things which gives rise to a new situation for mankind'.[10] This document is rooted within a renewed ecclesiological perspective. It is able to determine authentic principles of practice, and to recognize the need for the involvement of every member of the Church in mission activity. The first chapter of the decree is the most important to a study of contemporary pastoral theology. It resembles a theological treatise and contains more patristic references than any other chapter of the document.[11] These resources of tradition are important. They ensure that socio-cultural considerations are founded upon a coherent theological system.

There was a synodal examination of the relationship between mission and justice in 1971. This was followed three years later by a Synod on Evangelization. The fruit of this synodal investigation was not resolved in a synodal statement. The debate findings were presented to Paul VI. He published the subsequent apostolic exhortation four years later. This was called *Evangelization in the Modern World*. It is an important source text for pastoral theological reflection. This document contains a particular analysis of the means by which evangelization must influence current socio-cultural attitudes. The Church's mission can be fully understood only within the context of the transformation of humanity. On the twenty-fifth anniversary of the Council's *Decree on the Church's Missionary Activity*, John Paul II published an encyclical letter *On the Permanent Validity of the Church's Missionary Mandate*. This points to the future of mission. On the eve of

9. Cf. Schreiter R. *Changes in Roman Catholic Attitudes toward Proselytism and Mission* in eds. Scherer J. and Bevans S. *New Directions in Mission and Evangelization* 2 (New York: Orbis Books, 1994) p.116

10. *Ad Gentes* (1965) art.1

11. Analysis of this lengthy chapter points to the detailed attention to tradition. There are more footnotes in chapter one than any other chapter in the document.

a new Millennium it declares that 'the whole Church is invited to live more intensely the mystery of Christ by gratefully cooperating in the work of salvation.'[12] These three documents together form the theological foundation for an investigation into the theme of mission.[13] The testimony of Avery Dulles is apposite: 'In my judgement the evangelical turn in the ecclesial vision of Popes Paul VI and John Paul II is one of the most surprising and important developments in the Catholic Church since Vatican II.'[14] Dulles is a Professor of Theology at the Catholic University of America in Washington D.C.

The Church is missionary by nature. This statement has a firm foundation within the Trinitarian plan of salvation. Thus, the Church's missionary activity finds its source in the mission of the Trinity. Cardinal Jozef Tomko, Prefect of the Congregation for the Evangelization of Peoples, suggests that this foundational truth relates to divine nature itself. Mission has its ultimate source 'within the Blessed Trinity that extends from within the intimate life of God into the mission of the Son in virtue of the Holy Spirit'.[15] The Father wanted 'to establish a relationship of peace and communion with himself.'[16] He sent his Son 'into the world as the true Mediator between God and men.'[17] The Church continues the mission of Jesus: 'To do this, Christ sent the Holy Spirit from the Father to exercise inwardly his saving influence, and to promote the spread of the Church.'[18] John Paul II reflected upon this conciliar teaching at the beginning of his mission encyclical: 'The Council emphasized the Church's "missionary nature", basing it in a dynamic way on the Trinitarian mission itself.'[19] This Trinitarian understanding provides the necessary motivation for renewal of missionary activity. Furthermore: 'This definitive self-revelation of God is the fundamental reason why the Church is missionary by her very nature.'[20] The consequences of

12. *Redemptoris Missio* (1990) art.92
13. The documents referred to are *Ad Gentes, Evangelii Nuntiandi and Redemptoris Missio*
14. Cf. Martin R. *The Catholic Church and the End of an Age* (San Francisco: Ignatius Press, 1994) p.104
15. Tomko J. *Catechism shows God's salvific will requires Church to be missionary* in *L'Osservatore Romano* 3 March 1993, p.7
16. *Ad Gentes* (1965) art.3
17. Ibid. art.3
18. Ibid. art.4
19. *Redemptoris Missio* (1990) art.1
20. Ibid. art.5. Cf. also: 'Missionary activity is nothing else, and nothing less, than the manifestation of God's plan' (*Ad Gentes* art.9)

the Trinitarian origin of mission are understood and developed by Schreiter. Mission 'is no longer simply a duty incumbent upon Christians, but becomes part of the very nature of being a Christian.'[21]

An authentic understanding of mission is also fundamentally Christological: 'Christ, whom the Father sanctified and sent into the world (cf. John 10:36), said of himself: "The Spirit of the Lord is upon me, because he anointed me; to bring good news to the poor, he sent me to heal the broken hearted, to proclaim to the captive release, and sight to the blind" (Luke 4:8); and on another occasion: "The Son of man has come to seek and to save what was lost" (Luke 9:10).'[22] The mission of Christ creates the ecclesial community and its mission. Authentic missionary activity is born out of a true communion with Jesus Christ. This Christocentric dimension forms a paradigm that is developed further in the two post-conciliar documents. Dulles writes of the two papal authors of these documents: 'For them, as for the kerygmatic theologians, the heart and center of evangelization is the proclamation of God's saving love as shown forth in Jesus Christ. Where the name of Jesus is not spoken, there can be no evangelization in the true sense.'[23]

Paul VI positions Christ's evangelizing activity within the dynamic reign of God: 'Only the Kingdom therefore is absolute, and it makes everything else relative.'[24] The nature of Christ's Kingdom is suggested in the two Gospel texts quoted above. This is developed further in the encyclical letter: 'As the kernel and centre of his Good News, Christ proclaims salvation'.[25] This is clearly defined, on the one hand as 'liberation from sin and the Evil One'[26], and on the other as 'the joy of knowing God and being known by him'.[27] This not only suggests the nature of Christ's mission but also its purpose. There are pastoral reasons for a Christocentric synthesis of missionary activity. This pastoral necessity demands more attention, and needs a further critique of the Christological basis for its fuller understanding.

There is a further elaboration of the Christological symbol in John

21. Schreiter R. *Changes in Roman Catholic Attitudes toward Proselytism and Mission* in eds. Scherer J. and Bevans S. op.cit. pp. 116-117
22. *Ad Gentes* (1965) art.3
23. Cf. Martin R. (1994) op.cit. p.104
24. *Evangelii Nuntiandi* (1975) art.8
25. Ibid. art.9
26. Ibid. art.9
27. Ibid. art.9

Paul II's encyclical. In an age of inter-religious dialogue and focus on human development, it is essential not only to affirm the salvation offered by Christ, but also his unique role as Saviour: 'If we go back to the beginnings of the Church, we find a clear affirmation that Christ is the one Saviour of all, the only one able to reveal God and lead to God.'[28] The salvation offered by Christ is universal. It is able to bring about a fundamental change in every human life: 'The urgency of missionary activity derives from the radical newness of life brought by Christ and lived by his followers.'[29] In this sense, Christian mission does not proclaim a relativistic Gospel, but a Kingdom that makes absolute claims upon all human beings. The Kingdom cannot be conceptualized, or reduced to programmatic proportions. It is 'before all else a person with the face and name of Jesus of Nazareth, the image of the invisible God.'[30] The process of secularization has led some contemporary thinkers to a nihilist position. This fruit of post-Enlightenment secularism can be interpreted as a negative reaction to the centrality of the person of Christ in the Christian tradition.[31] Within a post-modernist view of society, without teleological purpose or historical focus, missionary activity is currently in a state of crisis. There may be many methods for the renewal of ecclesial evangelizing purpose. However, it is essential that this issue is addressed with a firm focus on the person of Christ.

This Christological focus is crucial for an authentic understanding of ecclesial mission. The Church believes that Christ is the centre and meaning of human history, and his very personhood defines the way in which the Church enters into relationship with him. Jesus' mission radically defines his personality. His obedience to the Father's will actually gives meaning to his identity. An authentic encounter with this mystery of the person of Jesus leads to a response of wonder and awe. It can be boldly proclaimed that ecclesial mission is born and sustained out of a faith-filled encounter with the person of Jesus Christ.

What about those who have never had the Gospel proclaimed to them, or belong to other religious traditions? An ancient patristic formulation declared *extra ecclesiam nulla salus*.[32] For centuries, this

28. *Redemptoris Missio* (1990) art.5
29. Ibid. art.7
30. Ibid. art.18
31. Cf. Scola A. *The event of Jesus Christ today* in *Communio* vol.xxi, no.4, Winter 1994, p.569ff.
32. Meaning, 'outside the Church there is no salvation'.

statement provided fuel for missionary endeavour. It is possible to argue about the boundaries of the Church and to suggest an ever-widening and more inclusive circle. However, there is still a sense in which humanity is divided into those who are 'inside' the circle and those, at least theoretically, who are 'outside' of it. The *Dogmatic Constitution on the Church* speaks of 'the Church as the universal sacrament of salvation'.[33] This ecclesiological development has revealed new perspectives. However, it has not changed the fundamental reality. John Paul II writes of those of good will who have not come to explicit Christian faith, and yet may still find salvation: 'This grace comes from Christ; it is the result of his Sacrifice and is communicated by the Holy Spirit.'[34] Later, he states: 'To the question, "why mission?", we reply with the Church's faith and experience that true liberation consists in opening oneself to the love of Christ.'[35] Dulles confirms that 'the Council repeatedly and emphatically taught that the procurement of salvation is the most important task of the Church. Far from doing away with the ancient doctrine that salvation is given only to those united to the Church, Vatican II reasserted this doctrine.'[36] With reference to the Council's constitution on the Church and the missionary decree, Dulles writes: 'In all these passages there is no minimizing of explicit faith and adherence to the Church.'[37] In the *Declaration on the Relation of the Church to Non-Christian Religions*, the Council Fathers declared that the Church 'rejects nothing of what is true and holy' in other religions, but then declared: 'Yet she proclaims and is in duty bound to proclaim without fail, Christ who is the way, the truth and the life (John 1:6). In him, in whom God reconciled all things to himself (2 Cor. 5:18-19), men find the fulness of their religious life.'[38] This doctrine is affirmed in the Catechism of the Catholic Church: 'Because she believes in God's universal plan of salvation, the Church must be missionary.'[39]

The nature and purpose of mission cannot be understood outside of this Christological context. Missionary activity is an extension of the

33. *Lumen Gentium* (1964) art.48
34. *Redemptoris Missio* (1990) art.10
35. Ibid. art.11
36. Dulles A. *Vatican II and the Church's purpose* in *Theology Digest* vol.32 no.4 Winter 1985, p.345
37. Ibid. p.347
38. *Nostra Aetate* (1965) art.2
39. *Catechism of the Catholic Church* (1994) art.851

divine plan of salvation. It is a continuation of the evangelizing ministry of Jesus Christ, who is the message as well as the messenger. Schreiter describes the decade after the Council as 'the period of the missionary crisis'.[40] The Council had caused a ferment of doubt and confusion by admitting that salvation is not restricted to those who believe in Christ Jesus. Johannes Schutte, the Superior General of the Divine Word Missionaries, provided the theological means for resolving this dilemma. Schutte proposed three Christological resolutions to the problem: the eschatological fulfilment, offered in the 'fullness' of Christ; the realization of the Incarnation through every cultural expression; and the striving for peace and reconciliation, which expresses Christ's dominion over creation and prepares for his Second Coming.[41] Leslie Newbigin was a bishop in the ecumenical Church of South India. This humble man ended his days as the pastor of a small West Indian fellowship in the inner city of Birmingham. His non-Catholic perspective also makes some pertinent points in this area. It is possible to introduce the idea of inclusivity, which suggests that all those of 'good will' would find salvation in Christ. Newbigin believes that 'this scheme is vulnerable at many points. The devout adherent of another religion will rightly say that to call him or her an anonymous Christian is to fail to take the other faith seriously... Its most serious weakness, however, is one shared in some degree by the other views we have examined: it assumes that our position as Christians entitles us to know and declare what is God's final judgment upon other people.'[42] Mission, then, has its source and fulfilment in God. Now, it is necessary to examine the place of the Church in all of this.

The missionary decree of the Council builds upon the *Dogmatic Constitution on the Church*, in recognizing the establishment of the Church as the purpose of Christ's missionary activity. It states that 'the Lord, who had received all power in heaven and on earth (cf. Matt. 28:18), founded his Church as the sacrament of salvation'.[43] This teaching is affirmed in post-conciliar papal encyclicals. Paul VI declares that 'the Church is born of the evangelizing activity of Jesus and the Twelve. She is the normal, desired, most immediate and most visible

40. Cf. Schreiter *Changes in Roman Catholic Attitudes toward Proselytism and Mission* in eds. Scherer J. and Bevans S. op.cit. p.120

41. Cf. ibid. p.121

42. Newbigin L. *The Open Secret* (London: SPCK, 1995) pp.172-173

43. *Ad Gentes* (1965) art.5

fruit of this activity'[44] John Paul II confirms this in his statement that 'the first beneficiary of salvation is the Church. Christ won the Church for himself at the price of his own blood'.[45] The bishops at the Second Vatican Council decreed that the Church acts 'in obedience to Christ's command', and in response to his missionary mandate, when 'the Church makes itself fully present to all men and peoples in order to lead them to the faith, freedom and peace of Christ'.[46] The purpose of this missionary activity is 'the evangelization and the implanting of the Church among peoples or groups in which it has not yet taken root.'[47] There is the clear assertion that 'the principal instrument in this work of implanting the Church is the preaching of the Gospel of Jesus Christ.'[48] This teaching represents the amalgamation of the two missionary perspectives discussed in the introduction to this chapter.

As individuals become disciples of the Lord, so they are impelled to 'gather together in Jesus' name in order to seek together the Kingdom, build it up and live it.'[49] This becomes the nature and purpose of the Church. If the Church is 'the community of believers, the community of hope lived and communicated, the community of brotherly love'[50], then there is a need for constant openness to the radical demands of the Kingdom. However, John Paul II warns that 'the Kingdom cannot be detached either from Christ or from the Church.'[51] This is because the intrinsic nature of the Kingdom 'is one of communion among all human beings – with one another and with God.'[52] This brings together the fundamental themes of mission. The 'insertion of missiology into ecclesiology, and the integration of both areas into the Trinitarian plan of salvation, have given fresh impetus to missionary activity'[53]

44. *Evangelii Nuntiandi* (1975) art.15
45. *Redemptoris Missio* (1990) art.9
46. *Ad Gentes* (1965) art.5
47. Ibid. art.6
48. Ibid. art.6
49. *Evangelii Nuntiandi* (1975) art.13
50. Ibid. art.15
51. *Missio Redemptoris* (1990) art.18
52. Ibid. art. 15. cf. also: 'The disciples are to live in unity with one another, remaining in the Father and the Son, so that the world may know and believe' (ibid. art.23) and: 'One of the eternal purposes of mission is to bring people together in hearing the Gospel, in fraternal communion, in prayer and in the Eucharist.' (ibid. art. 26)
53. Ibid. art.32

6.2 The Means of Mission

A contemporary understanding of the nature and purpose of mission leads us to reflect upon the question of how this mission can be accomplished. This section is concerned with evangelization as the principal means of fulfilling the missionary mandate. In the action of evangelization, the Church discovers 'her deepest identity. She exists in order to evangelize, that is to say in order to preach and teach, to be the channel of the gift of grace.'[54] Carlo Martini, the Archbishop of Milan, acknowledges that evangelization is the primary responsibility of the Church.[55] The documents propose two kinds of activity. First of all, there is an evangelization that is directed towards individuals, 'transforming humanity from within and making it new'.[56] It is an 'adherence to the Kingdom', which 'reveals itself concretely by a visible entry into a community of believers.'[57] This can be accomplished only by conversion of life.[58] Secondly, there is the evangelization of societies and cultures, 'bringing the Good News into all strata of humanity'.[59] This means allowing the Gospel message to affect 'mankind's criteria of judgment, determining values, points of interest, lines of thought, sources of inspiration and models of life, which are in contrast with the Word of God and the plan of salvation.'[60] Thus, both individuals and whole societies are recipients of evangelization. This integrated holistic picture must be complete in an authentic understanding of evangelization.

The bishops at the Second Vatican Council declared that all 'ought to be converted to Christ, who is known through the preaching of the Church, and they ought, by baptism, to become incorporated into him, and into the Church which is his body.'[61] This statement provides the instrument for understanding the place of evangelization as the primary means of undertaking the missionary imperative. There can never be true evangelization, without 'a clear and unequivocal proclamation of the Lord Jesus.'[62] This means a communication of 'the

54. *Evangelii Nuntiandi* (1975) art.14
55. Cf. Martini C. *Catechism responds to desire and needs of Church today* in *L'Osservatore Romano* 31 March 1993, p.9
56. *Evangelii Nuntiandi* (1975) art.18
57. Ibid. art.23
58. Cf. *Redemptoris Missio* (1990) arts. 46-47
59. *Evangelii Nuntiandi* (1975) art.18
60. Ibid. art.19
61. *Ad Gentes* (1965) art.7
62. *Evangelii Nuntiandi* (1975) art.22

name, the teaching, the life, the promises, the Kingdom and the mystery of Jesus of Nazareth'.[63] It was necessary for Paul VI to strengthen the Christocentric focus for evangelization, in 'this time of uncertainty and confusion'.[64]

Furthermore, this focus on Christ ensures that faith is understood primarily as a relationship with the Lord, rather than intellectual knowledge of formulated truths. John Paul II affirms this in his declaration that 'salvation consists in believing and accepting the mystery of the Father and of his love, made manifest and freely given in Jesus through the Spirit.'[65] Both Paul VI and John Paul II develop the Council's fundamentally Christological understanding of mission. The Christological symbol of the incarnation is considered to be the model of all authentic ecclesial mission.[66] Sometimes, the incarnation is reduced to a social concept of inculturation. However, it must be understood here in its more profound Catholic sense of the 'analogy of being'. This means that there is a direct ontological continuity between the world and its Creator. This reality is also acknowledged in some non-Catholic definitions of evangelization. Bosch, for example, suggests that 'evangelism is the proclamation of salvation in Christ to those who do not believe in him, calling them to repentance and conversion, announcing forgiveness of sin, and inviting them to become living members of Christ's earthly community and to begin a life of service to others in the power of the Holy Spirit.'[67]

The mission documents also make suggestions about the process of evangelization. The most important means is found in the quality of Christian life lived out by believers. Paul VI suggests that 'modern man listens more willingly to witnesses than to teachers, and if he does listen to teachers, it is because they are witnesses.'[68] It is by the quality of 'her living witness of fidelity to the Lord Jesus'[69], that the Church gives this witness. The seeds of this sentiment are to be found in the Council's document: 'All Christians, by the example of their lives and the witness of the word, wherever they live, have an obligation to

63. Ibid. art.22
64. Ibid. art.1
65. *Redemptoris Missio* (1990) art.12
66. Cf. Richard L. *Mission and Inculturation: The Church in the World* in ed. Richard L. et.al. *Vatican II The Unfinished Agenda* (New York: Paulist Press, 1987) p.108
67. Bosch D. (1991) op.cit. pp.10-11
68. *Evangelii Nuntiandi* (1975) art.41
69. Ibid. art.41

manifest the new man which they put on in baptism, and to reveal the power of the Holy Spirit by whom they were strengthened at confirmation, so that others, seeing their good works, might glorify the Father.'[70] By rooting evangelical witness in the sacraments of inititiation, every single Christian disciple is invited to become involved in missionary evangelization.

Articles eleven and twelve of the *Decree on the Church's Missionary Activity* provide some examples of how the community of believers can witness to the Gospel in love. These have been summarized by John Paul II. He believes that 'the evangelical witness which the world finds most appealing is that of concern for people, and of charity towards the poor, the weak and those who suffer.'[71] This involvement in pastoral care, and its source in Christian initiation, will be developed more thoroughly in chapter seven. In many respects, the ministry of charity may be described as the teleological purpose of evangelization. However, this cannot be accomplished apart from the full preaching of the Gospel: 'Proclamation is the permanent priority of mission.'[72] Only when individuals accept the mystery of Christ, and enter into relationship with him, will they 'satisfy all their inner hopes'.[73] Paul VI defines this relationship, not as 'an immanent salvation', but as communion with the 'divine Absolute: a transcendent and eschatological salvation, which indeed has its beginning in this life but which is fulfilled in eternity.'[74] The Church considers 'her contribution to liberation is incomplete if she neglects to proclaim salvation in Jesus Christ.'[75]

It is important to examine the place of human development in the process of evangelization. Witness to the Kingdom cannot be effective, if evangelization is not concerned with 'justice, liberation, development and peace in the world. This would be to forget the lesson which comes to us from the Gospel concerning love of our neighbour who is suffering and in need.'[76] Paul VI insisted on the need to include the struggle for justice and peace in an understanding of ecclesial

70. *Ad Gentes* (1965) art.11
71. *Evangelii Nuntiandi* (1975) art.42
72. *Redemptoris Missio* (1990) art.44
73. *Ad Gentes* (1965) art.13
74. *Evangelii Nuntiandi* (1975) art.27
75. Ibid. art.34
76. Ibid. art.31

evangelization.[77] In other words, it is not possible to offer evangelization in the name of Jesus Christ, without attention to those who are marginalized and alienated. However, this commitment to the work of development must be situated within a theological tradition that contains an eschatological understanding of redemption.[78] John Paul II situates the Church's concern for justice within the vision of the Gospel Beatitudes: 'In fidelity to the spirit of the Beatitudes, the Church is called to be on the side of those who are poor and oppressed in any way.'[79] When the Church bears witness to this agenda, then Christ is manifested to all peoples.

Evangelization is an ecclesial activity. It is directed towards the whole of human life, and involves every aspect of human existence. In this sense, evangelization is the supreme means of mission, and can only be sincerely enacted within the community of faith. The work of evangelization makes that community credible, as the Church desires conversion of life and the human condition.[80] As conversion begins to take place, then there is a period of evangelization 'which involves a progressive change of outlook and morals' and 'should be manifested in its social implications'.[81] Although these words of the Council Fathers were directed towards the catechumenate, it is clear that the work of evangelization is never actually completed in the community of believers. The work of evangelization concerns pastoral ministry to the whole community of disciples.[82]

In a post-conciliar pastoral theological reflection, evangelization is clearly an activity within established churches. Some examples of its recipients are listed in *Evangelization in the Modern World*: those who live in a secularized culture, those who have received sacramental inititiation, but have not been brought to faith, those who have faith without knowledge of the truths, those who need to develop this knowledge beyond that given them in their childhood.[83] This activity is

77. Cf. Johnstone B. *The European Synod: The Meaning and Strategy of Evangelization* in *Gregorianum* vol.73 no.3 1992, p.471
78. Cf. McGregor B. *Commentary on Evangelii Nuntiandi* in ed. Flannery A. (1977) op.cit. p.73
79. *Redemptoris Missio* (1990) art.60
80. Cf. Mette N. *Evangelization and the Credibility of the Church* in *Concilium* no.114, (New York: The Seabury Press) p.54
81. *Ad Gentes* (1965) art.13
82. Cf. Dhavamony M. *Evangelization and Dialogue in Vatican II and in the 1974 Synod* in ed. Latourelle R. *Vatican II Assessment and Perspectives* (New York: Paulist Press, 1989) p.268
83. Cf. *Evangelii Nuntiandi* (1975) art.52

named as evangelization rather than catechesis. In the context of a believing community, evangelization stands against the secularist and atheistic forces, which rob catechesis of its ability to 'deepen, consolidate, nourish and make ever more mature the faith'[84] of believers. John Paul II acknowledges this need too. He believes that 'the boundaries between pastoral care of the faithful, new evangelization and specific missionary activity are not clearly definable, and it is unthinkable to create barriers between them or to put them into water-tight compartments.'[85]

6.3 The Ministry of Mission and Evangelization

The missionary decree of the Second Vatican Council suggests that 'various types of ministry are necessary for the implanting and growth of the Christian community.'[86] Elsewhere, the communications media are considered a particularly important means of evangelization. Every member of the Church 'should make a concerted effort to ensure that the means of communication are put at the service of the multiple forms of the apostolate'.[87] Within a study of pastoral theology, it is particularly appropriate to investigate the ministerial elements that are concerned with mission in the Church. Besides the witness of ordained and committed religious ministry, the missionary document also refers to the important testimony of the lay faithful.[88] Article seventeen mentions the work of catechists and the need for their formation. Conciliar debate suggests that their ministry be understood within the narrow context of fewer clergy. There is a systematic development of lay ministry in the post-conciliar documents.

The dependency of this decree upon the *Dogmatic Constitution on the Church*, is shown in its insistence that the whole Church is missionary. The work of evangelization is 'the fundamental task of the People of God'.[89] And, for this reason, Paul VI states that 'evangelization is for no one an individual and isolated act; it is one that is deeply ecclesial.'[90] John Paul II declares that 'without witnesses there can be no witness,

84. Ibid. art.54
85. *Redemptoris Missio* (1990) art.34
86. *Ad Gentes* (1965) art.15
86. *Inter Mirifica* (1963) art.13
88. Cf. *Ad Gentes* (1965) art.15
89. Ibid. art.35
90. *Evangelii Nuntiandi* (1975) art.60

just as without missionaries there can be no missionary activity.'[91] This does not mean that every Christian has the same task to perform.[92] An important role is given to all those who exercise presbyteral ministry: 'They are educators of the People of God in the faith and preachers, while at the same time being ministers of the Eucharist and of the other Sacraments.'[93] Indeed, the evangelizing proclamation of the Gospel is said to give an identity to all presbyteral service, and to provide the 'distinct character on our activities'.[94]

The specific task of the laity is to evangelize 'politics, society and economics, but also the world of culture, of the sciences and the arts, of international life, of the mass media.'[95] Dulles writes of this task: 'Only if the Church is faithful to its evangelical mission can it hope to make its distinctive contribution in the social, political, and cultural spheres.'[96] Alongside these professional areas, there are more fundamentally personal and human situations, such as family life, love and suffering. Most areas of human activity and life can only be evangelized by the efforts of the lay faithful.[97] Walter Hollenweger is the former Professor of Mission at the University of Birmingham. He describes this evangelizing activity, as the 'establishment of organizational and social forms which are on the way to the humanization of man revealed by the Gospel.'[98] In all of this, authentic missionary evangelization will always point to the transcendent potential within every human event.[99] O'Meara's understanding of ministry is most appropriate within a context of ecclesial mission. He believes that ministry is 'doing something; for the advent of the kingdom; in public; on behalf of a Christian community; which is a gift received in faith, baptism and ordination; and which is an activity with its own limits and identity within a diversity of ministerial actions.'[100]

---

91. *Redemptoris Missio* (1990) art.61
92. Cf. *Evangelii Nuntiandi* (1975) art.66
93. Ibid. art.68
94. Ibid. art.68
95. Ibid. art.70
96. Cf. Martin R. (1994) op.cit. pp.104-105
97. Cf. McGregor B. *Commentary on Evangelii Nuntiandi* in ed. Flannery A. (1977) op.cit. p.54
98. Hollenweger W. *The Aims of Evangelization* in *Concilium* no.114, (New York: The Seabury Press) p.41
99. Cf. *Evangelii Nuntiandi* (1975) art.70
100. O'Meara T. *Theology of Ministry* (New York: Paulist Press, 1983) p.136

6.4 Within a Secular City

This pastoral theological reflection must be applied to the parish community. In order for this to be effective, theological reflection must be contextualized within the negative effects of the secularized society. The post-conciliar *Pastoral Instruction on the Means of Social Communication* gives expression to this. Through the 'work of the communications media, Christians are better able to understand the state of contemporary world society, a society which is frequently alienated from God.'[101] This does not suggest that socio-cultural expressions are, of themselves, in conflict with the values of the Kingdom of God. On the contrary, 'whatever goodness is found in the minds and hearts of men, or in the particular customs and cultures of peoples, far from being lost is purified, is raised to a higher level and reaches its perfection, for the glory of God.'[102] The Second Vatican Council called for a positive appreciation of culture and the different cultural manifestations of ecclesial life.[103] All forms of religion, even the most transcendental, are influenced by cultural factors.[104] Ecclesial mission, through the operative means of evangelization, enables culture to attain its doxological purpose.

The Council's missionary document does not directly address the problems of secularization. This is because the text is directed primarily at those regions of the world which have never heard the Gospel message. A conciliar analysis of this issue is given some critique in the *Pastoral Constitution on the Church in the Modern World.* The bishops of the Second Vatican Council point to the 'accelerated pace of history'[105] as the fundamental cause for spiritual upheaval. Society is becoming more enigmatic, as scientific and technological change mean 'that many of our contemporaries are prevented by this complex situation from recognizing permanent values'.[106] Industrialization and urbanization, without personal development, are also seen as causes for concern. Human beings are described as 'the meeting point of many conflicting forces.'[107] There is a confusion of purpose and meaning, which leads to

101. *Communio et Progressio* (1971) art.97
102. *Ad Gentes* (1965) art.9
103. Cf. Komonchak J. *The Local Realization of the Church* in ed. Alberigo G. *The Reception of Vatican II* (Tunbridge Wells: Burns & Oates, 1987) p.79
104. Cf. Starkloff C. *Inculturation and Cultural Systems* in *Theological Studies* vol.55 no.1 March 1994, p.75
105. *Gaudium et Spes* (1965) art.5
106. Ibid. art.4
107. Ibid. art.10

an unstable foundation for the work of evangelization. These are the fundamental topics that constitute the conciliar theme of secularization.

There was certainly an awareness of contemporary secularism in the Council's debate. There are no suggestions in conciliar documents that secularism is to be applauded. Harvey Cox is a Baptist Minister who was Professor of Divinity at Harvard. In *The Secular City* Cox considered that 'secularization and urbanization do not represent sinister curses to be escaped, but epochal opportunities to be embraced.'[108] Others are of the same opinion. Bernard Häring taught moral theology in a number of Catholic universities in Rome and Germany. He was also involved in an extensive pastoral ministry. He believes that 'secularization may be seen in the future as one of the most beneficial events in the history of salvation.'[109] Cox is the original proponent of the idea that secularization can be used positively in theological reflection. He betrays his hand in the statement that 'pluralism and tolerance are the children of secularization.'[110] Wittingly, or otherwise, he demonstrates the authentic nature of secularization. It is difficult to understand how this phenomenon can provide a comfortable environment for a life of faith: 'The forces of secularization have no serious interest in persecuting religion. Secularization simply bypasses and undercuts religion and goes on to other things.'[111] Christianity 'will become even more peripheral, and that means we can now let go and immerse ourselves in the new world of the secular city.'[112] Urbanization is understood to mean 'a structure of common life in which the diversity and the disintegration of tradition are paramount.'[113] Finally, faith issues are reduced to footnotes in a social scientific setting: 'The reason speaking about God in the secular city is in part a sociological problem is that all words, including the word God, emerge from a particular sociocultural setting.'[114]

Secularization can never provide a correct understanding of Christian anthropology. There can be no autonomous history which is outside the unfolding drama of salvation history.[115] Acceptance of

108. Cox H. *The Secular City* (Middlesex: Penguin Books, 1968) p.11
109. Häring B. *Sin in the Secular Age* (Slough: St Paul Publications, 1974) p.4
110. Cox H. (1968) op.cit. p.17
111. Ibid. p.16
112. Ibid. p.18
113. Ibid. p.18
114. Ibid. p.253
115. Cf. O'Grady C. *The Secular City* in *Doctrine and Life* vol.20 July 1970, p.357

secularization as a legitimate theological model is certainly not universal. John Habgood was the Archbishop of York. He asks if it is 'possible to reap the benefits of modernization without its attendant disadvantage, secularization?'[116] Secularism has found firm and steady growth in the past few centuries. Habgood suggests that this is not a modern phenomenon. It is 'an age-old cosmological type, a product of definable social experience, which need have nothing to do with urban life or modern science.'[117] This is an important statement in the context of a chapter which views secularization from the perspective of mission. Unfortunately, Habgood does not follow through his initial thoughts to a satisfactory resolution. His ambivalence demonstrates an inability to define the necessary conclusions in terms of evangelization: 'My defence of establishment, for instance, was based fundamentally on an assessment of the needs of the nation, and a view of the church as not confined to those whose religious commitment is most explicit and most ready to express itself in overt religious activity.'[118]

Allan Bloom understands this liberalism and names it as 'relativism'. Bloom has an academic background in adult education. He believes that contemporary students 'are unified only in their relativism and in their allegiance to equality.'[119] Thomas Dubay advances the proposition even further. He writes about 'a wonderless education' that is 'more concerned with facts than with amazement'.[120] Within this secularized climate, we find that 'country, religion, family, ideas of civilization, all the sentimental and historical forces that stood between cosmic infinity and the individual, providing some notion of a place within the whole, have been rationalized and have lost their compelling force.'[121] Their analysis of secularism does not sit comfortably with Habgood's position. Bloom suggests that 'there is no doubt that value relativism, if it is true and it is believed in, takes one into very dark regions of the soul and very dangerous political experiments.'[122]

How does the Church respond to this phenomenon of secularism? Paul VI refers to the 'true secularism' that has no 'need for recourse to

116. Habgood J. *Church and Nation in a Secular Age* (London: DLT, 1983) p.14
117. Ibid. p.16
118. Ibid. p.176
119. Bloom A. *The Closing of the American Mind* (London: Penguin Books, 1987) p.25
120. Dubay T. *Faith and Certitude* (San Francisco: Ignatius Press, 1985) p.12
121. Bloom A. (1987) op.cit. p.85
122. Ibid. pp.150-151

God'.[123] The phenomenon is widespread: 'Atheistic secularism and the absence of religious practice are found among adults and among the young, among the leaders of society and among the ordinary people, at all levels of education, and in both the old Churches and the young ones.'[124] Articles eighteen to twenty of this document contain an important conclusion about secularized societies. These societies no longer contain cultures that sustain or promote Christian faith. The issue of media communication is central to this debate. Hence, the bishops at the Second Vatican Council looked to a post-conciliar document that would promote the pastoral implications of the *Decree on the Means of Social Communication.* The *Pastoral Instruction on the Means of Social Communication* was published on 29 January 1971. The foreward of the text declares that 'more than ever before, the way men live and think is profoundly affected by the means of communication.'[125] Media communications are not neutral. The community of disciples often 'have to watch social communications used to contradict or corrupt the fundamental values of human life.'[126] John Paul II understands the contemporary struggle for the material advancement of mankind. Nevertheless, he is also able to talk of 'man who is truncated, reduced to his merely horizontal dimension.'[127] In addition to the problem of urbanization, there is a very real sense of alienation encountered by many in the world's 'megalopolises'.[128] This is both a religious and social phenomenon. Unfortunately, none of these topics are fully developed in these texts.

Christian witness is a minority viewpoint. There is an isolation of Christian cultural values and a discrepancy between the language of doctrine and that of contemporary European society.[129] Evangelization has to face the reality of a post-Christian mindset and those who have rejected the Gospel and the life-style it offers. This reality is profoundly contrary to the Gospel. Newbigin notes that faith is interpreted within a 'social conditioning of belief'.[130] He recognizes the ways in which faith is considered unreasonable within the 'plausibility structures' of

123. *Evangelii Nuntiandi* (1975) art.55
124. Ibid. art.56
125. *Communio et Progressio* (1971) art.1
126. Ibid. art.9
127. *Redemptoris Missio* (1990) art.11
128. Cf. ibid. art.37
129. Cf. Jossua J-P. *Believers and Unbelievers Today* in ed. Flannery A. (1977) op.cit. p.99
130. Newbigin L. *The Gospel in a Pluralist Society* (London: SPCK, 1989) p.8

contemporary Western society. In this society, faith statements are likely to be dismissed as being 'ignorant, arrogant, dogmatic'.[131]

Christian mission activity often followed in the aftermath of political colonialism.[132] When Christianity is too closely identified with one particular political system, rejection of the latter may lead to hostile antipathy towards the former. The establishment of ecclesial activity often meant the replacement of indigenous cultures with a European culture.[133] Newbigin confirms this widely held view, and affirms the need 'to discover the form and substance of a missionary church in terms that are valid in a world that has rejected the power and the influence of the Western nations. Missions will no longer work along the stream of expanding Western power.'[134] There is certainly some truth in these statements. However, the true nature of evangelization can never be disguised. Ecclesial missionary activity has a defined purpose of establishing the Church. Before the Council, mission may have been considered as 'the centripetal movement of assimilation.'[135] Since the Second Vatican Council, there has been a growth in legitimate spontaneity, within a rediscovery of the local ecclesial community.

6.5 Towards a Missionary Vision of Parish Community

After the Council's treatment of missionary activity, there was an incontrovertible dialectical tension between two viewpoints. This became most apparent in the Synod of 1974 and with the publication of the subsequent post-synodal apostolic exhortation. On the one hand, evangelization was an activity seen in a very broad and almost cosmological context. Anything that promoted the values of the Kingdom, and enabled God's creating and saving activity to be manifested, was considered part of the Church's missionary mandate. On the other hand, there was a narrower perspective which understood the specific proclamation of the Gospel to be the only means of authentic evangelization. Those who adopted this viewpoint only

131. Ibid. p.10
132. Cf. Frohnes H. *Mission in the Light of Critical Historical Analysis* in *Concilium* no. 114 op.cit. pp. 9-16
133. Cf. Amalorpavadass D. *Evangelization and Culture* in *Concilium* no.114, (New York: The Seabury Press) p.61
134. Newbigin L. (1995) op.cit. p.5
135. Dhavamony M. *Evangelization and Dialogue in Vatican II and in the 1974 Synod* in Latourelle R. (1989) op.cit.vol.3, p.267

recognized the traditional ecclesial activities of preaching and teaching to be genuine evangelization.[136] Analysis of John Paul II's letter *On the Permanent Validity of the Church's Missionary Mandate* suggests that in the magisterial forum, this post-conciliar tension has been resolved in favour of the second approach.[137] In the language of Bosch, the resolution of this tension might be described as the consequence of a 'paradigm shift' which 'always means both continuity and change'.[138] This does not mean a complete denial of the wider context, for example, with regard to the means of social communication: 'They inform a vast public about what goes on in the world and about contemporary attitudes and they do it swiftly.'[139] Their value as a tool of evangelization is appreciated.

If the Kingdom of God is the focal point of all evangelization, then this leads to 'a consciousness of the radical newness and irreducibility of the saving message of the risen Christ.'[140] Furthermore, the action of evangelization is a central feature of living within the reign of this Kingdom. There are those who propose that this is a new concept to many individuals and parish communities. In the words of one local Catholic evangelist, 'we engaged our people, in the past, in a very private faith, and now we are asking them to have a direct witnessing faith.'[141] This investigation into the notion of conciliar ecclesial mission clearly suggests that evangelization does not only bring an individual into relationship with Christ. It must engage that individual with the community of faith.

Patrick Lynch is a Diocesan priest from Nottingham and the founder of the Sion Community for evangelization. Lynch advances a very particular understanding of the subject. He suggests that 'being evangelized means meeting Jesus in a personal relationship, and then, of necessity, I will have my own way of sharing that encounter with others.'[142] There is a need for caution here. Evangelization cannot take place in a culturally neutral environment. There are always a number of

136. Cf. McGregor B. *Commentary on Evangelii Nuntiandi* in ed. Flannery A. (1977) op.cit. p.62
137. The *magisterium* is the name given to the official teaching body of the Roman Catholic Church.
138. Bosch (1991) op.cit. p.366
139. *Communio et Progressio* (1971) art.6
140. Ganoczy A. *The Absolute Claim of Christianity: The Justification of Evangelization or an Obstacle to it?* in *Concilium* no.114 *Evangelization in the World Today* (New York: The Seabury Press) p.25
141. Lynch P. *Awakening the Giant* (London: DLT, 1980) pp.6-7
142. Ibid. p.10

different cultural expressions and contexts within contemporary Western societies.[143] Evangelization demands a careful analysis of local cultural expressions within the parish community. It is justifiable to question the meaning of 'meeting Jesus in a personal relationship'. It is perhaps even more important to examine the precise nature of the 'encounter' with others. Even personal relationships cannot be culturally indeterminate. So often, we are dealing here with issues of cultural language. The suitability of one particular evangelizing method in one situation may not be as appropriate in another. The key is surely charity and respect for others: 'Communication is more than the expression of ideas and the indication of emotion. At its most profound level, it is the giving of self in love.'[144] There is a tendency, in some circles, to limit the cultural context in which evangelization can take place. Lynch is not the only advocate of this. Some would prefer to abandon dialogue with culture altogether. Culture is 'at its very root hostile to the act of definition and prefers an endlessly fluid reality, capable of being endlessly manipulated to serve the purposes of history.'[145]

Ecclesial communities are not essentially concerned about structures. These are important, but must be directed towards the life of the Church as a communion of faith. Another title might be 'communion of hope'. Ecclesial mission needs to be faithful to the Incarnation, which provides the theological basis for an authentic understanding of inculturation. Pedro Arrupe was a former Superior General of the Society of Jesus. He understood this well in his invention and definition of the term 'inculturation'.[146] This is an understanding of the incarnate life and message of the Gospel 'in a particular local cultural context, in such a way that the experience not only finds expression through elements proper to the culture in question (this alone would be no more than a superficial adaptation), but becomes a principle that animates, directs, and unifies a culture, transforming and remaking it so as to bring about a "new creation".'[147] This definition of

143. Cf. Richard L. *Mission and Inculturation: The Church in the World* in ed. Richard L. et.al. (1987) op.cit. p.94
144. *Communio et Progressio* (1971) art.11
145. Cf. Dubay T. (1985) op.cit. p.49
146. *Letter on Inculturation* i.e. a reflection on the *Pastoral Constitution on the Church in the Modern World* and *Evangelization in the Modern World*, after the thirty-second General Congregation of 1974-1975.
147. Quoted by Starkloff C. *Inculturation and Cultural Systems* in op.cit. p.69

inculturation is not only sympathetic to the mission problems which confront any Christian community, it is also faithful to the Church's tradition. Noujeim recognizes the influence of the Eastern tradition upon the *Catechism of the Catholic Church*. He suggests that this is a legitimate form of inculturation. It accounts for 'the multiplicity of traditions which, although very close to one another, have their own spiritual and theological visions.'[148]

Within every cultural context, mission needs to be accountable to the redemptive mission of Christ. This provides the fundamental paradigmatic model for contemporary pastoral theological reflection. The Church is invited to allow Christ's death and resurrection to inform its life and mission.[149] Only when this life and witness is present in a parish can it be truly a community of hope. It is clear from our consideration of conciliar and post-conciliar pastoral theology, that there cannot be a dualistic opposition between the Church and society. However, neither can the proclamation of the Gospel be reduced to a mere programme of social action. The parish participates in liturgy as a celebration of faith. This celebration then becomes the catalyst for a hope-filled action of evangelization to the rest of society. The liturgical act is fundamentally remembrance. When liturgy fails this purpose, *anamnesis* is soon reduced to amnesia.[150]

Contemporary Christianity needs to resource itself in a radical learning situation. This becomes the basis for pastoral ministry in any parochial situation. The parish needs to be an expression of the Trinitarian life in a dynamic of giving and receiving. Newbigin recognizes the importance of this model in understanding the mission of Christ. Jesus 'speaks of his words and works as not his own but those of the Father.'[151] The work of evangelization belongs to the Trinity. It cannot be grasped by the Church as an action which belongs to herself. There is a sure consequence of this. The Church not only gives something in mission, but receives too. In order for a community of faith to share its hope with others, it must be learning from the Spirit who will lead the disciples into the fullness of

148. Noujeim G-P. *Eastern tradition reflected in new catechism's spirituality in L'Osservatore Romano* 24 March 1993, p.10
149. Cf. Amalorpavadass D. *Evangelization and Culture* in op.cit. p.69
150. *Anamnesis* is the act of making present the reality of the paschal mystery in liturgical celebration.
151. Newbigin L. (1989) op.cit. p.117

truth.[152] Newbigin makes two observations that help us to understand mission within a parish community. He suggests that 'the Church is not so much the agent of the mission as the locus of the mission.'[153] He also states that 'the Church is not the source of the witness; rather, it is the locus of witness.'[154] In order to be faithful to Christ's mandate, the Church must be open to learning. This is because mission 'is based not on human abilities but on the power of the Risen Lord.'[155] Furthermore, there is 'a pluralism which reflects different experiences and situations within the first Christian communities.'[156] This pluralism is still present today, and suggests the reason why there can never be a universal blueprint for parish-based mission.

There have been many attempts to interpret the Council's movement towards ecclesial reform.[157] It is possible to situate the current pluralistic nature of communities at the centre of contemporary pastoral theology, especially as this pluralism is applied to the local church. Those commentators who espouse this pluralism must argue for an attainable unity within a pluralistic ministerial diversity. They need to focus on the elements of communion shared by a variety of different communities.[158] The conversation between theologians and practitioners of pastoral ministry is a vital part of this process. This promotion of pluralism offers an invitation for parish communities to recognize their diverse needs and give uninhibited expression to them. The response to these needs is the development of new ministries and structures.[159] This analysis appears quite attractive, as a method for renewing a community's ability to engage in mission. However, there is a danger. An exaggerated focus on structures does not necessarily lead to renewal of mission-life. Secondly, the Church's fundamental self-understanding is aligned to the missionary nature of Christ. This means that ministries can be understood only as received gifts and charisms.

---

152. Cf. John 16:12-15
153. Newbigin L. (1989) op.cit. p.119
154. Ibid. p.120
155. *Redemptoris Mission* (1990) art.23
156. Ibid. art.23
157. Cf. Durkin M. *Pluralism and Church Reform: Pastoral Theology looks to the future* in ed. Tracy D. et.al. *Toward Vatican III The work that needs to be done* (Dublin: Gill and Macmillan, 1978) p.179ff.
158. Cf. ibid. p.180
159. Cf. ibid. p.186

How then does a parish community discover its vision of mission? The Gospel provides a fundamental hermeneutic for every life. For 'it must be shared universally. It cannot be private opinion.'[160] From this certain truth, Newbigin correctly warns that 'there will always be the temptation, even for those within the Christian community, to find the clue in the success of some project of our own'.[161] Any missionary process must have first entered into a sincere and thorough analysis of the socio-cultural situation. The bishops at the Second Vatican Council rightly declared that 'the differences which must be recognized in this activity of the Church, do not flow from the inner nature of the mission itself, but from the circumstances in which it is exercised.'[162] This is a more correct understanding of ecclesial pluralism. Within an authentic notion of pluralistic diversity, there is a need to adapt methods and activities to a particular situation.

Finally, the mission of any ecclesial community must always be understood within a pneumatological context: 'Techniques of evangelization are good, but even the most advanced ones could not replace the gentle action of the Spirit.'[163] This is followed by a warning against reliance upon psycho-social programmes. Evangelization is fundamentally a work of the Holy Spirit, 'who, today just as at the beginning of the Church, acts in every evangelizer who allows himself to be possessed and led by him.'[164] The Spirit also 'predisposes the soul of the hearer to be open and receptive to the Good News and to the Kingdom being proclaimed.'[165] John Paul II also discusses the important work of the Holy Spirit, in his encyclical letter *On the Permanent Validity of the Church's Missionary Mandate*.[166] In particular, he suggests that 'the Spirit's presence and activity affects not only individuals but also society and history, peoples, cultures and religions.'[167] This mission has always been 'difficult and complex, and demands the courage and light of the Spirit.'[168] John Paul II affirms this constant post-conciliar assertion in a recent encyclical letter

160. Newbigin L. (1989) op.cit. p.125
161. Ibid. p.126
162. *Ad Gentes* (1965) art.6
163. *Evangelii Nuntiandi* (1975) art.75
164. Ibid. art.75
165. Ibid. art.75
166. Cf. *Missio Redemptoris* (1990) arts. 21-30
167. Ibid. art.28
168. Ibid. art.87

concerning moral teaching. He states that 'at the heart of the new evangelization and of the moral life which it proposes and awakens by its fruits of holiness and missionary zeal, there is the Spirit of Christ, the principle and strength of the fruitfulness of Holy Mother Church. As Paul VI reminded us, "Evangelization will never be possible without the action of the Holy Spirit".'[169] This is an important corrective principle in an understanding of ecclesial mission that is often dominated by a debilitating focus on limited human resources.

169. *Veritatis Splendor* (1993) art.108, quoting *Evangelii Nuntiandi* (1975) art.75

CHAPTER SEVEN

The Laity

7.0 Introduction

The previous chapter investigated the theme of ecclesial mission as a fundamental element of pastoral theological reflection. The Church's missionary activity defines the primary meaning and purpose of ecclesial life. Indeed, the theme of mission provides an even more fundamental contribution to this investigation. It contains an inherent definition of Christian anthropology. To be human 'means to undergo the adventure of eternity'.[1] This understanding of ecclesial mission suggests the need to focus on the ministry of the lay faithful, and on the development of that pastoral ministry since the Second Vatican Council. An investigation of contemporary pastoral theology would be incomplete if it failed to reflect upon the vocation and mission of the lay faithful. The absence of such reflection from this study would lead to a very truncated view of the parish community.

Bernier situates the sacerdotalization of ministry in an early patristic era. This is a time when sacramental ministry became cultic and was centralized on the ministry of the ordained.[2] Nevertheless, focus on the hierarchical elements of ministry should never distort a parallel tradition. Attention was always given to the development of the apostolate and spirituality of the laity. Analysis of the readings appointed for the calendar of saints in *The Divine Office* suggests that much care was taken in this matter. For example, there is a sermon which is attributed to Peter Chrysologus, the fifth century Archbishop of Ravenna.[3] His reflection on the need to work for justice and peace in charity is read in connection with the political reconciling apostolate of Elizabeth of Portugal. Stephen of Hungary and Louis of France both exhorted their sons to live and rule in a virtuous manner and to see their kingship as a Christian apostolate.[4] Many sermons,

1. Balthasar H. *Bernanos: An Ecclesial Existence* (San Francisco: Ignatius Press, 1996) p.121
2. Cf. Bernier P. *Ministry in the Church* (Mystic: Twenty-Third Publications, 1992) p.63
3. Congregation for Divine Worship *The Divine Office* vol.3 (Collins, London, 1974) p.99*
4. Ibid. p.201* and 216*

instructions and other sources, are also quoted. Often, these directly address the importance of fidelity to the Gospel and witness to its values in the lives of all lay men and women.

Joseph Cardijn was a Belgian priest and spent his whole life and ministry with young workers. These are the people 'who are actually living and working in the ordinary circumstances of everyday life . . . and it is up to them to carry out Christ's mission in all the different temporal sectors of life and to make the whole Church present there.'[5] Cardijn's personal vision of the lay person's contribution to the task of ecclesial mission was not universal. However, there are other enlightened reflections on the lay apostolate before the Second Vatican Council. Pius XI declared: 'I write encyclicals, and I'm very glad to do it, but it's impossible for me to transmit all that they contain to the workshops and factories, because I'm just not there . . . Neither bishops nor priests can do it because they aren't in these environments'.[6] In 1905, Georges Bernanos, the French novelist and essayist, wrote: 'If I don't have the intention of becoming a priest it's, first of all, because I don't think I have the vocation for it, but then too because a layman can fight on many levels where the cleric cannot accomplish much.'[7]

This evidence belongs to a generation before the Second Vatican Council which certainly promoted the lay apostolate. The Second Vatican Council received this inherited tradition and provided a theological foundation for further development. And in this theme too, the Council's renewal took place within a revisitation of biblical and patristic themes.[8] Neither could the bishops at the Council ignore the myriad of witnesses throughout Christian history. The powerful theme of the universal call to holiness in the *Dogmatic Constitution on the Church* was not entirely new. In a post-conciliar text John Paul II wrote of 'Francis de Sales, who promoted lay spirituality so well. In speaking of devotion, that is, Christian perfection or life according to the Spirit, he presents in a simple yet insightful way the vocation of all Christians to holiness'.[9] The doctrine of this seventeenth century Bishop of Geneva certainly prefigures the themes of the Second Vatican council

5. Cardijn J. *Laymen into Action* (London: Geoffey Chapman, 1964) p.114
6. Ibid. p.114
7. Cf. Balthasar (1996) op.cit. p.155
8. Despite Bernier's assertion that the ministerial 'chasm' was opened up between ordained and the laity in these early centuries.
9. *Christifideles Laici* (1988) art.56

which are further explored in the post-synodal apostolic exhortation on *The Vocation and the Mission of the Lay Faithful in the Church and in the World*. The final part of this chapter will explore the eschatological nature of collaborative ministry. All models of collaboration within pastoral care must be weighed against the sanctifying nature of pastoral ministry. For authentic ministry is inevitably to be understood within the depths of the sacramental mystery.

7.1 The Development of Catholic Action

During the 1930s, Pius XI promoted the development of an apostolate known as 'Catholic Action'. He defined this movement as 'the participation of the laity in the apostolate of the Church's hierarchy.'[10] However, there is a fundamental flaw in the pre-conciliar understanding of Catholic Action. The laity did not possess a ministry of their own. Their apostolate was a share in the pastoral ministry of the ordained. Thus, Catholic Action became subservient to clerical initiative and organization.[11] Catholic Action was a clearly defined spiritual work and a 'participation' in the practice of pastoral care. It was organized by the bishops. This apostolate of the laity had firm structures for single-sex groups, and was exercised in territorial areas. Furthermore, so-called 'temporal' activity did not have any place within Catholic Action whatsoever. Under these guidelines, some lay movements were never truly gathered under the umbrella of Catholic Action. Even in these early days, however, Congar was able to focus on Pius XI's hopes that 'lay activity was the answer to worldwide secularization.'[12]

Pius XII published the encyclical letter *On the Mystical Body of Christ* in 1943. The ecclesiological sentiments of this document, albeit tentatively, contained some recognition of the obligations of the laity to the need for ecclesial mission. First of all, there was a traditional reference to the hierarchy: 'It is certainly true that those who hold sacred power in this body are its first and chief members. It is through them, in accordance with the plan of the divine Redeemer Himself, that Christ's functions as Teacher, King and Priest endure forever.'

10. Newman J. *The Background to Vatican II* in ed. Newman J. *The Christian Layman* (Dublin: Scepter Books, 1966) p.24
11. Cf. Shaw R. *To Hunt, to Shoot, To Entertain: Clericalism and the Catholic Laity* (San Francisco: Ignatius Press, 1993) p.75
12. Congar Y. *Laity, Church and World* (London: Geoffrey Chapman, 1960) p.56

Then there are important comments on the role of the laity: 'However, when the Fathers of the Church mention the ministries of this body. . . they rightly have in mind not only persons in sacred orders, but . . . those also who, though living in the world, actively devote themselves to spiritual or corporal works of mercy; and also those who are joined in chaste wedlock.'[13] This is a maturing approach which cannot be understood outside of a developing understanding of the Church. Catholic Action was part of the ecclesiological renewal taking place at Tübingen. This exciting centre of theological renewal had begun to investigate an important patristic source of ministry in sacramental initiation.[14] Lay participation in the Church's mission was firmly on the agenda. And in a war-time Christmas message of 1943, Pius XII offered this invitation to the community of disciples: 'Get to work then, dear children! Close your ranks! Don't lose heart or sit idle among the ruins. Go out and build a new social world for Christ.'[15]

With the encouragement of Monsignor Léon-Josef Suenens, Pius XII sought to widen the Church's understanding of Catholic Action. This expanded vision was offered to the Second World Congress for the Apostolate of the Laity in October 1957. Jeremiah Newman[16] describes this gathering as the official catalyst for the renewed understanding of Catholic Action.[17] The Congress witnessed the beginning of a debate that lasted until the Council. During the 1957 Congress, Archbishop Giovanni Battista Montini[18] raised the question of 'graduated representativeness'. He suggested that as Catholic Action became more involved in the temporal order, 'it progressively loses its capacity to represent the Church and to share in the Church's direct mission.'[19] Monsignor Emile Guerry, Archbishop of Cambrai, was a leading figure in a generally radical French Catholic Action. However, in March 1956 prior to the Second World Congress, he affirmed the specifically spiritual nature of this movement, and warned against '*la tentation politique*'.[20]

13. Ed. Neuner J and Dupuis J. *The Christian Faith* (London: Collins, 1983) pp. 237-238
14. Cf. Keightley G. *Laity* in ed. Komonchak J. et.al. *The New Dictionary of Theology* (Dublin: Gill & Macmillan, 1987) p.559
15. Congar Y. *Lay People in the Church* (London: Geoffrey Chapman,1965) p.469
16. This is Jeremiah Newman: professor of sociology at Maynooth at the time when this book was published. He is not to be confused with John Henry Cardinal Newman from the previous century.
17. Cf. Newman J. *The Background to Vatican II* in ed. Newman J. (1966) op.cit. pp. 27-28
18. The future Paul VI.
19. Ibid. p.29
20. Ibid. p.32

The view of these two prelates was not universal. Joseph Comblin was a French priest who had given some thought to the lay apostolate. In 1961 he developed a critique of Catholic Action in *The Failure of Catholic Action*. He proposed the thesis that ecclesiology was over-spiritualized, and that the lay apostolate must find ways of influencing society and culture. He believed that the transformation of contemporary civilization was a necessary condition for authentic evangelization. The tension between these two viewpoints has historical significance: 'This question, in fact, was one of the principal ones which exercised the Commission for the Lay Apostolate which prepared the schema on the laity for Vatican II.'[21]

7.2 The Second Vatican Council and the Laity

The Second Vatican Council was the first Ecumenical Council to examine a specific theology of the laity. Furthermore, 'it was the first to consider the question of the Church's understanding of itself in such a way as to give prominence or restore prominence in a positive sense to all the potential dignity of the laity to be found in revelation.'[22] In his plan for the Council, Suenens demanded a serious conciliar engagement with this subject. The 1917 Code of Canon Law suggested the importance of this need. Suenens resented the Code's devotion of a mere three lines to the lay faithful.[23] In his preliminary plan, he suggested the basis for a renewed understanding of the lay vocation, 'recognizing their rights and duties by virtue of their baptism, which incorporates them into the Church.'[24]

Yves Congar was an influential theologian of the Second Vatican Council. This event was a time of theological renewal even for him. In particular, Congar had not fully rooted his theological reflection in an understanding of the Church as communion. The consequences of this were seen in his *Lay People in the Church*. The distinctions between the ordained and the lay faithful were too distinct.[25] For Congar, the Council's reform 'concerned the entire manner in which the Christian

21. Ibid. p.29
22. Magnani G. *Does the So-Called Theology of the Laity Possess a Theological Status?* in ed. Latourelle R. *Vatican II Assessment and Perspectives vol.1* (New York: Paulist Press, 1989) p.593
23. Suenens L-J. *A Plan for the Whole Council* in ed. Stacpoole A. *Vatican II by those who were there* (London: Geoffrey Chapman, 1986) p.100
24. Ibid. p.100
25. Cf. McBrien R. *Church and Ministry: the achievement of Yves Congar* in *Theology Digest* vol.32 no.3 Autumn 1985, p.205

faith is embodied in the Church community in the world of today'.[26] However, it is worth noting the nuance to this viewpoint provided by Aiden Nichols: 'Congar's theology in the post-conciliar period would register no change. The development of his own theological doctrine was placid, and his view of what theology in the Catholic tradition ought to be knew no interruption.'[27]

The documents of the Second Vatican Council situate any discussion of ministry within an ecclesiological perspective. The *Dogmatic Constitution on the Church* has a number of pertinent articles concerning the laity. The second chapter of this constitution concerns the nature of the People of God. It is God's will 'to make men holy and save them, not as individuals without any bond or link between them, but rather to make them into a people who might acknowledge him and serve him in holiness.'[28] This people is 'established by Christ as a communion of life, love and truth, it is taken up by him also as the instrument for the salvation of all'.[29] Thus, reflection upon the *nature* of the Church begins to suggest how all its members are involved in its mission. Later, this document states that 'all in the Church, whether they belong to the hierarchy or are cared for by it, are called to holiness'.[30]

The nature and mission of the Christian disciple find their sources in sacramental Baptism. The Church is an apostolic community that receives the life of the Spirit for mission. The Spirit 'distributes special graces among the faithful of every rank. By these gifts he makes them fit and ready to undertake various tasks and offices for the renewal and building up of the Church'.[31] This text clearly teaches that Baptism into Christ means a share in his mission. This is developed further in the fourth chapter of the constitution, which contains specific articles on the laity. The Council teaches that 'the faithful who by Baptism are incorporated into Christ, are placed in the People of God, and in their own way share the priestly, prophetic and kingly office of Christ, and to the best of their ability carry on the mission of the whole Christian people in the Church and in the world.'[32] The Council affirms that

26. Nichols A. *Yves Congar* (London: Geoffrey Chapman, 1989) p.173
27. Nichols A. *From Newman to Congar* (Edinburgh: T & T Clark, 1990) p.262
28. *Lumen Gentium* (1964) art.9
29. Ibid. art.9
30. Ibid. art.39
31. Ibid. art.12
32. Ibid. art.31

'there is a common dignity of members deriving from their rebirth in Christ, a common grace as sons, a common vocation to perfection, one salvation, one hope and undivided charity.'[33] Kenan Osborne is the Professor of systematic theology at the Franciscan School of Theology in the Graduate Theological Union at Berkeley, California. He has noted that before the Second Vatican Council, the Christological offices of priest, prophet and king belonged exclusively to the ordained ministry: 'Vatican II has, however, widened this view of the *tria munera*. Sharing in the threefold office of Jesus is now a hallmark of the baptized-confirmed and eucharistic Christian'.[34] This focus on the three-fold office of Christ can be dated to the fourth century work of Eusebius of Caesarea. The trilogy received renewed attention twelve centuries later, when the Protestant reformer John Calvin applied the notion to all the baptized.[35]

Articles ten, eleven and thirty-four of this constitution outline the priesthood of all the laity. The bishops of the Second Vatican Council make an important distinction here between the priesthood and apostolate of the laity. The former is concerned with their participation in liturgical worship: 'The faithful indeed, by virtue of their royal priesthood, participate in the offering of the Eucharist. They exercise that priesthood, too, by the reception of the sacraments, prayer and thanksgiving, the witness of a holy life, abnegation and active charity.'[36] Those who are joined to Christ's life and mission are given 'a share in his priestly office, to offer spiritual worship for the glory of the Father and the salvation of man.'[37] The apostolate of the laity is concerned with evangelization. The redeemed children of God 'must profess before men the faith they have received from God through the Church . . . Hence they are, as true witnesses of Christ, more strictly obliged to spread the faith by word and deed.'[38] This apostolate truly belongs to the priestly office of Christ, 'worshipping everywhere by their holy actions, the laity consecrate the world itself to God.'[39] This doctrine is expressed by Osborne in his assertion 'that there is a

33. Ibid. art.32
34. Osborne K. *Ministry: Lay Ministry in the Roman Catholic Church* (New York: Paulist Press, 1993) p.548
35. Cf. Drilling P. *Trinity and Ministry* (Minneapolis: Fortress Press, 1991) p.29
36. *Lumen Gentium* (1964) art.10
37. Ibid. art.34
38. Ibid. art.11
39. Ibid. art.34

common matrix of gospel discipleship, which the documents of Vatican II call "priesthood of all believers," is an official teaching of the Roman Catholic Church.'[40]

The lay faithful have a prophetic ministry when 'they manifest a universal consent in matters of faith and morals.'[41] Faith that is appropriated leads to a life of charity. This too, belongs to the prophetic ministry of the laity. It 'spreads abroad a living witness to him, especially by a life of faith and love'.[42] Later, the constitution acknowledges the vocation of all 'living members' to the 'building up of the Church and to its continual sanctification all the powers which they have received from the goodness of the Creator and from the grace of the Redeemer.'[43] This text very specifically defines the prophetic ministry of the laity. There is no confusion here with the prophetic ministry of the ordained ministry. The laity are called 'to make the Church present and fruitful in those places and circumstances where it is only through them that she can become the salt of the earth.'[44] Specific reference is made to the family and to social life.[45]

The kingship of Christ is realized, above all, in his humble obedience to the Father. Through this obedience, Christ is exalted and 'all things are subjected to him until he subjects himself and all created things to the Father'.[46] The laity share in this royal office through Baptism. 'The Lord also desires that his kingdom be spread by the lay faithful: the kingdom of truth and life, the kingdom of holiness and grace, the kingdom of justice, love and peace.'[47] Indeed 'the laity enjoy a principal role in the universal fulfilment of this task.'[48] In this aspect of baptismal sharing in Christ's three-fold office, there is also a clear theological basis for including temporal business in the lay apostolate, 'since not even in temporal business may any human activity be withdrawn from God's dominion.'[49] Osborne supplies a conclusion to this part of our investigation, in his suggestion that 'the Christocentric center of all

40. Osborne K. (1993) op.cit. p.536
41. *Lumen Gentium* (1968) art.12
42. Ibid. art.12
43. Ibid. art.33
44. Ibid. art.33
45. Cf. ibid. art.35
46. Ibid. art.36
47. Ibid. art.36
48. Ibid. art.36
49. Ibid. art.36

ecclesial mission and ministry provides the basis for both non-ordained and ordained mission and ministry in the church. This is found in Vatican II's teaching on the *tria munera* of Jesus.'[50]

There is a reference to Catholic Action in this document, as a means of exercising the lay apostolate. Within the universal call to involvement, 'the laity can be called in different ways to more immediate cooperation in the apostolate of the hierarchy.' And a little later we read that 'they have, moreover, the capacity of being appointed by the hierarchy to some ecclesiastical offices with a view to a spiritual end.'[51] However, their 'secular character' defines the particular contribution of the laity to the Church's mission.[52] Here, there is a resolution of the earlier debate concerning Catholic Action, for 'by reason of their special vocation it belongs to the laity to seek the kingdom of God by engaging in temporal affairs and directing them according to God's will.'[53] By full engagement with temporal things, the laity 'contribute to the sanctification of the world' and 'manifest Christ to others.'[54] Here, the Second Vatican Council confirms the doctrine of Francis de Sales, who insisted over three hundred years previously that 'devotion is possible in every vocation and profession'.[55] Through Baptism into Christ, the lay faithful share in a universal call to holiness: 'In the Church not everyone marches along the same path, yet all are called to sanctity and have obtained an equal privilege of faith through the justice of God'.[56] Furthermore, the contribution of the hierarchy to Catholic Action has also developed in its treatment by the Council. The ordained ministers 'should recognize and promote the dignity and responsibility of the laity in the Church.'[57] These same pastors should give the laity 'the courage to undertake works on their own initiative.'[58] Indeed, the pastors 'must respect and recognize the liberty which belongs to all in the terrestrial city.'[59]

Despite the presentation of these theological insights in the

50. Osborne K. (1993) op.cit. p.558
51. *Lumen Gentium* (1968) art.33
52. Ibid. art.31
53. Ibid. art.31
54. Ibid. art.31
55. Tr. and ed. Ryan J. *Introduction to the Devout Life by St Francis de Sales* (New York: Image Books, 1972) p.43
56. *Lumen Gentium* (1964) art.32
57. Ibid. art.37
58. Ibid. art.37
59. Ibid. art.37

Dogmatic Constitution on the Church, the Council was compelled to produce a fuller *Decree on the Apostolate of Lay People*. This document certainly extends the implications of the decree on the Church. It also calls for a deeper appreciation of lay ministry, because 'present circumstances, in fact, demand from them an apostolate infinitely broader and more intense.'[60] It is little wonder that Congar struggled to appropriate a renewed theological understanding. The draft schema of the document on the apostolate of the laity produced more debate than any other in the third session of the Council.[61] The reason for this may be found in the emerging ecclesiological models. Only when these were fully mature, could a theological understanding of the laity find clear articulation.

The first chapter of this document is a summary of the fourth chapter of the Constitution on the Church. It defines the purpose of the Church as 'founded to spread the kingdom of Christ over all the earth for the glory of God the Father, to make all men partakers in redemption and salvation'[62] There is a clear eschatological dimension to this statement. The kingdom is not fully established yet, and the Church has an important work to fulfil in this regard. Every member of the ecclesial community has some work to accomplish. The Council Fathers stated that 'the Christian vocation is, of its nature, a vocation to the apostolate as well.'[63] The lay Christian is active in society in many different ways. In what sense can this secular activity be called apostolic?[64] Despite the opposition of many Fathers, the document confirms 'the conviction that the worldly activities of the Christian, as a penetration of temporal things with the Christian spirit, represent a participation in the mission of the Church.'[65]

There is further evidence to support this viewpoint. The Christological foundation of contemporary pastoral theology is presented as a fundamental principle of theological reflection in this study. In the context of this chapter, this element supports a wider understanding of the apostolate: 'Christ, sent by the Father, is the

---

60. *Apostolicam Actuositatem* (1965) art.1
61. Cf. McNicholl A. *The Lay Apostolate* in *Doctrine and Life* vol.14 December 1964, p.573
62. *Apostolicam Actuositatem* art.2
63. Ibid. art.2
64. Cf. Klostermann F. *Decree on the Apostolate of the Laity* in ed. Vorgrimler H. *Commentary on the Documents of Vatican II vol.3* (London: Burns & Oates, 1969) p.311
65. Ibid. p.313

source of the Church's whole apostolate. Clearly then, the fruitfulness of the apostolate of lay people depends on their living union with Christ.'[66] Christ's redemptive work is said to involve 'the renewal of the whole temporal order.' This means that 'the mission of the Church, consequently, is not only to bring men the message and grace of Christ but also to permeate and improve the whole range of the temporal.'[67] As we have seen, the lay faithful are inserted into 'the Mystical Body of Christ by baptism and strengthened by the power of the Holy Spirit in confirmation'.[68] Sacramental initiation provides the basis for a Christological understanding of the apostolate. This union with Christ is developed more fully in a post-synodal apostolic exhortation called *On the Vocation and the Mission of the Lay Faithful in the Church and in the World*.[69] However, even in the Council's document on the laity, initiation is presented as a vehicle for understanding the specific Christian contribution of the laity in secular affairs. In terms of lay spirituality, the Blessed Virgin Mary is given as a perfect example, precisely because 'she remained intimately united to her Son and cooperated in an entirely unique way in the Saviour's work.'[70]

This document definitively teaches that 'laymen ought to take on themselves as their distinctive task this renewal of the temporal order.'[71] The mandate for this understanding of the lay apostolate finds a focus within a theological understanding of Creation and the Fall. The world was created with a 'natural goodness'.[72] However, 'in the course of history the use of temporal things has been tarnished by serious defects.'[73] Only the redemptive work of Christ could bring about the restoration of creation, and right order in socio-cultural life. The Church is called by Christ to share in this unfolding work of redemption: 'It is the work of the entire Church to fashion men able to establish the proper scale of values on the temporal order and direct it towards God through Christ.'[74] This is an aspect of evangelization that has been discussed in chapter six of this study. The *Decree on the*

66. *Apostolicam Actuositatem* (1965) art.4
67. Ibid. art.5
68. Ibid. art.3
69. Usually known as *Christifideles Laici* (1988)
70. *Apostolicam Actuositatem* (1965) art.4
71. Ibid. art.7
72. Ibid. art.7
73. Ibid. art.7
74. Ibid. art.7

Apostolate of Lay People confirms the role of the laity in this important missionary apostolate.

The bishops at the Second Vatican Council understood the need to discern authenticity within lay apostolic action. The document points to four different types of activity: 'Some look to the general apostolic end of the Church; others aim specifically at evangelization and sanctification; others work for the permeation of the temporal order by the Christian spirit; and others engage in works of mercy and of charity as their special way of bearing witness to Christ.'[75] In all types of action, the text teaches that 'their apostolic value depends on their conformity with the Church's aims, as well as on the Christian witness and evangelical spirit of each of their members and of the association as a whole.'[76] The apostolate is to be exercised within a collaborative framework: 'it is the hierarchy's place to put proper system into this collaboration.'[77] The theme of collaboration will be examined later in this chapter.

7.3 The Post-Conciliar Development

The Council's treatment of the laity was well received. At the end of the debate, the bishops were addressed by Pat Keegan, International President of the Young Christian Workers, and the first lay person to address a General Congregation of the Council. Keegan's response to the bishops was a strong affirmation of the discussion and the final document on the laity. He believed that the document provided vision and insight into the ecclesial mission of the lay faithful.[78]

Twenty years after the conclusion of the Second Vatican Council, the 1987 Synod considered the vocation and mission of the laity. The final text of the bishops is worthy of analysis, as well as the post-synodal apostolic exhortation. The bishops were concerned that 'the end for which this Synod was convoked was the celebration, verification and promotion of Vatican Council II.'[79] In this context, the bishops also wanted to state the Council's legitimate authenticity and authority within the tradition of the Church. Once again, there is the assertion

75. Ibid. art.19
75. Ibid. art.19
77. Ibid. art.23
78. Cf. McNicholl A. *The Lay Apostolate* in op.cit. p.582
79. *Final relatio of the Synod* in *L'Osservatore Romano* 16 December 1985, p.6

that 'communion is the very mystery of the Church.'[80] There have been problems too: 'In truth there certainly have also been shadows in the post-conciliar period: in part due to an incomplete understanding and application of the Council'.[81] The Church is more than an institutional structure. Sometimes, conciliar teaching has been interpreted within a secularized context. This has led to difficulties and misunderstandings. The bishops suggested a pastoral programme of formation, in which the theology of the conciliar constitutions and decrees could be appropriated and assimilated into ecclesial life.

From the above analysis of conciliar texts, it is clear that the lay apostolate has made a positive move into temporal affairs. Nevertheless, since the conclusion of the Council, there has been a failure to understand secularism as one of the fundamental 'signs of the times'. The affirmation of the 'legitimate autonomy of temporal realities' should not become the 'secularism that consists of an autonomist vision of man and the world, one which leaves aside the dimension of mystery'.[82] The sense of the sacred is still present in the heart and mind of contemporary men and women. However, the reduction of this sense of the sacred to sect and cult involvement becomes a challenge to all of Christ's faithful. The bishops in Synod offer a response to this challenge: 'The Church makes herself more credible if she speaks less of herself and ever more preaches Christ crucified and witnesses with her own life.'[83] This statement forms the Christological critique of all pastoral theology. It is particularly apposite to an understanding of pastoral care practice. The Christological response to the secularism of our contemporary world is presented by the Synod on the lay faithful as the hermeneutical principle for understanding the life and ministry of the laity: 'In our day above all, when so many people feel an interior void and spiritual crisis, the Church must preserve and energetically promote the sense of penance, prayer, adoration, sacrifice, self-giving, charity and justice.'[84] It is possible that all Christ's faithful can desire institutional reform, and ignore this fundamental vocation of all those who are Baptized into Christ. The purpose of holiness and ecclesial devotion is

80. *Christifideles Laici* (1988) art.18
81. *Final relatio of the Synod* in op.cit. p.6
82. Ibid. p.6
83. Ibid. p.6
84. Ibid. p.7

realized, when lives are transformed 'with the light and life of Christ'.[85]

The bishops reminded pastors of their fundamental duty towards the laity. They stated that 'the true intent of pastoral work consists in actualizing and making concrete the truth of salvation'.[86] Thus, ecclesial life finds its source in the saving events of the Trinity God. The Church is the work of the Lord, and the community of faithful are those who have responded to this work. From an ecclesiological viewpoint, a theology of communion is essential to reception of God's soteriological action. In their final synodal document, the bishops wrote: 'Fundamentally it is a matter of communion with God through Jesus Christ, in the Holy Spirit . . . The communion of the eucharistic Body of Christ signifies and produces, that is, builds up, the intimate communion of all the faithful in the Body of Christ which is the Church'.[87] A theological vision of communion needs promotion in the post-conciliar Church, if ecclesiological understanding of lay ministry is not to be reduced to a struggle for power. This doctrine also allows a genuine pluriformity and diversity, that does not descend into a secular pluralism of 'dissolution, destruction and the loss of identity.'[88]

Twelve months after the Synod, John Paul II published the apostolic exhortation *On the Vocation and the Mission of the Lay Faithful in the Church and in the World*. This document has fully appropriated the Second Vatican Council's understanding of communion, and presents this theology within the biblical image of the vine. Besides the vine model of the Church in the fourth Gospel[89], there is also the vineyard model of ministry in the synoptic tradition.[90] Peter Coughlan was a priest of the Shrewsbury Diocese and worked as a theological consultor to the Pontifical Council for the Family. He believed that this image of the vineyard 'is intimately connected with the evangelization theme that runs throughout the document. The world is seen as an immense vineyard that must be transformed according to the plan of God in view of the definitive coming of the kingdom of God.'[91] These two

85. Ibid. p.7
86. Ibid. p.7
87. Ibid. p.7
88. Ibid. p.7
89. John 15
90. Matt. 20
91. Coughlan P. *The Emerging Role of the Laity* in ed. Boyack K. *The New Catholic Evangelization* (New York: Paulist Press, 1992) p.74

biblical images are used to demonstrate the call of all Christ's faithful to involvement in mission. This is the dominant motif of the post-synodal apostolic exhortation. The invitation to involvement in mission 'is addressed to everyone: lay people as well are personally called by the Lord, from whom they receive a mission on behalf of the Church and the world.'[92] This is the specific doctrinal development of the Council, which has 'written as never before on the nature, dignity, spirituality, mission and responsibility of the lay faithful.'[93] In article three of the exhortation, there is the familiar recognition that this arises from 'a new state of affairs today'.[94] However, it is important to note the theological basis for the mission of the laity. This is built upon a renewed understanding of their participation in the mission of Christ, as Priest, Prophet and King.

Their 'secular character' determines the specific manner of lay involvement in Christ's mission. This is a profoundly theological reality, 'for the lay faithful, to be present and active in the world is not only an anthropological and sociological reality, but in a specific way, a theological and ecclesiological reality as well.'[95] In this post-conciliar document, conciliar teaching has reached maturity. However, all commentators do not acknowledge this maturity. William Rademacher teaches theology at Duquesne University in Pittsburgh. He also directs the pastoral ministry programme in this university. He believes that this document 'does not provide anything more than a descriptive definition of the laity: "A secular quality is proper and special to laymen".'[96] This chapter will attempt to demonstrate the proposition of this study that, from a theological perspective, such an interpretation is misplaced. The mission of the laity cannot be understood apart from that secular character, which is focused on 'the act of God the creator and redeemer'.[97] John Paul II writes: 'The lay faithful's position in the Church, then, comes to be fundamentally defined by their newness in Christian life and distinguished by their secular character.'[98] This character obliges the laity 'in their proper and irreplaceable way, to

92. *Christifideles Laici* (1988) art.2
93. Ibid. art.2
94. Ibid. art.3
95. Ibid. art.15
96. Rademacher W. *Lay Ministry* (Slough: St Paul Publications, 1991) p.81.
97. *Christifideles Laici* (1988) art.15
98. Ibid. art.15

work towards the Christian animation of the temporal order.'[99] The secular character of lay ministry has an ecclesial purpose too: 'It fulfils an ecclesial service in bearing witness and, in its own way recalling for priests, women and men religious, the significance of the earthly and temporal realities in the salvific plan of God.'[100] In this sense, secular character is the specific contribution of lay ministry to contemporary pastoral theology. It is also the means of avoiding two problems discussed at the beginning of this document, 'the temptation of being so strongly interested in Church services and tasks that some fail to become actively engaged in their responsibilities in the professional, social, cultural and political world; and the temptation of legitimizing the unwarranted separation of faith from life.'[101]

This mission is achieved above all when the laity respond to the common vocation to holiness offered in the sacramental life. Thus, 'the vocation to holiness is intimately connected to mission and to the responsibility entrusted to the lay faithful in the Church and in the world.'[102] Once again, Baptism is understood to be the source of this vocation and the fountain of all ministry, 'in acknowledging and in conferring various ministries, offices and roles on the lay faithful, the Pastors exercise the maximum care to institute them on the basis of Baptism in which these tasks are rooted.'[103] Indeed, the text recognizes the right of the faithful to form associations, which may help them to grow in holiness and missionary awareness. This activity 'flows from the Sacrament of Baptism, which calls the lay faithful to participate actively in the Church's communion and mission.'[104]

Once again, it is clear from our investigation of these documents, that pastoral theology is built upon an ecclesiology of communion. This theme is particularly discussed in the second chapter of the document. However, the apostolic exhortation makes an important association here: 'Communion and mission are profoundly connected with each other, they interpenetrate and mutually imply each other, to the point that communion represents both the source and the fruit of mission: communion gives rise to mission and mission is accomplished

99. Ibid. art.36
100. Ibid. art.55
101. Ibid. art.2
102. Ibid. art.17
103. Ibid. art.23
104. Ibid. art.29

in communion.'[105] The identity, fundamental dignity, vocation and mission of the laity are found within the 'mystery of communion'.[106] The theological reason for this is found at the heart of conciliar documents, 'the mystical unity of Christ with his disciples and the disciples with each other, presenting it as an image and extension of that mystical communion that binds the Father to the Son and the Son to the Father in the bond of love, the Holy Spirit.'[107] Intimate communion with Christ, then, directs the nature of ecclesial community and the need for communion amongst the disciples. An understanding of communion also provides the context for understanding participation in Christ's three-fold mission of Priest, Prophet and King.[108] Through Baptism, a Christian enters into Trinitarian and ecclesiological communion, and is given the dignity of a share in Christ's three-fold office. This dignity is 'the source of equality for all members of the Church, guarantees and fosters the spirit of communion and fellowship, and at the same time, becomes the hidden dynamic force in the lay faithful's apostolate and mission.'[109] This communion does not lead to uniformity, but rather 'is characterized by a diversity and a complementarity of vocations and states in life, of ministries, of charisms and responsibilities.'[110]

7.4 Collaborative Ministry

The purpose of the apostolic exhortation, in the words of John Paul II, is 'to stir and promote a deeper awareness among all the faithful of the gift and responsibility they share, both as a group and as individuals, in the communion and mission of the Church.'[111] This is the context for understanding collaborative ministry, as one of the commanding topics in contemporary pastoral theological reflection. Collaboration is a fruit of an ecclesiology of communion: 'Episcopal Conferences are called to evaluate the most opportune way of developing the consultation and collaboration of the lay faithful . . . so that they may consider well the problems they share and manifest better the communion of the whole

105. Ibid. art.32
106. Ibid. art.8
107. Ibid. art.12
108. Cf. ibid. art.14
109. Ibid. art.17
110. Ibid. art.20
111. Ibid. art.2

Church.'[112] In this study, collaborative ministry will be considered within the particular context of parish community. It has already been noted in chapter four, that the parish is the theatre for the practice of most pastoral care ministry.

The Bishops' Conference of England and Wales responded to the invitation of the post-synodal apostolic exhortation with the publication of *The Sign We Give*. This report from the working party on collaborative ministry seeks to develop a statement made by the bishops after a time of reflection: 'We are convinced that the manner and style of relationships in the Church are part of the sign it gives and, for this reason, we must develop patterns of collaborative ministry as a key feature of Church life to come.'[113] The report acknowledges the many diverse interpretations of collaboration. Also, the necessity of further development in this concept of ecclesial ministry: 'These relationships and patterns are the practical implications of the vision of the Church expressed in the teaching of Vatican II and deepened in later documents.'[114] Indeed, the Council's invitation to ecclesiological renewal has found a clear response in this report. Unfortunately, the Christological foundation lies dormant and undeveloped. The issue of authority can only be understood within a Christological context of servanthood.[115] If this is the case, the exploration of authority within a Christological symbol would enable a wider reception of this document.

In the exhortation *On the Vocation and the Mission of the Lay Faithful in the Church and in the World*, the parish is defined as 'a community of faith and an organic community'.[116] As a eucharistic community, the parish is a theological reality. Thus 'it is necessary that in light of the faith all rediscover the true meaning of the parish, that is, the place where the very "mystery" of the Church is present and at work'.[117] Indeed, parish structures must be adapted in order for the laity to exercise a collaborative ministry. Smaller communities must be developed, in order that Christ's faithful can encounter ministry

112. Ibid. art.25
113. Bishops' Working Party on Collaborative Ministry *The Sign We Give* (Bishops' Conference of England and Wales, 1995) from the Foreword
114. Ibid. p.9
115. Cf. O'Leary D. *Water in the Wilderness – the Challenge of Collaborative Ministry* in *The Furrow* vol.46 no.10 October 1995, p.557
116. *Christifideles Laici* (1988) art.26
117. Ibid. art.26

received and given.[118] Collaborative ministry is very much concerned, then, with the identification of the gifts of all baptized lay faithful. Nicholas Cooper was a priest in the Archdiocese of Edinburgh and St Andrews until his untimely death. He believed that 'collaboration in ministry is a response to the call received in baptism and confirmation to recognize the Spirit's charisms in all.'[119] The sacraments of initiation provide the lay faithful with a legitimate responsibility for involvement in the exercise of pastoral ministry.[120] Although, as always, Dubay's comment is worth noting: 'Pastoral care requires a competent knowledge of foundational theology.'[121]

A further warning note needs to be sounded here. If the parish is to be a truly missionary institution, then ecclesial communion must be authentic. Only then is it able to be a place, sign and instrument to 'the neighbourhoods of humanity'.[122] Rademacher recognizes that 'Vatican II recovered the New Testament teaching on *diakonia* (ministry) and the Pauline emphasis on charisms as they relate to the body of Christ.'[123] This is certainly true. Nevertheless, any exercise of ministry and charism must take place within a context of communion. To the present writer, there are two important areas of concern that emerge here. First of all, any discussion of collaborative ministry presupposes a mature faith-filled ecclesial community. This community must fit the broad theological brushstrokes painted above. Secondly, and within a Christological analysis, collaboration is never founded on a secular system of democratic rights. This is a challenge to Rademacher, who notes: 'It is worth recalling that most citizens today have a right to choose their own form of government'.[124] Collaborative ministry may only be viewed from a perspective of servanthood. Furthermore, this is a service which is received rather than chosen. Loughlan Sofield and Carroll Juliano conduct workshops on collaborative ministry throughout the United States. They suggest that 'the basis for all ministry is giftedness. A person's call to ministry is a direct response to

118. Cf. ibid. art.26
119. Cooper N. *Collaborative Ministry* (New York: Paulist Press, 1993) p.6
120. Cf. Duggan R. *Pastoral care from a Roman Catholic Perspective* in *Concilium* no.5 *Catholic Identity* (London: SCM Press, 1994) p.103
121. Dubay T. *Faith and Certitude* (San Francisco: Ignatius Press, 1985) p.20
122. Sofield L. and Juliano C. *Collaborative Ministry Skills and Guidelines* (Notre Dame: Ave Maria Press, 1987) p.27
123. Rademacher W. (1991) op.cit. p.169
124. Rademacher W. (1991), op.cit. p.177

the gifts God has bestowed on that person, and ministry should flow from those gifts.'[125]

The *Parish Project* has been sponsored by the Bishops' Conference of England and Wales. It is an attempt to work with the theology of the post-synodal apostolic exhortation. Furthermore, it seeks to implement the process of the *Rite of Christian Initiation of Adults*, with its challenge: 'What does it mean to be a community which truly celebrates and welcomes new members?'[126] The authors are aware of the difficulties in appropriating the Council's ecclesiology of communion: 'The Parish Project accepts that such renewal is not easy: growth means struggle; and real growth may be slow growth, but the Holy Spirit is at work at the heart of our life as a Church.'[127] The parish is still the primary place of ecclesial identity and belonging. This ecclesial community is the fundamental provider of pastoral care.[128] This programme of renewal seeks to deepen a parish's involvement with mission by using the process of the pastoral cycle. As a process, rather than a programme, the *Parish Project* uses a model of collaborative ministry. In this collaborative process, parishioners are invited 'to describe and explore their own experience, reflect on it in the light of Scripture and Church teaching and come to new levels of awareness and fresh insights into their identity and mission as individuals and as a parish.'[129] It is then, an attempt to put into practice conciliar and post-conciliar pastoral theological reflection. The *Parish Project* also contains a dynamic vision of what a parish can become. It enables the identification of ministerial gifts within the community.[130]

Can this process be fruitful? The *Parish Project* has not been in existence long enough for thorough empirical analysis. The lack of empirical evidence for this application of contemporary pastoral theological principles is a concern for any serious evaluation. Walter Forde's recent observations are important. He believes that 'there is very little detailed writing, research and discussion on the parish. There is no monitoring of individual initiatives or writing up of particular projects'.[131] However, the five elements of the pastoral cycle which

125. Sofield L. and Juliano C. (1987) op.cit. p.16
126. O'Shea J. et.al. *Parish Project* (London: Harper Collins Religious, 1992) p.3
127. Ibid. p.4
128. Cf. Forde W. *Adventuring in Priesthood* (Dublin: The Columba Press, 1993) p.34
129. O'Shea J. et.al. (1992) op.cit. p.14
130. Cf. Sofield L. and Juliano C. (1987) op.cit. p.72
131. Forde W. (1993) op.cit. p.33

inform the methodology of this process are not original. They are similar to the inquiry method of the successful pre-conciliar Catholic Action organization, called the Young Christian Workers. Founded by Cardijn, this movement uses a method of inquiry developed by the founder, and known as 'See – Judge – Act'. Examination of a situation is judged in the light of the Gospel, in order to produce an informed action. In the *Parish Project*, the members of a parish community are invited to 'describe' their life-situation, 'explore' this observation by sharing and listening to others, 'reflect' on this situation in the light of Christian tradition, 'act' in specific parish or group priorities, and 'celebrate' through liturgical and social events. It is difficult to offer an objective critique without the necessary data to evaluate the process. However, the openness to collaborative ministry within parish structures is obviously an indication of whether this process can be fertile.

The role of the parish priest is clearly defined in this process: 'His ministry, service and leadership shapes the way in which a parish understands itself, organizes itself, worships and responds to the local neighbourhood of which it forms a part.'[132] In terms of this experiment in collaborative ministry, the presbyteral role is highlighted further: 'Any process of parish renewal will be determined by the parish priest's understanding, commitment and involvement in the task in hand.'[133] This cannot mean 'a business model in which the pastor is the chief executive officer'. Instead, the Church 'needs to provide its own model that respects its tradition and gospel values, while engaged in a dialogue with society.'[134]

Real collaboration with the lay faithful does not diminish the need for effective presbyteral ministry. Indeed, collaborative ministry has appropriated an ecclesiology which understands the basis of ministry in Baptism, and the specific contribution made to the Church's mission by the secular character of the laity. This demands a presbyteral ministry that is able to recognize, name, enable, and facilitate the charisms present in the whole community.[135] Such a leadership-style is both creative and involves conflict. This arises, above all, from the

132. O'Shea J. et.al. (1992) op.cit. p.20
133. Ibid. p.20
134. Cooper N. (1993) op.cit. p.9
135. Cf. ibid. p.20

struggle to involve the *whole* community in collaborative ministry, and not just a vocal part of it.

Despite the lack of empirical evidence for the *Parish Project,* it is possible to offer some textual criticism of its process, within the principles of contemporary pastoral theology. In order for ministry to be truly responsive, Bernier believes that 'we need to become more aware of the social environment in which we live to see how we may respond to current needs for gospel values. We also need a knowledge of ourselves, of our own gifts and talents so that we might use these as best we can in our particular environment.'[136] If pastoral ministry is to be effectual, then it must be fully aware of the 'signs of the times'. If this ministry is to be sustained, then it must be firmly anchored in a personal knowledge of a baptismal share in Christ's priestly, prophetic and kingly offices. The principal problem here is described by Bernier as the 'dichotomy between life and religion.'[137] Unless Christian practice is holistic, and integrated along the lines suggested in the chapter on liturgical celebration, then this compartmentalization of life will continue. Through a dynamic of focused attention, the *Parish Project* attempts to bring faith and daily life together. This is certainly recognized in accounts of collaborative ministry: 'A major challenge confronting today's Church is how to translate the ideal concept of collaboration into the reality of daily life.'[138]

Within an authentic understanding of conciliar and post-conciliar teaching, a dominant symbolic ecclesial model is the 'People of God'. Clearly, this means that the basic root of Christian dignity is positioned within the Sacrament of Baptism. It also means a universal responsibility for the Church's mission in evangelization. However, this does not necessarily mean confusion between the priesthood of the faithful and the ordained ministry. Through the *Parish Project*, all members of the parish community have an opportunity to develop an understanding of their particular contribution. There is a differentiation of function and role, that is based upon a theological vision and a particular understanding of ministry. The encounter of one local church with the process of collaborative ministry suggests that the

136. Bernier P. (1992) op.cit. p.216
137. Ibid. p.216
138. Archdiocese of Milwaukee *Continuing the Journey Together: A Guidebook for Collaboration* (1991) p.71

fundamental problem is certainly not organizational. Those parish communities who wish to attempt the *Parish Project* need to listen carefully to this account: 'Many people who attempt to collaborate lack a spirituality that provides a context for working with others and that nourishes them as they collaborate. They start with great ideals of collaborating in ministry. They then experience severe conflicts and frustrations and question or terminate the collaborative effort.' Then we encounter the fundamental Christological symbol of all pastoral ministry: 'The death-resurrection mystery of Jesus is at the heart of collaboration. The trials and joys of working with others reflect the paschal mystery into which we have all been baptized.'[139]

139. Ibid. p.71

CHAPTER EIGHT

A Model of Ministry

8.0 Introduction

This inquiry has investigated a number of significant pastoral theological themes. They were chosen because of their specific application to presbyteral ministry within the Church today. Nevertheless, a substantial amount of this material may be applied to pastoral theological reflection in any pastoral care situation. These theological concerns were analysed within the doctrinal developments of the Second Vatican Council and of subsequent post-conciliar documents. There are two tasks remaining in this study. First of all, there is an attempt to create a methodological model for contemporary pastoral theology, leading towards a theological construction of the pastoral process itself. Then there is an application of this model to the process of pastoral theological reflection.

The journey towards methodological respectability contains an inherent problem. This may be described as the movement from neo-scholastic objectivity, through anthropocentric existential theology, towards a new sort of theological inquiry. This begins with a focus on human self-reflection and is developed, in an eschatological manner, on the future.[1] Claude Geffré suggests that the crisis of this shift is concerned with theological method. Hermeneutics starts 'from present factors that condition dogmatic theology in order to bring to light certain contents of contemporary theology and to open out onto problems of method.'[2] Gerald O'Collins agrees with this focus on hermeneutics.[3] Pastoral theology relies on the data of an ecclesiological reflection. It is substantially concerned with interpretation, and seeks to inform the expression of dogma with its findings. In order to be properly constituted as a theological discipline, pastoral theology is inevitably involved in the crisis of method that concerns other areas of theological inquiry.

1. Cf. Geffré C. *A New Age in Theology* (New York: Paulist Press, 1974) p.30
2. Ibid. p.3
3. Cf. O'Collins G. *Retrieving Fundamental Theology* (London: Geoffrey Chapman, 1993) p.8

In a later work, Geffré explores further the move from dogmatics to hermeneutics. He believes that in the past twenty years, theology 'has ceased to be treated as constituted knowledge and has become pluralistic interpretation.'[4] He discerns the source of this change in the move away from scholastic philosophy by the theologians of the Second Vatican Council. These theologians used the ideas and methods of existentialist philosophy and, above all, the behavioural sciences.[5] These changes, however, do not reflect the whole story. The documents of the Second Vatican Council offer a theological perspective that is rooted within scriptural and patristic sources. These sources contain the Christological and Trinitarian themes which are used to develop the ecclesial dimension of discipleship. Werner Jeanrond, a theology lecturer at Trinity College, Dublin, recognizes three principal paradigms in contemporary theology. There is 'one which defends dogmatic certainty, another which develops its own theological mode of participating in the wider human conversation on adequate theories of text-interpretation and world-interpretation, and a third which ultimately limits itself to intratextual considerations.'[6] Donald Gelpi, the Professor of Historical and Systematic Theology at the Jesuit School of Theology at Berkeley, California, has an even more poignant comment to make about contemporary theology. This is 'a confused age of theological eclecticism', in which theologians 'have despaired of systematic thinking and settle for a grab-bag of dubiously related theological ideas.'[7]

The effect of non-theological subjects on the study of theology must be acknowledged. Since the conception of pastoral theology two hundred years ago, these subjects have certainly influenced the nature of theological inquiry. The theological use of social scientific concepts has been considerably advanced through the influence of pastoral studies. Stephen Pattison is a practical theologian and a lecturer in Health and Social Welfare at the Open University. He recognizes that 'the most important feature of pastoral care in the USA since the last war has been the dominance of the counselling and pastoral psychology movements.'[8] He correctly points to the Clinical Pastoral

4. Geffré C. *The Risk of Interpretation* (New York: Paulist Press, 1987) p.11
5. Cf. ibid. p.18
6. Jeanond W. *Theological Hermeneutics* (London: SCM Press Ltd., 1994) p.164
7. Gelpi D. *The Turn to Experience in Contemporary Theology* (New York: Paulist Press, 1994) p.125
8. Pattison S. *A Critique of Pastoral Care* (London: SCM Press Ltd., 1993) p.19

Education movement as a major influence in pastoral studies' programmes.[9] Pattison's work is a useful resumé of the recent historical perspective. Nevertheless, it is difficult to discover where his own sentiment lies. On the one hand, he denigrates those pastors who are 'still wilfully and woefully ignorant and unskilled in counselling'.[10] He believes that 'much British pastoral care remains amateurish, traditional and unselfconscious in the pejorative senses of those words.'[11] On the other hand, American authors are seeking 'to address more general issues which are of enduring and universal interest and importance.'[12] Indeed, Pattison suggests that 'the whole nature and direction of pastoral care has come into question and criticism has particularly focused on the hegemony of secular counselling theories and methods.'[13] Counselling is no longer the only paradigm for pastoral care. There is now a 'new emphasis on the importance of the Christian theological tradition . . . the Christian community as the context of pastoral care . . . on the wider social and political context and implications of pastoral care.'[14] His own position is still confused. He recognizes the importance of this new trend, but regrets that 'little attention is paid to society outside the church'. He is concerned, 'if it means that pastoral care ceases to learn from, and dialogue with, secular insights and disciplines.'[15]

It is unfortunate that pastoral care practice, and the formation for pastoral ministry, should remain so heavily influenced by the non-theological pedagogical models developed elsewhere. Excessive dependence on other models may be the reason why pastoral theology has not vigorously sought the development of its own methodological model. Rather, it has been content to hold a semi-parasitic relationship with other disciplines. Ratzinger recognizes that 'even in the realm of spiritual exercises and pastoral counselling, the formal psychomontage replaces, more often than not, an objective content that is no longer trusted'.[16] This present study is an attempt to address this problem. Dietrich Ritschl, the former Professor of Systematic Theology at the

9. Ibid. p.19
10. Pattison S. (1993) op.cit. p.26
11. Ibid. p.26
12. Ibid. p.27
13. Ibid. p.27
14. Ibid. p.29
15. Ibid. p.31
16. Ratzinger J. *Principles of Catholic Theology* (San Francisco: Ignatius Press, 1987) p.319

University of Heidelberg, was able to state that 'in the last resort I do not trust any theological teacher – except perhaps a professional in exegesis and history – who has not spent a long time as a pastor, visited the old and sick, buried children and young people and had to preach to the congregation every Sunday, even when he had no new ideas.'[17] If pastoral theology is to move away from its recent course, then it must steer into the choppy waters of contemporary theological method. However, in order to discover the direction it must take, it may be worth revisiting another age of controversy. This was a time of emerging pluralism and dogmatic debate, a generation when the Church's leading theologians were also pastoral bishops.

8.1 Mystagogy Revisited

The technique of mystagogical reflection has a pre-Christian tradition within a hellenistic religious environment. The pagan mystagogue was a teacher-priest who initiated converts into the liturgical practices of secret religious rituals. Christian teachers, in the early centuries of Christian history, began to use the pedagogical techniques of mystagogy in post-baptismal catechesis. The patristic mystagogia was historically formed within an evolving catechumenate towards the end of the fourth century. This ancient catechumenal school endeavoured to use liturgical celebration as the basis for deepening a faith appreciation of revelation within the Christian community. This teaching took place in a school called the mystagogia. In many respects, this development was a reaction to a changing ecclesiological situation. The legal acceptance of Christianity within the Roman Empire created both benefits and challenges. The use of a new pedagogical technique also suggests an odour of crisis within a dying catechumenate. Any analysis of patristic mystagogical reflection must take place within a pastoral context. These pastor bishops were particularly concerned with the foundation and development of faith in the life of their ecclesial communities. Within this catechumenal context, it is possible to explore this movement further and to examine the potential contribution of mystagogy to a contemporary methodological model for pastoral theology.

The mystagogues were philosophically dependent upon a neo-

17. Ritschl D. *The Logic of Theology* (London: SCM Press Ltd., 1986) p.295

platonic world-view. Enrico Mazza, the Professor of Liturgical History in the Catholic University at Milan, suggests that these pastor theologians were conditioned by the cultural and philosophical ideas of their age.[18] Nevertheless, they were philosophical mavericks when it suited them. Cultural idiom was only a framework in which to organize their theological and pastoral concerns. Their primary concern was the revelation given by God in the person and life of Jesus Christ. Their generation witnessed a period of intense theological speculation, and innovation in liturgical practice. In this context, the specific insight of mystagogy associated dogma and liturgy, by interpreting the mysteries of the faith in the sacramental liturgy of the Christian community. In a move of blinding significance, the mystagogia became a school that focused on the liturgical celebration of the Church as a vehicle for revelation, rather than on the former sole emphasis on biblical exegesis.

For the mystagogical theologian, sacramental revelation is nothing less than the making present of the saving action of God in the liturgical event. Despite the varied approaches taken by these fourth and fifth century theologians, there was a common method in their work. Mystagogy 'is not so much a form of catechesis or spiritual theology as it is a way of doing theology in the true and proper sense of the term.'[19] In particular, it produced a method of theological inquiry that was based upon typology. Old Testament events and figures are understood to have direct reference to the events and figures of the New Testament. The older text prefigured the later soteriological event in salvation history. This event, then, is more perfectly understood in the light of the earlier text. Mystagogy continued this methodology beyond the New Testament, and into ecclesial liturgical life.

The mystagogues considered the scriptural text to be a 'type' which was actualized in the liturgical event. The mystery of salvation was once again made present to God's people, with all the power of Christ's dynamic presence: 'The *mysterium* is salvation, that is, the deeper content of history insofar as history is a series of saving events; and this content is now made available to human beings through the *sacramentum* or liturgical celebration.'[20] The cause for this

18. Cf. Mazza E. *Mystagogy* (New York: Pueblo Publishing Company, 1989) p.172
19. Ibid. p.6
20. Ibid. p.23. This insight is dependent upon Ambrose of Milan and his linguistic distinction between *mysterium* and *sacramentum*.

soteriological efficacy is fundamentally Christological. It is Jesus the Word of God, who is operative in theophanic saving events in the Old Testament. Jesus is the Incarnate Son of God whose activities are described in the New Testament. The same Christ is present in ecclesial sacramental liturgical celebration.

In the mystagogia school, knowledge of the mysteries was kept until after sacramental initiation. To some extent, this was due to a culture of liturgical reverence. There was also another reason. It is a consequence of a pedagogy that believes only those who have participated in something of what is being taught can appreciate truth.[21] This is particularly emphasized in John Chrysostom's mystagogy, where the sacraments are seen to be the source and power of a renewed life. This great pastor was made Bishop of Constantinople towards the end of the fourth century. He suffered no illusions about the disciple's struggle to appropriate the paschal mystery. Nevertheless, he knew that ecclesial communion was founded upon an individual's personal engagement with the mysteries of faith. Mystagogy affirms an understanding of theology as 'a sapiential knowledge which attended salvation.'[22]

The fruits of mystagogy may be obvious. First of all, it is a theological method that is essentially related to the pastoral purpose. It is concerned with the personal impact of the divine saving mystery within ecclesial life, and seeks to ensure that this engagement is effective. Contacts with philosophical and cultural elements outside the faith environment are used shrewdly. They are not allowed to interfere with the fundamentally theological nature and purpose of pastoral ministry. The unique integrity of Christ's role within history is non-negotiable. In these respects, it may be possible to use mystagogical typology as a theological paradigm of contemporary pastoral action. The mystagogical technique may offer an insight into the nature of authentic pastoral theological reflection. In other words, any valid pastoral theological method must seek to discover how Christ's saving work is truly present within the practice of pastoral care. This saving presence suggests that the pastoral moment is theologically determined, precisely because it contains a dynamic of divine

21. Even as early as the second century Hippolytus, progress in the catechumenate was not dictated by length of instruction, rather, by change in the catechumen's life-style. Cf. ed. Shrawley J. *St Ambrose On The Sacraments and On The Mysteries* (London: SPCK, 1950) p.17
22. Farley E. *Theologia* (Philadelphia: Fortress Press, 1983) p.81

revelation. Furthermore, the Church's pastoral ministry is able to provide the ontological condition for authentic theological reflection. In our understanding of pastoral theology, pastoral ministerial practice determines the a priori struggle for theological meaning.

8.2 The Contemporary Theological Climate

Marie-Dominique Chenu believes that pastoral theology became a dualistic survival of controversy after the First Vatican Council.[23] It needed to be reintroduced as 'a living substance'.[24] This need, in the mind of this theologian, created a defining historical moment, and 'was a preliminary episode of the present recasting of theology.'[25] The movement beyond neo-scholasticism has already been noted. There are other influences upon theological inquiry today. For example, there is the relationship of reciprocal effect between dogmatic theology and pastoral action. Also, as we have already seen in this study, there is the influence of secularism upon the Church's missionary activity. For Geffré, however, dogmatic theology has been influenced more by the phenomenon of secularization, than either ecclesiology or pastoral action.[26]

The introduction of pastoral theology in secular universities, and the need to provide it with academic respectability, was a prime mover in this secularist dominance. This demand upon theological research has enabled secularization to exert considerable influence. Ratzinger is convinced that this has led to 'the degeneration of theology first into historicism, then into sociologism and, at the same time, to the impoverishment of philosophy.'[27] This is particularly true of an existential method, espoused by those who advance a demythologizing critique of fundamental source texts. Despite the apparent foundation of theological research in the needs of the human subject, this existential approach 'fails to provide the critical ontological inquiry which is also necessary to an adequate theology.'[28] This may be due to

23. Cf. his Foreword in Geffré C. (1974) op.cit. p.3
24. Ibid. p.3
25. Ibid. p.3
26. Cf. Geffré C. (1974) op.cit. p.32
27. Ratzinger J. (1987) op.cit. p.316. Although, he suggests the problem really began with Abelard's movement of theology from the monastery to the school room, 'and so into the neutrality of academe.' (ibid. p.322)
28. Macquarrie J. *Existentialism and theological method* in *Communio* vol.vi, no.1 Spring (1979), p.15

the total concern with the immediate, often to the detriment of the transcendental nature and teleological purpose of the human being.

Geffré names the 'progressive diversification of communities'[29] as another concern. To the present writer, there is a similar methodological problem with both these influences. The assumption of correspondence between theological investigation and the pastoral enterprise is indistinct and seriously weakened. Contemporary theology 'is striving to be the stage for the dialogue between the Church and the modern world.'[30] The danger here is obvious, and recent theological research has paid a severe penalty. In the past twenty years, theology 'has ceased to be treated as constituted knowledge and has become pluralistic interpretation.'[31] Maybe this has been an attempt to move away from Ritschl's understanding of received theological method. This is 'a system of theological study inherited from late antiquity, leading to a lifelong professional activity, without being fully convinced of its rightness.'[32] Within an ecclesial community of faith, this is an understandably inadequate method. Furthermore, it is a method greatly different to that of the fourth century pastoral mystagogues. Ritschl's reaction to 'late antiquity' may be to the scientific idealism which originated in the Enlightenment.[33]

There is an impression that theological reflection has changed in other respects too. Hans Frei was Professor of Religious Studies at Yale University. He believes that theology is concerned with 'statements or proclamations made in the course of Christian practice and belief.'[34] In this sense, theology is very much an activity of the faith community. Geffré believes that theology 'no longer fulfils its essential function in the Church: the service of the proclamation of the faith.' He believes that 'we are witnessing a rather disturbing break between catechesis or preaching and learned theology'.[35] There is a need to overcome the divisions between theological reflection and pastoral care practice. Some recent theological inquiry has been offered within an

29. Geffré C. (1974) p.35
30. Ibid. p.93
31. Geffré C. (1987) op.cit. p.11
32. Ritschl (1986) op.cit. p.294
33. Cf. Farley E. (1983) op.cit. p.19
34. Frei H. *Types of Christian Theology* (New Haven: Yale University Press, 1992) p.2
35. Geffré C. (1974) op.cit. pp.32-33. Farley's study epitomizes this divorce, when he talks about the: 'problem of theology and faith' within 'contemporary theological education.' (Farley (1983) op.cit. p.12)

understanding of history that suggests there should be no distinction between the unfolding drama of divine saving action and what has often been termed secular history.[36] This understanding of historical event may suggest a solution to the problem of the dichotomy between theology and the practice of ministry.

There is some evidence that the tide may be turning. Geffré wonders how the theologian can 'decode contemporary human experience unless he is informed by the conscious or unconscious effects of centuries of the Judaeo-Christian tradition?'[37] Ratzinger defines the theological process as 'a mode of questioning that is entirely philosophical, that does not stop with apparent or real historical facts, with sociological diagnoses or with pastoral techniques but insists inexorably on the search for causes.'[38] This is a good definition, but still fails to engage with the fundamental problem. There was probably a time when pastoral ministers gave serious consideration to theological issues. This is not the case in the present age.[39] The response to this situation is not to return to the position of a former generation, but rather, to rediscover a serious engagement of theology and practice in a renewed theological reflection.

The present tension in all theological disciplines is a dialectic between acceptance by secular academic institutions and the need to remain closely in touch with the life of an ecclesial community. It is a fundamental assertion of the present writer that this tension should be resolved in favour of the latter. Only this approach will enable the creation of an authentic pastoral theological methodological model. There has certainly been some attempt to integrate the two approaches in the development of theological method. Friedrich Schleiermacher was a Protestant pastor who was influenced by the German Romantic Movement. This led him to build a pastoral theological system which was heavily influenced by emotional feeling rather than dogma. He understood theology as 'a discipline in which the two, academic method and Christian self-description, are correlated as two autonomous yet reciprocally related factors.'[40] John Thiel, who teaches theology at Fairfield University, argues that Schleiermacher's

36. Cf. ibid. p.40
37. Geffré (1987) op.cit. p.3
38. Ratzinger J. (1987) op.cit. pp.315-316
39. Cf. Colborn F. *Grace and Pastoral Practice* in *Chicago Studies* vol.33 no.1 April 1994, p.67
40. Cf. Frei. H. (1992) op.cit. p.35

theological method is consonant with a Catholic position. This method 'understands dogmatics as the ongoing task of bringing the Christian community's pious affection to doctrinal expression.'[41] However, Bradford Hinze, from Marquette University, correctly suggests that Catholic theology would abhor the promotion of practical theology over the source elements of Christian tradition.[42] An authentic pastoral theology would clearly respect both these constituents of a genuine theological reflection.

Schleiermacher certainly reacted against the philosophy of Immanuel Kant, and was critical of the distorted reductionistic approach to Christianity advanced by other rationalists.[43] Johann Sebastian Drey was the Catholic contemporary of Schleiermacher at Tübingen. Johannes Evangelist Kuhn was Drey's successor. One step removed from Schleiermacher, Kuhn agreed with the need to preserve the dimension of reflection on ecclesial ministry.[44] Nevertheless, 'he was also convinced of the need to preserve the critical element, if theology was to succeed as an academic discipline.'[45] Our own investigation suggests the reciprocal relationship between the disciplines of doctrine and pastoral theology. Perhaps Kuhn's fundamental concern lies in Schleiermacher's tendency to collapse one discipline into the other. Theology, from a scientific perspective, may contain a number of disciplines. The important point raised by Schleiermacher is to ensure the presence of *all* dimensions in the theological process.

From a pastoral theological perspective, this was an important historical moment. Frei identifies Schleiermacher's theological position in the context of a pastorally-minded business, 'whose unity lies in its aim, the training of people in the conceptual skills necessary for ministry in the community defined by specific Christian life and language use; and as an historical and philosophical inquiry into the "essence" of Christianity, that is, as an academic discipline grounded in a unitary theory of explanation for all disciplines and in human nature.'[46] Is this

41. Thiel J. *Schleiermacher as 'Catholic': A change in the rhetoric of modern theology* in *The Heythrop Journal* vol.37, no.1, January 1996, p.64
42. Cf. Hinze B. *Johann Sebastian Drey's critique of Friedrich Schleiermacher's theology* in ibid. p.19
43. Cf. ibid. p.2
44. Madges W. *Faith, Knowledge and Feeling: Towards an Understanding of Kuhn's appraisal of Schleiermacher* in ibid. p.56
45. Ibid. p.56
46. Frei H. (1992) op.cit. p.70. Ritschl suggests that this dichotomy is contrary to Schleiermacher's intentions (cf. Ritschl (1986) op.cit. p.296)

entirely Schleiermacher's position, or has Frei's editorial work created something even better? In either case, the synthesis of two viewpoints is absent and the complete integration still needs to take place. This has clearly not happened, if one observer of contemporary clerical education is able to talk of the need 'to restore the *habitus* of theological understanding to the course of study which prepares the leadership of the church.'[47] Theological understanding 'occurs in the life of faith itself'.[48] Maybe this is a necessary caution within an academic study of theology which is totally divorced from the ecclesial community of faith.

Is it possible to find contemporary ecclesially-rooted pastoral-minded theologians, whose interests are similar to those of the fourth century mystagogues? In this present generation, Avery Dulles is an ecclesiologist whose work manifests an obvious desire to advance theology in a culture of doubt and a climate of constant revision. He recognizes the need to move beyond the neo-scholasticism of theology before the Second Vatican Council, in particular its dependency upon Aristotelian constructs. At the same time, he does not accept the authenticity of a pluralism that constantly undermines doctrinal formulation: 'For the better health of theology I believe that its ecclesial character needs to be more clearly recognized. Theology must serve the Church and be accountable to it.'[49] He suggests that a post-critical theology is used, in which 'the affirmations of faith cannot be rightly probed except from within the horizons of faith.'[50] This theological method seeks to move beyond the scepticism of many theological styles which have been influenced by the rationalist approach of the Enlightenment. There are obvious similarities here with the theological method of fourth century mystagogy.

In the development of a methodological model for pastoral theology, the post-critical position has further advantages. It stresses the need for internal analysis rather than detached observation, and it recognizes the primary function of liturgical celebration in theological development. In a statement applied to liturgy, Dulles asserts that 'symbols have greater cognitive importance. They are signs imbued with plenitude or

47. Farley E. (1983) op.cit. p.195
48. Ibid. p.195
49. Dulles A. *The Craft of Theology – From Symbol to System* (Dublin: Gill & Macmillan, 1992) p.viii
50. Ibid. p.7. The introduction of post-critical thought did not originate within a theological context. Rather, it was first used in a philosophical environment e.g., Polanyi M. *Personal Knowledge: Towards a Post-Critical Philosophy* (London: Routledge & Kegan Paul, 1958)

depth of meaning that surpasses the capacities of conceptual thinking and propositional speech.'[51] The patristic mystagogues realized that symbols have the power to evoke mystery. Ritschl makes a complementary point about the language of worship: 'It always gives theology afresh the task of taking up its work of secondary verification, putting forward and justifying regulated thought and action, and carrying out its characteristic tests for the comprehensibility, coherence and flexibility of renewed discourse from and to God.'[52] Thus, the symbol has cognitional value in a theological framework that is focused more on experiential awe and wonder.[53]

For a post-critical theology, conversion provides the basic material of theological reflection. Dulles proposes an investigation from two perspectives. Obviously, there is the faith journey of the individual and the personal decision of faith. Also, there is the witness of the faith community 'that mediates the action of God bringing about conversion.'[54] The role of the community is vital, even though it is often neglected. Why is this communal dimension so important? The principal reason lies in the new identity given in the sacraments of initiation. This provides an integrity that is not individualistic, but rather an entering into relationship with others: 'I would insist that no Christian conversion is complete unless it situates the convert solidly within the community of faith.'[55]

The work of Bernard Lonergan, a competent philosopher as well as an accomplished theologian, is crucial for an understanding of post-critical theology. He provides the philosophical language for a mystagogical-type theological model. In particular, he has analysed the act of knowing and developed a cognitional theory that recognizes the many operations which combine together in the act of knowing. Lonergan has discovered that the operational elements in the subjective cogitional act are arranged in a 'method'. A method is defined as 'a normative pattern of recurrent and related operations yielding cumulative and progressive results.'[56] This method may be applied to

51. Dulles A. (1992) op.cit. p.18
52. Ritschl D. (1986) op.cit. p.99
53. The theology that results from this process, is named by Dulles as an 'ecclesial-transformative approach' (Dulles (1992) op.cit. p.20)
54. Ibid. p.56
55. Ibid. p.66
56. Lonergan B. *Method in Theology* (London: Darton, Longman & Todd, 1971) p.4

the practice of pastoral ministry. In this method, we seek not only to understand what is happening in ministry. We seek to evaluate the practice of ministry in a manner that leads to further consideration of alternative courses of action.[57] Clearly, the 'knowing subject' is the focus of Lonergan's cognitional structure. Indeed, it is the subject himself who verifies the factual authenticity of this structure. Theological reflection must always begin here, for the reality of existential thought always precedes the systematization of this existence. This is Lonergan's generalized empirical method. Placed within a system of data – hypothesis – verification, it confirms the operation of the human subject as knower.

Lonergan states that 'human knowledge, then, is not some individual possession but rather a common fund, from which each may draw by believing, to which each may contribute in the measure that he performs his cognitional operations properly and reports their results accurately.'[58] This assertion is true not only in the province of the empirical sciences. It is a finding of one whose principal task is doing theology. It is a foundation for any reflection on meaning, and in particular, the context of meaning within intersubjectivity. Symbols are communal precisely because they concern communication. Furthermore, 'symbols obey the laws not of logic but of image and feeling' and 'the symbol, then, has the power of recognizing and expressing what logical discourse abhors: the existence of internal tensions, incompatibilities, conflicts, struggles, destructions.'[59] The symbol finds its significant meaning and dynamic within an existential ecclesial community, rather than a doctrinal formulation. Nevertheless, this does not deny the need for individual internal assimilation.

Indeed, involvement in the practice of ministry alone is insufficient for the community or the individual to discover true knowledge. There is a need to question ministerial practice and to seek the insight of intelligent operations. Such insight demands the patient application of conceptualization, understanding and even imagination in the exercise of pastoral ministry. This challenges the current emphasis on the accumulation of data alone, and suggests the need for interpretation.

---

57. Cf. ibid. p.13. Barth proposed a theological phenomenology of three distinct yet united elements: *explicatio, meditatio and applicatio* (cf. Frei H. (1992) op.cit. p.92)
58. Lonergan B. (1971) op.cit. p.43
59. Ibid. p.66

Geffré suggests that 'since the emergence in the nineteenth century of a new "historical consciousness", we have had a better appreciation of the fact that every act of knowledge must be an act of interpretation.'[60] James Fowler, the Director of the Centre for Faith Development in the Candler School of Theology at Emory University, Atlanta, has analysed the process of faith development, and arrived at a similar conclusion: 'While the conceptual analysis and translation of the symbol make its meanings explicit, we may fail to notice that in the process of communicating meanings the initiative has shifted from the symbol to the analyst of the symbol.'[61]

There is no mandate in Lonergan's epistemology for a denial of the Christian tradition, in any construction of the pastoral process. However, 'the rock, then, is the subject in his conscious, unobjectified attentiveness, intelligence, reasonableness, responsibility.'[62] All data must be subjected to this level of reasonable operation. It demands an epistemological method if pastoral ministry is to be correctly understood. Until now, we have referred to pastoral ministry or the practice of pastoral care, and avoided the term 'experience'. Lonergan refers to 'the ambiguity of the word, experience. For that word commonly is used as a synonym for knowledge, and, indeed, for thorough and especially for practical knowledge.'[63] We will develop this theme later. Finally, Lonergan states that 'there are the particular methods adapted to the needs and opportunities of particular fields.'[64] Authentic pastoral knowledge can be gained only through a pastoral theological method, and not by indiscriminate borrowing from elsewhere. As this method must inform all pastoral action, it will probably be inspired by the symbolic rather than the logical. This does not mean the symbolic is insubstantial, or that it forms an ethereal element in a methodological proposition.

8.3 Towards a Methodological Model

This brief analysis of contemporary theological inquiry implicates Christology as the primary pastoral theological symbol. Furthermore,

60. Geffré C. (1987) op.cit. p.2
61. Fowler J. *Faith Development and Pastoral Care* (Philadelphia: Fortress Press, 1987) p.70
62. Lonergan B. (1971) op.cit. p.20
63. Ed. Crowe F. *A Third Collection. Papers by Bernard J.F. Lonergan SJ* (London: Geoffrey Chapman, 1985) p.116
64. Ibid. p.150

our investigation leads to the assumption that the incarnate life and work, the death and resurrection of Christ, may be truly understood only within the community of faith. The present day effectiveness of pastoral theology demands that pastoral action be firmly painted upon this canvas. The Christological symbol, then, provides the necessary hermeneutic for understanding the practice of pastoral ministry. It embodies the conceptual matrix of all authentic pastoral care. Clearly, there are consequences here for the goals of pastoral care. From outside a perspective of discipleship, this would probably be quite unacceptable to academic theology in a secular context.

The significance of our earlier reflection upon the mystagogia school may become clearer at this point. Mystagogy was developed against a background of vehement heterodoxy and Christological controversy. Debate and tortuous definition racked the first four centuries of the Church's life. Just when Platonism seemed to have the ascendancy, the whole hellenistic middle-platonist system was seemingly abandoned and orthodoxy assumed the mantle of paradox. The wounds were still opened when the mystagogical pastors developed their theological tools of reflection.

Symbols are filled with an inner power to evoke awe and wonder. They also contain an inherent tension, conflict and struggle. Examination of contemporary Christology provides evidence of this proposition. There is a profound crisis in the Church today, which is concerned with the ability of the communion of disciples to understand their symbols of faith and to communicate them to others.[65] Faith is not only 'intellectual affirmation of the truths of faith nor a simple decision of the will, and it is certainly not just a feeling devoid of content.'[66] Faith, it is proclaimed, is 'a declaration of love for God.'[67] Thus, faith involves knowledge, for the unknown cannot be loved. Furthermore, a faith-knowledge which is truly based on love, demands witness and relationship: 'Only faith as it is lived is convincing.'[68] Within this framework, the Church is more than a social institution open to social scientific scrutiny. Once again, disabled theological reflection is understood to be caused by the

65. Cf. Kasper W. *Transcending all Understanding: The Meaning of Christian Faith Today* (San Francisco: Ignatius Press, 1989) p.13
66. Ibid. p.58
67. Ibid. p.60
68. Ibid. p.14

Enlightenment's promotion of the 'rule of reason and of a completely determined empirical idea'.[69] The Enlightenment may be understood as the attempt 'to split up the interdependence of the figure believed in and the faith confessed, to try to reach a neutral "knowledge" about Jesus.'[70] Against this narrow perspective, the Church is known as a communion of disciples who understand faith and ministry from within the context of actively lived discipleship.

This notion of communion also involves the present age in a relationship with those disciples who have gone before us. In a passage reminiscent of Lonergan, Kasper writes: 'If we want to further our knowledge, we cannot always start anew. We must lay hold of the treasure of experience and knowledge of those who came before us.'[71] A major part of this communal inheritance is the knowledge and understanding gained from within a worshipping community. Prayer is more than an adjunct to faith knowledge and pastoral action. It is the very environment in which such action and knowledge survive and develop. Prayer within the communion of disciples, and this also relates to so-called private prayer, provides the context for the establishment and development of a life of faith and discipleship.[72]

Balthasar develops theological reflection within an environment of mysticism. He believes that 'the inflation of knowledge only becomes dangerous when, ceasing to be concerned about the integrity of the figure, it reproduces itself like a laboratory culture and regards its own hypotheses (and it rarely gets beyond them) as equal or even superior to the knowledge of faith.'[73] These are the words of one who believes that the Christological symbol should be approached with reverential awe and wonder. Faith knowledge is the generously given fruit of a revelation, that is always communicated within a context of divine initiative. The incarnation and redemption are the two focal points in an elliptic symbol. These are received with faith by the communion of disciples in every age, within a methodological model for pastoral theological reflection.

What does this mean for pastoral action? Within pastoral theological reflection knowledge of redemptive action is co-relative to the

69. Ibid. p.26
70. Balthasar H. *Does Jesus Know Us? Do We Know Him?* (San Francisco: Ignatius Press, 1983) p.62
71. Kasper (1989) op.cit. p.43
72. Cf. ibid. p.63
73. Balthasar H. (1983) op.cit. pp.66-67

scriptural accounts of these events in the life of Jesus. He is the full manifestation of God's covenant with his people. Balthasar believes that in the covenant event, Christ 'sees there is nothing other than God's totally committed action.'[74] This covenant manifests the Lord as 'the absolutely free life of love which, if it is to be known, must of itself reveal, communicate itself.'[75] Through the dynamic relationship of charitable love towards others, the pastor discovers a knowledge of Jesus and his Father in the Spirit. To be sure, this kind of faith knowledge is more 'a hope which is not yet fulfilled' than 'in experience and sight'.[76] Nevertheless, this limited vision should not distract us from the essential reality. It is only within the Christological symbol of covenant love that we can truly understand the nature of authentic pastoral action.

Here, we arrive at the essential meaning of the Christological symbol within pastoral ministry. It is the uncompromising subjection of faith knowledge and pastoral action to the dynamic of conversion and a changing life. In the presence of Christ, knowledge and action are found in one reality. This is why Balthasar begins his reflection with the question of how *we ourselves* are known by Jesus, and not the other way round. Christ's insights were not simply intuitive, but 'a *saving knowledge* which, in God's light, takes cognizance of man's involvement with guilt and his need for redemption.'[77] Jesus discovers authentic knowledge of our condition, precisely through entering into suffering. In the events of his passion and cross, Christ enters fully into that human suffering, in such a way that his knowledge of us is authentic.

James Alison taught theology at the Catholic University of Bolivia. From the pastoral context of a society that is filled with obvious human need and intense suffering, he explored Christ's knowledge of suffering in *Knowing Jesus*. His Christological symbol becomes an ecclesiological event, as he examines 'a way of talking that can now be found at the very centre of the Church, and talk of an experience, or set of experiences, which are thought to be at the very centre of what it means to be a Christian at the end of the twentieth century.'[78] At the heart of Alison's thesis is the understanding of Christian experience in

74. Ibid. p.78
75. Ibid. p.85
76. Ibid. p.85
77. Ibid. p.19
78. Alison J. *Knowing Jesus* (London: SPCK, 1993) p.4

terms of the paschal mystery. This is the only source of true knowledge. It is 'the centre from which any talk of knowing Jesus, or having a personal relationship with him, flows.'[79] In the pastoral action of the paschal mystery, Jesus has become a victim of suffering, and so understands our human condition from the inside. This perspective of openness to the full finiteness of the human condition is the only way we can truly know Christ. The community dimension is present too: 'A private experience, called "knowing Jesus" can never be a substitute for a public change in ways of relating, within the public framework by which Jesus makes himself to be known – the sacraments, and victims.'[80] Thus, the place of the ecclesial communion of disciples is once again assured.

The bishops at the Second Vatican Council declared that 'in reality it is only in the mystery of the Word made flesh that the mystery of man truly becomes clear.'[81] This statement affirms the symbolic primacy of Christology in the development of a methodological model for contemporary pastoral theology. This means that the person of Christ must be found at the heart of the pastoral enterprise. His person is the inspiration, his methods are the means, and his glorification is the end. This teleological purpose of pastoral action may appear strange to some. However, the great parable of judgment in Matt. 25 suggests that what is done to the least brother or sister, is actually done to the person of Christ himself. In the parable, Jesus suggests that this will be a cause of much surprise.

The word 'experience', as we have already indicated, is indeed ambiguous and contains several meanings. We now have the pastoral theological tool to use the term in relationship to that practice of pastoral ministry which is fully informed by the Christological symbol. This leads to an investigation of pastoral ministry, as a mystery to be integrated into, and informed by, a Christological symbol. Ratzinger declares that the question of pastoral ministry and faith 'has acquired more and more urgency in the theological dialogue of recent years'.[82] There is an obvious agreement here with the nature of contemporary theological reflection. This affirms that 'religious experience in its most

79. Ibid. p.17
80. Ibid. p.103
81. *Gaudium et Spes* (1965) art.22
82. Ratzinger J. (1987) op.cit. p.343

exalted form bears the mark of the cross. It embraces the basic model of human existence, the transcendence of self. The cross redeems, it enables us to see.'[83] This implies that the law of the cross is operative within the very intentionality of the pastoral minister. The paschal mystery acts from within the subject's intellectual, moral and religious self. What is being suggested here transcends a notion of pastoral care that is not theologically informed by a Christological symbol. This symbol is an invitation to place ministry within a tradition of faith, and enable it to find an eschatological purpose within a theological vision of saving history. When pastoral ministry rediscovers its teleological vision, then it also serves the purpose of necessary theological renewal. Eschatology desperately needs to be decosmologized, stripped of its non-Christian accretions, and integrated within an authentic Christological context.[84]

Therefore, the mystery of authentic pastoral experience must be distinguished from those incidents and events of pastoral care which have not appropriated a Christological symbol. Pastoral care may be found in many diverse human and institutional situations. It may be an event that is filled with care and compassion. As such, this practice of pastoral ministry may even be described as 'life-changing'. It is not our intention to deny the importance of such pastoral care practice. However, this pastoral care is not necessarily a pastoral experience that is rooted in the Christological symbol. For this care to become authentic pastoral ministerial experience, the nature of transcendence needs to present itself to the incident of pastoral care. This care becomes a pastoral experience when there is a manifest involvement and participation in the paschal mystery. This refers to the mystery in its fullness. Only an experience of the resurrection enables the disciple to undergo the cross.

Mystagogical typology suggested that the saving efficacy of the paschal mystery is present in liturgical celebration. This typology has the potential to provide a theological paradigm for the practice of pastoral care. The soteriological ministry of Christ, foretold in the Old Testament types, has passed into the sacramental life of the Church. Could the same claim not be made in the wider exercise of pastoral ministry? In particular, this is a reference to that pastoral care which is

83. Ibid. p.350
84. Cf. Balthasar *Explorations in Theology vol.1* (San Francisco: Ignatius Press, 1989) p.270

fully immersed in a Christological symbol. To contradict this assertion might amount to a distinction between the testimony of the Word made flesh, and the Lord who testifies. This separation does not appear to be present in the New Testament. In Christ, who is both testimony and testifier, the Father has revealed the 'mystery of his purpose'.[85] The mystagogue pastors understood the implication of this great mystery: that the scriptures reveal the Lord himself and how he relates to his creation in a saving manner. The whole of human history is to be understood within this self-revelation of the Lord. The word of God is not only read in created things, or on the pages of scripture, it is witnessed in the pastoral ministry of his chosen people. Thus, a pastoral care that is informed by the paschal mystery contains that same creative and saving reality. And furthermore, as the highest note of this divine revelation is sounded in the death and resurrection of Jesus, pastoral experience can truly claim possession to this most profound revelation.

This study is particularly concerned with the exercise of pastoral ministry within the context of a parish community. This ministry involves a large variety of pastoral care situations. By using a concept of pastoral care practice that is informed by the Christological symbol, priests, and all others who are involved in pastoral ministry, are able to understand a particular pastoral incident as a theological reality. Our whole investigation of contemporary pastoral theological themes is brought to bear on this moment. Balthasar believes that for too long the tradition has created an antithesis between action and contemplation. This reflects the ancient opposition of *actio* and *passio*.[86] There is some difference, in that 'action means simply external activity, in fact activity restricted to meeting the needs of the present life... Contemplation, on the other hand, is occupation with the truth for its own sake, and insofar as it is beyond time; ultimately divine truth and everything that stands in relation to it.'[87] Nevertheless, the true practice of one demands its exercise in relationship with the other. Throughout the history of the Church, an early ascetical influence has always sought to create a hierarchical structure, in which contemplation was more important than action.[88]

85. Eph. 1:9
86. Cf. Balthasar (1989) op.cit. p.227
87. Ibid. p.227
88. Cf. Ibid. p.230

By striving to ensure that the practice of pastoral care becomes experience, this study seeks to bring action and contemplation together. Indeed, this relationship between the two is an important component of our methodological model. Balthasar suggests that contemplation and action 'condition each other mutually, as do intellect and will, between which there exists a reciprocal priority, contemplation being a prerequisite of true action, and action the indispensable condition of true contemplation.'[89] Obviously, this relationship is understood most clearly within the Christological symbol. There was no action of Jesus that did not flow from his hours of prayer with the Father. Furthermore, this pastoral experience truly pointed beyond itself to the Father's will. In another place, Balthasar defines contemplation from within a particularly poignant Christological symbol. Contemplation is 'the presaging vision of transparent glory in the form of the Servant.'[90] In this way, the contemplation of his pastoral ministry has always been paradigmatic for the Church's subsequent ministry. From within this necessary symbol, faith is understood only in a context of love. This love discovers itself in a knowledge that is not content until it has fulfilled itself in action.

The eschatological nature of ministry has already been observed. Within our theological symbol, pastoral action receives other structural elements too. The Johannine discourses of the Fourth Gospel may be used here to illustrate the systematic development of these structures. In the conversation with Nicodemus, Jesus proclaims 'In all truth I tell you, we speak only about what we know'.[91] Here, the communion of disciples identifies its pastoral ministry with that of the Lord. Christ's saving work is made present through ecclesial pastoral action, precisely because the Church knows the mind of its Saviour. Having entered into this reality, the disciples echo the next lesson: 'My food is to do the will of the one who sent me, and to complete his work.'[92] Pastoral ministry is a continuation of the Lord's own ministry until the Kingdom is fully established. Knowledge of the Lord's will enables ecclesial ministry to exercise judgment in pastoral action.

89. Ibid. p.233
90. Balthasar *The Glory of the Lord vol.1: Seeing the Form* (Edinburgh: T. & T. Clark, 1982) p.39
91. John 3:11
92. John 4:34

Jesus declared that 'by himself the Son can do nothing; he can do only what he sees the Father doing.'[93] If pastoral ministry truly reflects this experience, then it continues to bring judgment upon human history. Where there is openness to the signs spoken through pastoral action, then 'such a person has passed from death to life.'[94] This is perceived only within the perspective of a faith community. Outside that community, human events are potentially isolated and unconnected, meaningless and futile, inconclusive and finite. The whole of the discourse in the synagogue at Capernaum is to be understood within the context of a community of liturgical celebration. Jesus is 'the living bread which has come down from heaven. Anyone who eats this bread will live for ever'.[95] The experience of this 'living bread', completely realized in the Eucharist, so often brings life to a particular moment of pastoral care. Authentic pastoral ministry not only satisfies the hunger within the human condition, but quenches the thirst too: 'From his heart shall flow streams of living water.'[96] This reference to the hour of Christ's passion reminds us that saving judgment is experienced above all in the paschal mystery: 'When you have lifted up the Son of man, then you will know that I am He.'[97] Thus, in the Church's eucharistic celebration, disciples not only know the Lord, but are substantially united with his transcendental ministry.

It is possible to discern the fullest scriptural model of all pastoral ministry in the imagery of the Good Shepherd. Jesus declares 'I have come so that they may have life and have it to the full.'[98] This fullness of life, however, is discovered only when 'the good shepherd lays down his life for his sheep.'[99] This narrative determines how pastoral experience must be completely informed by the paschal mystery. In a Johannine theology, this is called the Hour of Glory. If the single grain dies, 'it yields a rich harvest.'[100] There is no pastoral effectivity outside this central Christological symbol of the passion. Furthermore, because of Christ's return to the Father, the disciples 'will perform the same works as I do myself, and will perform even greater works, because I

93. John 5:19
94. John 5.:24
95. John 6:51
96. John 7:38
97. John 8:28
98. John 10:10
99. John 10:11
100. John 12:24

am going to the Father.'[101] In this manner, the paschal mystery enables ministry to become pastoral experience.

Viewed through the lens of a Christological symbol, pastoral ministry is also prophetic. The heart of this prophetic dimension is a ministry that is open for all to see: 'I have spoken openly for all the world to hear; I have always taught in the synagogue and in the Temple where all the Jews meet together; I have said nothing in secret.'[102] Christ's prophetic ministry is given to the disciples. They will also act in a way that can be witnessed by the world. The testimony of their ministry will be accepted or rejected by others. The fruitfulness of this ministry is a different matter. Balthasar suggests that 'the source whence it springs lies in the inward, invisible sphere. When it flows outward and produces a visible change, the connection is such that it can only be felt and glimpsed in faith; it can never be established by the methods of ordinary experience.'[103] This sentiment indicates the need for a precise and informed use of the term 'experience'.

It is now possible to propose a methodological model for pastoral ministry that is truly theological and not founded upon the method of other non-theological disciples. It is clear from our discussion so far, that pastoral care activity is dependent upon the saving action of the Trinity God.[104] The model proposed here is built upon a Christological symbol in its most profound sense. When an incident of pastoral care has become pastoral experience, it is possible to discern and outwardly observe the presence of the incarnate Word. The Word made flesh entered into the suffering of the cross and was glorified because of his obedience. This paschal mystery must remain the source and model of all ministry within the community of disciples. Pastoral ministry is always rooted in the Christian community within an ecclesiological model of communion. Therefore, contemporary ministry should demonstrate a truly collaborative typology. This is not only an ecclesiological consideration. It is an essential component of a Christological symbol that is rooted in the relationships of the Trinity. Pastoral care becomes pastoral experience when it responds to an essential contemplation of the Christian community's tradition. This

101. John 14:12
102. John 18:20
103. Von Balthasar H. *Explorations in Theology vol.2* (San Francisco: Ignatius Press, 1991) p.12
104. Cf. Drilling P. *Trinity and Ministry* (Minneapolis: Fortress Press, 1991) p.26

community is determined by the redemptive love of its Saviour. It follows then, that this same experience remains at the centre of the Church's pastoral ministry.

8.4 Construction of the Pastoral Process

Our methodological model may now be tested in the construction of an informed process for the exercise of pastoral ministry. The model will then be applied to the development of a pattern of pastoral theological reflection. This method is founded upon a post-critical theological model. (Other elements in the contemporary theological climate have already been noted.) Before this application is made to the process of reflection, it will be useful to investigate four writers, who all offer different perspectives on the theme: Stephen Pattison, George Furniss, David Deeks and Alastair Campbell. Finally, the model will be tested against a contemporary document issued by the Congregation for Catholic Education.[105]

Pattison's work, already cited in this study, is an attempt to provide professional direction to the practitioner of pastoral care. He suggests that 'it seems almost incredible that theological students spend years studying the Bible and ethics, for example, yet there are no widely available detailed discussions of the relationship of these areas to the practical work of pastoral care.'[106] While this statement is correct, the real issue concerns the methodology of the relationship. There is evidence that Pattison would not accept the methodological model proposed above. For example, a description of pastoral care that focuses on the Gospel and consequent 'theological commitments' is described as an 'indigestible definition'.[107] However, this does not necessarily lead to the total acceptance of non-theological models. Post-war material from the United States reflects the 'enormous influence of existentialist ideas there at that time.'[108] Furthermore, the 'Christian community and its tradition are not seen as important either in terms of context or resource.'[109] Pattison does not support this viewpoint.

Pattison rejects the American trend and is able to arrive at his own definition of pastoral care. It is 'that activity, undertaken especially by

105. A department of the Roman Curia.
106. Pattison S. (1993) op.cit. p.1
107. Ibid. p.5
108. Ibid. p.12
109. Ibid. p.12

representative Christian persons, directed towards the elimination and relief of sin and sorrow and the presentation of all people perfect in Christ to God.'[110] This definition appears to be influenced by a Christological symbol. The various elements of the symbol, detailed above in the preparation of our model, are present by implication but not necessarily appreciated or developed. After a review of contemporary material, Pattison states that 'pastoral theologians seem to have almost completely avoided considering the Bible.'[111] And then, the revelation of his hand, the 'most obvious reason for the relative neglect of the Bible in pastoral care theory and practice is that the Bible is not itself much concerned with this area. Pastoral care is largely a product of the post-biblical church.'[112] However, reference to the community of disciples and its tradition is practically non-existent in Pattison's definition of pastoral care. He does provide a useful survey of the ways in which scriptural material is used in post-Enlightenment academic practical theology. Unfortunately, there is no unambiguous presentation of his own model. This may be because of his limited appreciation of ecclesial tradition.[113]

Later, Pattison demonstrates a confused understanding of pastoral experience and pastoral care that is not theologically informed. He states that 'the inclusion of experience and the social sciences as full partners in the dialogue or conversation is particularly significant; traditional theological methods have often given a very subordinate place to contemporary experience as a significant element in discerning the truth.'[114] The problem here is obvious. The methodology of the social sciences is not consonant with that of 'traditional theology'. The inclusion of a social scientific understanding of contemporary pastoral care leads to the critical analysis of a practical theology – rather than the pastoral theology, which is the research matter of this investigation. Once again, there is confusion about where Pattison's real predilection is to be found. He acknowledges the idea that pastoral care based on

110. Ibid. p.13
111. Ibid. p.106
112. Ibid. p.107
113. Pattison does acknowledge some of these issues, in an 'Afterword' cf. pp.195-196. However, he still fails to understand the need for a strong central Christological symbol. One consequence of this is his total ambiguity and eventual openness to *any* definition: 'it is not necessary to adopt any one to the exclusion of others, particularly if doing so limits one's ability to discern and affirm practical pastoral care in whatever form when it is actually being performed.' (Ibid. p.196)
114. Ibid. p.41

the methods of secular counselling tends to promote 'harmful modernistic values such as individualism, narcissism and hedonism.'[115]

This critical appreciation of Pattison's work must not be construed as a denigration of the social sciences, or their methodologies, in themselves. An example from pastoral care practice may illustrate the dilemmas involved. In the course of pastoral ministry, someone may be presented for pastoral care. It becomes clear that this person is suffering advanced stages of physical and psychological stress. Medical treatment of a virus may attend to the first area of concern. How can the pastoral minister respond to the second? The one receiving ministry reveals that she had been abused twenty years previously. The guilt of this relationship is always present to her. More recently, loved members of the family have died. There are indications that the grief of this loss has been severely repressed. Pastoral care can certainly be offered to this person. It is a ministry which is interpreted within a Christological symbol. It calls upon the rich resources of ecclesial tradition. There may also be a need for professional psychotherapeutic help, in order that this person can be aided to deal with her emotional burdens. This, however, is not usually the domain of the pastoral minister. Neither should there be a confusion of methodology. Indeed, it is necessary to recognize the irreconcilable conflict between these two models of care in a particular pastoral incident.

Pattison's work is a good example of contemporary practical theological material. It is well researched, and provides a comprehensive survey of a wide constituency. Nevertheless, it is clearly from the stable of academic respectability. It is an attempt to flirt with the methodological approaches of other disciplines, in particular, the behavioural sciences. Above all else, there is no certain clarity about the author's own position. This is not a problem with Furniss' work, *Sociology for Pastoral Care*.[116] George Furniss is a Presbyterian minister who is involved in pastoral care practice in a hospital situation. He has also taught sociology to students preparing for pastoral ministry. As the title of his book suggests, this study is an unambiguous attempt to import the structural mechanisms of sociology into pastoral care. Aimed primarily at ministers of religion and candidates for this ministry, Furniss believes 'sociology has existed as a largely unheralded

115. Ibid. p.36
116. Furniss G. *Sociology for Pastoral Care* (London: SPCK, 1994)

tributary of the pastoral tradition.'[117] Its principal cultural hermeneutic is deconstructionalist, and a glossary of sociological terms is provided. This is needed, as the author 'asserts that sociology is a key resource for resolving the identity struggle confronting pastoral care today.'[118]

Furniss' book deliberately seeks to move away from every element in our methodological model for pastoral theology. He approves of a pastoral care that has 'bought heavily into the cultural pluralism and cognitive relativism of modern culture.'[119] The claim that pastoral care 'happens in a highly pluralistic social context',[120] is not offered as a mere statement of fact. Pluralism is lauded precisely because it creates 'the psychological context for modern life, the shift from fate to choice.'[121] The religious element in this caring diversity is acknowledged. However, pastoral ministry is never offered within the unique perspective of a Christological symbol. Indeed, 'unhealthy religion may contribute to persons' inadequate definitions of the situation.'[122] And 'religious uncertainty is a key aspect of the modern "homeless mind".'[123]

Our concept of pastoral experience finds no place in this system of pastoral care. Sociology offers 'the empirical realm of observable phenomena', while theology is concerned with 'the non-empirical or metaphysical realm.'[124] Hence, the practitioner of pastoral ministry is invited to buy into 'a new paradigm of pastoral care that unites psychology, theology, and sociology'.[125] However, this marriage is too one-sided. Following Don Browning, one of the founding fathers of clinical pastoral education, practitioners of this method of education believe that recent theories of pastoral care are meant to be altogether free of ecclesiological value.[126] Culture is 'the complex of a society's definitions of reality'.[127] Nevertheless, there is no attempt in this study to promote a specific Christian ethos, or its theological interpretation in the revelation of the incarnation and redemption. Such an ethos has

117. Ibid. p.vi
118. Ibid. p.x
119. Ibid. p.2
120. Ibid. p.16
121. Ibid. p.4
122. Ibid. p.6
123. Ibid. p.25
124. Ibid. p.9
125. Ibid. p.11
126. Cf. ibid. p.12
127. Ibid. p.20

an inherent capacity to challenge a contemporary mindset which is 'secularistic, capitalistic, individualistic, and rationalistic'.[128] Sadly, the opportunity of judgment within a Christological symbol is lost, and any criticism is reduced to the framework of a sociological model.

Furniss argues that most contemporary pastoral care models are rooted in a sociological functionalist tradition. In this system, 'religion benefits the society by generating in its members the motivation to play needed roles and by instilling commitment to the social order.'[129] There is no reference whatsoever to the redemptive and soteriological data of theological reflection. Prior to this statement about religion, the author recounts an event from his hospital chaplaincy experience: 'In one case, the heart monitor of a patient who was talking with me about major emotional and spiritual issues revealed marked irregularity to staff at the nursing station. In the other case, a patient had a cardiac arrest a few minutes after a significant pastoral conversation.'[130] Perhaps such 'sociological data' provide the appropriate response to such an empirical view of pastoral ministry. Later, Furniss outlines his theological understanding of pastoral care. It is a promotion of Peter Berger's 'inductive' theological approach to the 'problem' of religion in contemporary society.[131] In this approach 'the context impels choice-making among alternative worldviews where orthodoxies no longer are determinative. Compared to a deductive style, the inductive approach to pastoral care stresses the dialogical character of pastoral interaction and does not suppress full realization of modernism's challenge to religious viewpoints.'[132] Perhaps such a practitioner of 'pastoral care' should not be allowed into a cardiac care unit too often.

Furniss' pastoral care examples are mostly taken from his ministry in a hospital chaplaincy. In the context of preparation for ministry, clinical pastoral education models are highlighted.[133] The hospital chaplain must relate to many groups (he uses Merton's role-set figure to describe the complex web of relationships). The 'patients' are one of these groups. There is a list of eight other groups: nurses, social

128. Ibid. p.23
129. Ibid. p.85
130. Ibid. p.85
131. Cf. ibid. p.97
132. Ibid. p.104
133. Referred to at the beginning of this chapter, and introduced into training for ministry by James and Evelyn Whitehead.

workers, administrators, volunteers, other chaplains, pastors, physicians and psychiatrists. And then, as though this group does not appear elsewhere in the list, conservative Christians.[134] In Furniss' reflection on role-conflict, this final group stand isolated and alienated, without further discussion. We might presumptively conclude that these 'conservative Christians' are those who represent the ecclesial tradition. These are the ones who draw upon that tradition for their inspiration and insight. They stand against Furniss' understanding of pastoral care, and the sociological methodology that forms it.

Furniss suggests that 'the move in recent years toward differentiation of pastoral identity around *theological* diagnosis has been immensely positive.'[135] However, this is not followed through. The statement provides no serious threat to a sociological methodological model. He prefers a 'professional' approach that recognizes five stages of the pastoral care process.[136] Earlier, he acknowledges that 'the theological critique of the "professional" model stresses the need for *formation* of the pastoral caregiver. Formation is a concept with strong roots in the Roman Catholic tradition'.[137] However, in Furniss' study, a pastoral theological model of formation is not developed beyond this initial statement.

David Deeks is a Methodist minister and a tutor at Wesley House, Cambridge. In his *Pastoral Theology: An Inquiry*, he uses resources from many diverse disciplines. In many respects, this study is a weak illustration of our own pastoral theological model. Although, he actually recommends 'the intermingling of metaphors (from the sciences, the Christian tradition and everything else culture and history can supply) as a *necessary* path to understanding needs to be given structured expression.'[138] Nevertheless, this work is worth investigation as an attempt to take the theological tradition seriously. This pastoral theologian begins his work with the statement that 'the primary longing of the Christian is to live the faith of Christ.'[139] This faith is lived primarily in 'the practice of love, in words and deeds.'[140]

134. Cf. Furniss (1994) op.cit. p.124
135. Ibid. p.137
136. Defining pastoral identity; pastoral assessment; pastoral plan; pastoral intervention; pastoral evaluation (cf. ibid. p.144)
137. Ibid. p.135
138. Deeks D. *Pastoral Theology: An Inquiry* (London: Epworth Press, 1987) p.247
139. Ibid. p.1
140. Cf. ibid. p.9

However, pastoral theology 'begins with the search we all make for meaning in life.'[141] And in an easily misunderstood statement, he states that 'a pastoral theologian appears to live in the first instance as if there were no God.'[142]

Deeks is prepared to demonstrate the need for a contemplative attention of the Christological symbol: 'Prayer is the "heart" exploring and critically examining things; it is the means by which we attend and respond to God as he continues to love all that he has made. It is the interior task without which the exterior activity of pastoral care cannot function well.'[143] Later, he states that 'reflection can enable us to dig deeper into experience and disclose hidden levels of meaning.'[144] As an example of his own reflection, Deeks has developed the theme of alienation which is common to pastoral ministry and psychology alike. Within the methodologies of both disciplines, the discussion extends to the three themes of: contradiction, failure and exhaustion. He is prepared to draw upon scriptural resources, and uses the biblical paradigms of the prophets and Romans as the models and instruments for his reflection. The task of a pastoral theologian, he believes, is to establish a conversation between the drama of human existence and the Christian tradition.[145] This tradition is understood within an appropriate breadth: 'It includes poetry and hymns, art and architecture, wisdom and proverbs, community rules, prayers and liturgies, stories of faith and martyrdom, of individuals and institutions serving the world and being corrupted by it'.[146]

With regard to pastoral care, Deeks accepts the assertion that 'a common tradition, a common way of life, is not sustained by discussion alone. It requires the structuring of common experience, and the pursuit of agreed goals and purposes in common action.'[147] Underlying his work is the idea of a social community. Unfortunately, the potential of this common experience within the ecclesial community remains unformed and undeveloped. He does acknowledge that 'one of the consequences of secularization may be that we are

141. Ibid. p.67
142. Ibid. p.67
143. Ibid. p.1
144. Ibid. p.2
145. Cf. ibid. p.69
146. Ibid. p.79
147. Ibid. p.27

alienated from spiritual experience, represented by the mystic.'[148] A statement about science appears to contradict his methodological model. He believes that science 'cannot make sense of why anything should exist at all. It cannot contribute to discussions of any purpose that nature and society might be thought to have.'[149] None of these observations are thoroughly investigated, and the dichotomous relationship between two disciplines is not fully resolved.

Pastoral care has a clear purpose in this study. It is 'to assist men and women and boys and girls to live as disciples of Jesus.'[150] In this context, pastoral ministry involves a challenge to what is trivial or evasive, fantasy or illusion within the incident of pastoral care.[151] Deeks' study is a refutation of the professionalism that 'means to engage in a relatively detached way in a limited area of human experience'.[152] On the contrary, the pastor's principal call is 'to be human, to work with risk at an agenda that is as wide as life itself.'[153] In practice, the pastor may not be able to 'make a difference to human situations.'[154] How is one prepared for pastoral ministry? Deeks understands the practice of ministry to be the locus for this learning process. Learning takes place within ministerial tasks 'which are puzzling, challenging or unexpectedly inspiring and revelatory.'[155]

Alastair Campbell is an experienced pastoral theologian who operates in an academic context. He was the Senior Lecturer in the Department of Christian Ethics and Practical Theology in the University of Edinburgh. He does not write from a Catholic perspective. However, of all the works investigated, he offers the greatest sympathy to our methodological model. For Campbell, 'pastoral care overlaps virtually all the other theological disciplines at one point or another.'[156] As the title suggests, his work is an attempt to rediscover the nature of pastoral care within a theological framework. The heritage of ecclesial tradition is valued, 'the temptation to discard everything from the past as irrelevant to our present situation must be

148. Ibid. p.35
149. Ibid. p.55
150. Ibid. p.81
151. Cf. ibid. p.82
152. Ibid. p.82
153. Ibid. p.83
154. Ibid. p.233
155. Ibid. p.239
156. Campbell A. *Rediscovering Pastoral Care* (London: Darton, Longman & Todd, 1981) p.xii

resisted.'[157] There is recognition of the pluralistic foundation of contemporary thinking. This, however, is not welcomed with the same enthusiasm as Furniss. Campbell notes the unifying element of all pluralism as the reaction against 'all claims to an inerrant teaching authority.'[158] This produces conclusions already noted in our reflection on ecclesial mission. They are 'tolerance of ambiguity, and awareness that all theoretical formulations only approximate to the reality they attempt to describe are regarded as marks of the educated intellect.'[159]

Diverse theologies and the growth of the science of psychology have conspired to produce uncertainty within pastoral ministry. Through examples from literature, Campbell develops the need for what he names as 'integrity' within pastoral care. The pastoral minister is also 'a human being who must face desolation and vulnerability, despair and disillusionment, guilt and uncertainty.'[160] This is what Campbell means by integrity. Beyond care and compassion, this theologian points to other important elements in the pastoral relationship. There are other elements 'not achieved through the trivial glorification of "self-realization" so common in contemporary popularized versions of psychotherapy.'[161] This is the 'mysterious centre to our being, hard to describe or discuss, yet indispensable to our integrity.'[162] Indeed, this centre involves the 'contemplative aspects of Christian experience.'[163] Here is a theologian who has understood the synthesis of contemplation and action within the Christian tradition. He has struggled with the paschal mystery, and discovered a construct of pastoral care immersed within the glorious messiness of the Christological symbol.

Campbell does not use Lonergan's notion of symbol. Although, again using a literary construct, he has instead developed a theological concept of 'image'. He suggests that 'it is in the intuitive grasp of non-logical interrelationships that the image plays a unique role.'[164] The primary image of pastoral care is that of the Good Shepherd. It is necessary to penetrate the mystery of this image, and to apply it to the

157. Ibid. p.1
158. Ibid. p.4
159. Ibid. p.4
160. Ibid. p.12
161. Ibid. p.14
162. Ibid. p.14
163. Ibid. p.14
164. Ibid. p.19

pastoral relationship. Within Campbell's theological exposition, this produces a desire to abandon the 'stress on *competence* which has dominated pastoral care since the emergence of a literature devoted to pastoral counselling.'[165] In its place, he wants to restore a pastoral care that is 'embodied care, care incarnate.'[166]

This renewed concept of pastoral care demands a contemplative and exegetical focus on the biblical images. Campbell devotes a whole chapter to the image of the shepherd. Through attention to the primary source of the scriptures, he discovers that a central feature of the biblical shepherd is 'courage to the point of risking one's own life.'[167] This leads him to the conclusion that 'it is this element of courage based on trust in God which seems most obviously neglected in modern accounts of pastoral relationships.'[168] There are other elements: tenderness, skill, self-sacrifice, care of the despised and leadership.[169] Others have developed this biblical theme. Campbell, however, reflects upon the courage of Jesus as he enters his hour of passion. An important comparison is made and a critical conclusion attained. The pastoral relationship demands emulation of Christ's sacrificial love, and 'we know before we begin that the goal is unattainable. Yet perhaps it is no bad thing that the central image in pastoral care, when properly appreciated, has this humbling effect. It must surely finally dispose of all self-confident "management models" for pastoral care.'[170] There is humility in his discussion of pastoral ministry that will not compromise the form of an authentic theological understanding of pastoral care.

Indeed, the importing of methodological models from elsewhere is unreliable and unlikely to produce the fruit of pastoral effectivity. Campbell believes that 'preparation for pastoral care must avoid the danger of superficiality, of dealing only with techniques or with the more obvious dimensions of human need. We struggle to plumb the depths of human experience in pastoral care.'[171] His understanding of experience resonates with the model we have proposed. It demands a

165. Ibid. p.16
166. Ibid. p.16
167. Ibid. p.26
168. Ibid. p.26
169. Cf. ibid. pp.27-30
170. Ibid. p.35
171. Ibid. p.107

process of formation rather than training in professional skills: 'Formation for pastoral care must therefore encourage people to pay attention to the "inner life", in times of quiet reflection which give leave for light or dark to enter in.'[172]

In order to enter into the woundedness of a pastoral situation, a pastoral minister must allow himself to be wounded. This is certainly part of the Christological symbol in its fullness. It also allows pastoral care to become authentic experience: 'A wound is an opening in the walls of our body, a breaking of the barrier between us and the world around us.'[173] In this sense, pastoral care does not offer cheap palliative grace, but only the folly of the cross. In this context, Campbell can proclaim the return to steadfast integrity. He declares that 'the need of the helper and the helped are one: in life, in death in the midst of life, we can give and receive care only by discovering those things which alone enable us to stand firm against every threat to faith.'[174] At this moment, pastoral ministry is firmly rooted where it belongs, in the ecclesial community of faith.

Finally, our methodological model will be tested against a Catholic pastoral theological text. On 19 March 1995, the Congregation for Catholic Education published its *Directives on the Formation of Seminarians Concerning Problems related to Marriage and the Family*. The context of these directives is clearly defined within the ecclesial community of faith. It is imbued with a personalist anthropology, which understands the human being as created in the image and likeness of a Trinitarian God. Therefore, the human being is called to vertical and horizontal communion with others. Both marriage and family life issues are good examples of the pastoral events, open to duplex disciplinary methodologies. Furthermore, the diversity of marriage and family styles provides social phenomenological data. The important contribution of 'the human sciences'[175] is firmly acknowledged. Nevertheless, the principal foundation of this document is within an informed theological tradition. It certainly manifests elements of the Christological symbol.

The document concludes that 'in order to confront the enormous

172. Ibid. p.107
173. Ibid. p.39
174. Ibid. p.97
175. Congregation for Catholic Education *Directives on the Formation of Seminarians Concerning Problems related to Marriage and the Family* (1995) art.8

difficulties which they meet today, families need expert spiritual guides and sound doctrine.'[176] This can be found only in a synthesis of ministerial care, in 'new doctrinal, moral, spiritual, and pastoral developments and new emphases responding to the reality and urgency of the present situation.'[177] These directives are offered in the context of formation for presbyteral ministry. The text is observably compatible with a post-critical understanding of theological method. This demands that academic reflection remain faithful to the tradition. The Congregation's research suggests that this is not always the case. Indeed, 'this subject-matter is not being treated with that accuracy and fullness which is necessary in order to provide the Church with pastors who are well-prepared'.[178]

There must be integrity of pastoral care and theological reflection, if this preparation is to be effective. The suggestion that an individual is 'pastoral' is sometimes opposed to the assertion that someone else is 'rigidly theological'. This distinction creates a false confrontation and leads to an ineffective ministry. The text suggests that pastoral effectiveness 'depends to a great extent on the quality of the intellectual formation'[179] received during preparation for pastoral ministry. Pastoral formation has received much theological attention in recent magisterial teaching. However, 'the practical fruit of this teaching is at times diminished due to doctrinal uncertainty and instability'.[180] Against this situation, the Congregation asserts that pastoral theology needs to be 'deeply rooted in dogma and sound moral principles'.[181]

Pastors are to be 'sensitive towards human weaknesses, and also seriously concerned for the respect due to the inviolable divine laws.'[182] To understand this requirement, pastoral ministry needs to be fully immersed in a Christological symbol. Jesus understands our human condition because he is truly incarnate and shares our human nature. In his redemptive sacrifice, he not only enables healing of this condition, but also opens all human nature to eschatological judgment. Within practical pastoral ministry, there must be the 'possibility of testing and

176. Ibid. art.64
177. Ibid. art.1
178. Ibid. art.5
179. Ibid. art.7
180. Ibid. art.10
181. Ibid. art.39
182. Ibid. art.64

refining the capacity for communication and authentic human relationships.'[183] This statement reflects the call of the apostolic exhortation, *I will Give You Shepherds*, that the priest has 'the capacity to relate to others'.[184] This pastoral capacity is founded upon an ecclesiology and anthropology of communion, which is, rooted itself within the relationships of the Trinity. This communion dimension is of course a profound manifestation of the Christological symbol.

Unfortunately, an appreciation of pastoral care practice which is rooted within an understanding of Christo-Trinitarian communion is not fully developed in the ecclesiological dimension of this document. There is an emerging need for theological academic disciplines to work together. There is even recognition of the success in practical pastoral care that takes place 'in dioceses which are rich in initiatives on behalf of families (counsellors, groups and movements)'.[185] However, the full acceptance of collaborative ministry remains dormant. It is precisely in these areas of marriage and family life that contemporary pastoral ministry needs to be exercised in a collaborative manner.[186] In conclusion, we might note the absence of this element of our methodological model, in all five models of pastoral ministry that have been investigated.

183. Ibid. art.11
184. *Pastores Dabo Vobis* (1992) art.43
185. Congregation for Catholic Education (1995) op.cit. art.11
186. This is a broader concern than ministry alone. Collaboration also has implications for a contemporary theology of the priesthood.

CHAPTER NINE

Pastoral Theological Reflection

9.0 Introduction

The final task of this study of pastoral theology involves an application of the methodological model developed in the previous chapter to the practice of pastoral ministry and theological reflection. The immediate problem has already been identified. It is the inherent tension caused by the use of different methodologies in the exercise of pastoral care and the attempt to reflect on the practice of ministry. The pastoral theological model developed in this study claims fidelity to the theological process of the Second Vatican Council. It returns to the foundational biblical and patristic sources of the Christian tradition. In order to achieve this, it is necessary to disengage with certain post-Enlightenment theological and epistemological developments. The problems with these developments are grounded in the exaggerated emphasis on reason, as the *exclusive* foundation for authentic knowledge. Against this supposition, the methodological model developed in this study proposes that pastoral ministry itself can provide substantive knowledge. O'Collins suggests that there is a common theological scepticism about the suggestion that pastoral ministry can provide this knowledge.[1]

Other theological disciplines may not have adopted this particular model of practice and reflection. The Congregation for Catholic Education accepts the idea of methodological pluralism.[2] Nevertheless, this is accompanied by an important qualification. The Church 'must deplore arbitrary and chaotic pluralism which uses philosophies far removed from faith, and very disparate terminology thus making understanding between theologians ever more difficult, if not impossible.'[3] The ferment caused by this dialectic ensures the continued

1. Cf. O'Collins G. *Retrieving Fundamental Theology* (London: Geoffrey Chapman, 1993) p.108
2. Cf. Congregation for Catholic Education (1976) *The Theological Formation of Future Priests* in National Conference of Catholic Bishops *Norms for Priestly Formation vol. 1* (Washington: United States Conference, 1993) p.77
3. Ibid. p.78

confused uncertainty about the nature of pastoral ministry and theological reflection. Our study maintains the need to overcome an attitude of reductionism in the process of reflection on pastoral care practice. Pastoral ministry cannot be objectified in order to provide material for clinical analysis. It is important here to reflect upon the nature of pastoral ministry. The exercise of pastoral ministry is unable to begin with the dominant assumption that all true knowledge is neutral in value. This proposition of post-Enlightenment secularism does not sit comfortably within a post-critical Christological symbol. We must assume that the methodological model developed in the previous chapter provides a different purpose and direction to pastoral ministry. This in turn leads to a more mature understanding of reflection and appraisal.

9.1 The Practice of Pastoral Ministry

The pastoral minister's involvement in the practice of pastoral care is an important tool for developing an understanding of a theologically informed ministry. This means that the pastoral minister, presbyteral or otherwise, learns best about ministry from reflection on examples of pastoral care. The primary issue in this practice of ministry is effectiveness rather than efficiency. The pastoral minister has an effective involvement in pastoral care when there is a desire to accept the responsibilities of pastoral ministry. Pastoral ministers are able to develop this attitude through an authentic theological reflection and the witness of good practice. The pastoral minister's involvement in pastoral care practice does provide a real knowledge. In the Thomistic tradition, 'this second, connatural or sympathetic way of knowing is no less intellectual than abstractive, conceptual knowing.'[4] This does not necessarily mean that more participation in pastoral care practice, of itself, provides an increase of knowledge. Pastoral ministry may be simply reduced to a catalogue of unrelated and disparate incidents. It may never become authentic pastoral experience. There needs to be a full attention to the methodological model proposed in the previous chapter.

It is possible to consider spiritual development as a symbolic revelation of the Christian Mystery.[5] This area of spiritual growth does

4. Nichols A. *From Newman to Congar* (Edinburgh: T & T Clark, 1990) p.203
5. Cf. chapter nine of O'Collins G. (1993) op.cit.

not necessarily include pastoral care practice. Nevertheless, some of the elements in the area of spiritual development may be applied to pastoral ministry. These illustrate how such ministry can communicate real knowledge. Pastoral ministry is a process which includes many elements. Involvement in pastoral care situations may open the mind of the pastoral minister to the further elements of learning and reflection. In this manner, the knowledge gained from the practice of ministry is useful in the new and unencountered situation. This leads to the need for an *interpretation* of ministerial practice and the discovery of its *meaning*.[6] Only through such interpretation can pastoral care move beyond a catalogue of unrelated events. The meaning of experience, according to O'Collins, may take years to emerge. In a sense, it is created through this reflection. This fits our model comfortably. It also highlights the need for a methodological integrity, if reflection on pastoral care practice is to achieve theological awareness. Experience has an inherent *communicability*. The symbolic nature of experience makes this an inevitable dynamic. This symbolic nature is essential if pastoral ministry is to become a revelation of soteriological mystery. O'Collins also believes experience is 'undeniable' and 'imposes itself directly'.[7] This is qualified by a reference to the need for discernment. However, it suggests that many incidents of pastoral care are often mistaken for pastoral experience.

Clearly, any authentic pastoral experience must be totally informed by the Christological symbol. Balthasar states that 'the only way the Christian can commend himself to mankind today is through right action and determined commitment to the world in which he lives and to building the future.'[8] The particular action looked for here needs to be contextualized within a pastoral theological framework. It is the testimony of authentic Christian witness. The social sciences have successfully introduced the concept of 'roles' (and therefore 'role-play'). The notion is already becoming outdated. There is a tendency to replace 'role' with the even more pragmatic idea of 'function'.[9] Inevitably, psychology and sociology have introduced a dualism 'between what I represent and what I am in

6. Cf. ibid. pp.114-115
7. Cf. O' Collins G. (1993) op.cit. p.112
8. Balthasar H. *Theo-Drama. Theological Dramatic Theory, vol.1: Prolegomena* (San Francisco: Ignatius Press, 1988) p.32
9. Cf. ibid. p.481

reality'.[10] Through involvement with pastoral ministry, however, the pastoral minister needs to confront this professional duplicity, and achieve a personal synthesis of methodological model and pastoral behaviour. Henri Nouwen taught theology at the Harvard Divinity School. He spent the final five years of his life with a l'Arche community for the handicapped in Toronto. He has explored the themes of pastoral ministry in many published works and achieved similar insights to Campbell. The identity of the pastoral minister, for Nouwen, is defined by vulnerability and social irrelevance. Through life and ministry amongst mentally-handicapped people, he observed that 'these broken, wounded, and completely unpretentious people forced me to let go of my relevant self – the self that can do things, show things, prove things, build things – and forced me to reclaim that unadorned self in which I am completely vulnerable, open to receive and give love regardless of any accomplishments.'[11]

This understanding of pastoral ministry calls for a state of being in relationship, rather than a situation of detached and clinical observation. Within pastoral ministry practice, it means dealing with the dichotomy between the ecclesial leaders' 'own most private world and the good news they announce.'[12] Therefore, pastoral ministry experience is most fruitfully found within a radically communitarian framework in all dimensions. This fundamental observation has been made in every chapter of this study. Unfortunately, it does not always translate into the programme of pastoral care practice in many situations. The presbyteral minister and others often perceive pastoral ministry within the functional and individualistic settings, inherited from the skill-building agendas of behavioural sciences and the prevalent contemporary culture. Against this tendency, the practice of ministry and reflection on this ministry needs to attend more closely to an ecclesiology of communion: 'Community is a goal of social life; it points to the possibility of a shared vision that can move us to action in a public sphere, undertaken in a context of mutual concern.'[13]

Community, and its derivative concepts, are ambiguous. Community 'is not a univocal term.'[14] There is a need for caution here. James and

10. Ibid. p.481
11. Nouwen H. *In the Name of Jesus* (London: DLT, 1989) p.16
12. Ibid. p.48
13. Whitehead E. and J. *Community of Faith* (Minneapolis: The Winston-Seabury Press, 1982) p.23
14. Ibid. p.31

Evelyn Whitehead are consultants to the Centre for Pastoral and Social Ministry at the University of Notre Dame, Indiana. The work of the Whiteheads has made a significant contribution to contemporary models of pastoral theological reflection. However, in their understanding, pastoral ministry has to flourish in the soil of the behavioural scientific methodologies. In *Community of Faith*, they suggest a critical awareness of the limitations to these approaches. Nevertheless, their examination is 'an attempt to "befriend" the social sciences so that their power may be put at the service of the mission and ministry of Christian people.'[15] Later, they state that 'a vision of the community of faith emerges from our sociological analysis.'[16] Exactly how this vision is dependent on such analysis is not clearly discerned or even proved.

In another place, the Whiteheads state that 'a maturing faith community is itself generative of faith.'[17] Within a context of community that is neither passive nor neutral, this vision of pastoral ministry is seductive. However, their understanding of 'generativity' is provided in another work, *Christian Life Patterns*.[18] Here, their work is unequivocally dependent upon the psychological theory of Erikson. (This symbiosis is particularly acknowledged in an essay elsewhere.[19]) Thus, generativity is the third element of a developmental process, also involving identity and intimacy. In this investigation, the methodological problems involved in such a dependency have been noted in several places. In *Community of Faith*, these two pastoral counsellors complete their inter-disciplinary confusion. The *sensus fidelium* is a theological term belonging to ecclesiology. In the Whiteheads' understanding, it is interpreted within an alternative behavioural scientific environment. It is dominated by a sociological and psychological meaning, in which 'the maturity of a community of faith will be related to its developing sense or instinct about Christian values and how these are to be practically lived.'[20] The practitioner of pastoral care may use this definition within pastoral ministry. However, when

15. Ibid. p.xii
16. Ibid. p.59
17. Ibid. p.153
18. Whitehead E. and J. *Christian Life Patterns* (New York: Doubleday & Company Inc., 1982)
19. Cf. Whitehead J. *Priestliness: A Crisis of Belonging* in ed. Goergen D. *Being a Priest Today* (Collegeville: The Liturgical Press, 1992) p.20
20. Whitehead E. and J. *Community of Faith* (1982) p.154

'sense' and 'value' are rooted within the human sciences rather than ecclesial tradition, it is difficult to understand how the pastoral care can be transformed into authentic pastoral experience.

It is necessary to name the fundamental problem that underlies this behavioural scientific understanding of pastoral ministry. In our investigation, much has been made of the Enlightenment's need to ensure the sole criteria of rational plausibility in matters of religious faith. Our previous examination of contemporary pastoral theologies suggests that this has also influenced pastoral care, catechetics and evangelization itself. Thus, the problem is essentially concerned with the overt and misapplied application of professional training in programmes of preparation for pastoral ministry. There are indications of a theological movement away from this secular programme. Within his work as a pastoral theologian, Campbell uses classical literature to provide appropriate interpretative models. This paradigm is developed further by Balthasar's use of theatrical drama as a methodological tool within fundamental theology. He is not the first theologian to use this technique. Within a mystagogical tradition, William Harmless, a patristic scholar, suggests that 'catechesis is an art, or more precisely, a performing art. It was no accident that Augustine compared his efforts to the theaters he so often denounced.'[21] The forms of literature and the arts contain revelation material, and also important tools for interpretation and understanding of this material.

Within the context of our own model, it is suggested that pastoral care is an art discipline rather than a science. The demonstration of this hypothesis may be made from the evidence of hagiographical experience. Lonergan believes that genuine experience 'is orientated to the mystery of love and awe.'[22] Indeed, faith 'is the knowledge born of religious love.'[23] Clearly, this is not a rational form of knowledge. It involves the movement of understanding and judgment, but there is an epistemological difference between the knowledge of scientific experiment and artistic expression. To gaze upon a work of art with appreciation and wonder is both sensory and sensual. It is not necessarily subject to reason. It is proposed that a similar dynamic may be present in the development of faith.

21. Harmless W. *Augustine and the Catechumenate* (Collegeville: The Liturgical Press, 1995) p.349
22. Lonergan B. *Method in Theology* (London: Darton, Longman & Todd, 1971) p.119
23. Ibid. p.115

The experience of pastoral ministry belongs to the realm of faith. And 'in religious matters love precedes knowledge and, as that love is God's gift, the very beginning of faith is due to God's grace.'[24] This statement can find no better testing than the saintly experience of those who have responded most fully to divine grace. In this sense, faith resembles love. Both faith and love do not provide knowledge of something new. For the faith-filled subject, they constitute a new way of knowing. Rahner was a theologian who began his theological reflection with the idea of the self-transcendent human nature. Others have followed Rahner's lead, 'it is in the activities of knowledge and love that the subject really becomes itself.'[25] The purpose of pastoral care practice can never be directly concerned with the acquisition of further skills. It is the attempt, integrated within a discipleship of faith, to enter into a loving relationship with others. Pastoral care develops to maturity in a more profound knowledge of the Mystery of Christ and the salvation offered by him.

Within any programme of pastoral ministry, the minister must be brought to an effective appreciation of the paschal mystery. This is achieved when the minister deepens his or her capacity for an existential experience of the Cross. The aim of pastoral direction is therefore to enable pastoral ministers to discover the *meaning* of their involvement in pastoral ministry. This sense of meaning is not only found in the pastoral minister's own life, but in the one (or group) receiving pastoral care. If this meaning is determined by a Christological symbol, then 'successful practice' is not the objective. If the pastor has not entered into the interior anguish and deflated expectation of the Cross, then this minister is unable to understand pastoral ministry as Christ did. The key that unlocks the meaning of pastoral care is an understanding of weakness. This demands many internal spiritual resources, and the unambiguous identification of the pastor's own personhood with the action of pastoral ministry. This also involves the full application of our model to pastoral ministry practice. Furthermore, the *anamnesis*[26] of the paschal event in the Eucharistic liturgy becomes paradigmatic of what is happening in pastoral ministry. It is possible to enter fully into the matrix of pastoral involvement, only

24. Ibid. p.123
25. Drilling P. *Trinity and Ministry* (Minneapolis: Fortress Press, 1991) p.12
26. Or 'act of remembering'.

when one has discovered how to submerge oneself completely into this liturgical expression of the Mystery.

It has been suggested that this hypothetical model of pastoral ministry can be tested within the context of hagiographical evidence. It is appropriate to offer some examples. There are three: Thérèse of Lisieux, Jean-Marie Vianney and Francis de Sales. First of all, we can consider an important moment in the life of Thérèse of Lisieux: 'It was December 25, 1886, that I received the grace of leaving my childhood, in a word, the grace of my complete conversion.'[27] The scenario has all the elements of nineteenth century French bourgeois life. Thérèse is the spoilt youngest child in the motherless family home at *Les Buissonnets.* Her shoes were placed in the chimney-corner and packed with presents. A sharp comment was overheard from a tired father – producing the inevitable effect: 'I was going upstairs, at the time, to remove my hat, and Céline, knowing how sensitive I was and seeing the tears already glistening in my eyes, wanted to cry too, for she loved me very much and understood my grief.'[28] The event might pass unnoticed in the history of Christian spirituality or ministry. However, for Thérèse, it precipitates a conversion to pastoral charity and an all-consuming burden for missionary activity.

The importance of this experience is discovered in its interpretation and use within the pastoral ministry of this Carmelite nun. In this context, it becomes an exemplary paradigm of universal pastoral charity. Countless Christian disciples have imitated it within the past century. Furthermore, there are obvious implications for the contemporary practice of pastoral care and reflection on this ministry. Thérèse recognized her imperfections and weakness: 'I was really unbearable because of my extreme touchiness'.[29] Framed within the knowledge of divine love and grace, she also knew her own inability to overcome this tendency. It was an obstacle to any growth in ministry to others. Incapable of self-improvement, her conversion to pastoral love is situated within a Trinitarian and Christological symbol: 'On that luminous night which sheds such light on the delights of the Holy Trinity, Jesus, the gentle, little Child of only one hour, changed the night of my soul into rays of light. On that night when He made

27. Tr. Clarke J. *Story Of A Soul* (Washington D.C.: ICS Publications, 1976) p.98
28. Ibid. p.98
29. Ibid. p.97

Himself subject to weakness and suffering for love of me, He made me strong and courageous, arming me with His weapons.'[30] The subsequent growth in charity and heroic patient suffering suggests that this was no exercise in sentiment. Placed in a context of apostolic vocation, Thérèse's experience compels her to a true ministry: 'I experienced a great desire to work for the conversion of sinners, a desire I hadn't felt so intensely before. I felt charity enter into my soul, and the need to forget myself and to please others; since then I've been happy!'[31]

The same theme of happiness and complete dedication is found in the pastoral experience of Jean-Marie Vianney, the Curé of Ars. His life and ministry are offered to all parish priests as a model of presbyteral perfection. Nevertheless, the Abbé Monnin makes an important point about this saint at the outset of his parish priesthood. He was 'destitute of all natural means of attracting interest or commanding admiration. He had none of the ordinary graces of youth, nor had he yet attained that spiritual beauty which glorified his old age. His face was pale and angular, his stature low, his gait awkward, his manner shy and timid, his whole air common and unattractive.'[32] Monnin was a biographer with a privileged insight into the life and ministry of Jean Vianney. He spent some years as the saint's assistant. Despite the lack of many personal resources, Jean Vianney's phenomenal ministry is a paradigmatic example for all priests.

It is tempting to focus on the successful completion of a ministry lasting over forty years: the pilgrimages and devotions, the miracles and conversions. In the early years, however, the Curé's parish was careless and indifferent in its faith. His response was a demanding and rigorous pastoral programme, 'to persevere in prayer to God from whom all blessings flow; to sanctify himself so as to be able to sanctify others, and to offer expiation for the sins of those who refused to do penance for themselves.'[33] Accompanying a life of personal penance, there was an unassailable devotion to his pastoral ministry: 'He would shut himself up for days together in his sacristy, devoting to this employment every moment which he had to spare from his spiritual

30. Ibid. p.97
31. Ibid. p.99
32. Monnin A. *Life of the Blessed Curé D'Ars* (London: Burns, Oates & Washbourne Ltd.) p.42
33. Trochu F. *The Curé D'Ars* (Rockford: Tan Books and Publishers, Inc., 1977) p.114

exercises.'[34] And all this effort was to prepare a Sunday homily worthy of the occasion. He persisted in pastoral visitation and familiar conversation 'till he found an opportunity, without any abrupt or harsh transition, to speak to them of divine things.'[35] It was not easy. Towards the end, he mused: 'If on my arrival at Ars I had foreseen all that I was to suffer there, I should have died on the spot.'[36] There were humiliations and rejection, hostility and bitter trials. In the face of these experiences, the patron of parish priests planned and reflected upon his ministry. As he allowed the paschal mystery to become the focus of his presbyteral life, the more fruitful became his pastoral ministry.

The third example is Francis de Sales. As the Bishop of Geneva, he achieved fame for his wisdom, spiritual direction and pastoral writings. More important for the demonstration of our hypothesis, is an earlier period as missionary to the Calvinist Chablais. A biographer describes this period. Francis was 'for four years an itinerant, needy, poor, constantly threatened missionary who at certain critical times would not have recovered his 'breath' or courage except for the examples of Saint Francis Xavier or the recent English martyrs.'[37] Once again, a situation of personal weakness and dependence on grace produced fruit in an authentic pastoral ministry.

The papal nuncio of Savoy described the task of Francis as that of an 'explorer or a precursor, in order to examine the means to be taken so as to provide the country with remedies and physicians'.[38] This concerned the development of a shrewd pastoral strategy. It involved the complete integration of personhood and ministry, in a task which 'would cost him labours, contradictions, hatred, even setbacks – at least temporarily – harder than those that he would have known by walking through hamlets and villages as a simple missionary.'[39] Unlike Jean-Marie Vianney, here is a man from a very different social background. He is imbued with many natural graces. Despite the differences, however, the pastoral ministerial experience is similar.

In this enterprise, failure and even death were very real possibilities.

34. Monnin A. op.cit. p.45
35. Ibid. p.46
36. Trochu F. (1977) op.cit. p.173
37. Ravier A. *Francis de Sales Sage and Saint* (San Francisco: Ignatius Press, 1988) p.61
38. Ibid. p.63
39. Ibid. p.63

Twelve months after beginning his work in the Chablais, Francis de Sales wrote to his Bishop: 'We are marching, but in the manner of an invalid who – after having left his bed – finds that he has lost the use of his feet, and, in his frail health, no longer knows whether he is healthy or sick.'[40] In a letter to his former spiritual director, he is even more doubtful about the pastoral effectivity of his work: 'I am hardly good enough to preach to bare walls, which is what I am presently doing in this town.'[41] A few months later, he must have known extreme fatigue: 'The harvesting of Thonon is a yoke that surpasses my strength, but I have resolved to abandon it only with your agreement, by your order.'[42] And even when he left his successful missionary work in the Chablais, to become the coadjutor of Bishop de Granier, this area continued to concern him and cause profound anxiety.[43] The witness of his life bears testimony to a full appropriation of the paschal mystery.

9.2 Theological Reflection: The Exegesis of Pastoral Ministry

Balthasar writes of a theological dramatic theory: 'The task of the stage is to make the drama of existence explicit so that we may view it.'[44] This final section of the study is concerned with theological reflection. Don Browning understands reflection as the objectification of thought processes, 'in order to examine their logical validity or their claim to generate knowledge.'[45] On a deeper level, reflection is 'thinking designed to grasp symbolically the force or desire that comes to expression in the self.'[46] After the practice of pastoral care itself, this is the most creative tool available to enable the pastoral minister become more fruitful in the practice of pastoral care. The context for this reflection on pastoral ministry is a contemporary theological minefield. Critical reflection on pastoral care can change the nature of the pastoral practice. It assumes a new understanding. Decisions and actions are evaluated in the light of judgment.[47] There is a need to work within well-defined parameters of interpretation. Theological reflection is a

40. Ibid. p.71
41. Ibid. p.71
42. Ibid. p.74
43. Cf. ibid. p.95
44. Balthasar H. (1988) op.cit. p.17
45. Ed. Browning D. *Practical Theology* (San Francisco: Harper & Row, 1983) p.xvii
46. Ibid. p.xvii
47. Cf. Gelpi D. *The Turn to Experience in Contemporary Theology* (New York: Paulist Press, 1994) p.2

means of developing the practice of pastoral care into mature pastoral experience. There are, however, a number of models available for this work of reflection. It is difficult to recognize the specifically *theological* element in some of them. All models begin with the ministerial practice of the student. In the methodological model developed in chapter eight of this study, this may not be called experience. Indeed, explicit viewing of the 'drama of existence' suggests a lengthy paschal journey, before incidents of pastoral care become mature experience.

Anne Brotherton, the Director of Pastoral Field Education at the Jesuit School of Theology in Berkeley University, suggests that a good model of theological reflection creates a 'conversation' between pastoral care practice and theology.[48] For her, the means of this conversation are found in social analysis. In the model employed by her: 'The skilful integration of social analysis into the Theological Reflection process is perhaps, at this time, our greatest challenge, and one to which we are strongly committed.'[49] This is the present model used by the Field Education Department in the Jesuit School of Theology at Berkeley, California. It is built upon the foundational tri-polar model, developed by the Whiteheads in *Method in Ministry: Theological reflection and Christian Ministry*.[50] This joins together the three dimensions of personal response, the religious tradition and secular culture in an axial relationship. The means of theological reflection is a process of attending, asserting and pastoral response.[51] The model is offered as an example. The authors, themselves, do not expect that it will be followed in a totally slavish manner.

The Whiteheads have revised their earlier study in the light of criticism and further involvement in pastoral education. In the more recent edition, there is an explicit concern to relate theological reflection to 'the movement of discernment in spiritual direction' and 'the vitality of the tradition'.[52] The influence of these two elements does not, however, always find expression in their understanding of theological reflection. This process, it is claimed, is focused on action.

48. Cf. Brotherton A. *Theological Reflection at Jesuit School of Theology Berkeley* in Irish Association for Pastoral Formation *Guidelines for Pastoral Formation* (Dublin: IAPF, 1991) p.25
49. Ibid. p.26
50. Cf. Whitehead J. and E. *Method in Ministry: Theological Reflection and Christian Ministry* (London: Sheed and Ward, 1995)
51. To the present writer, this is remarkably similar to the Cardijn method of see – judge – act, mentioned in chapter seven of this investigation.
52. Whitehead J. and E. (1995) op.cit. p.vii

Their notion of theological reflection 'cannot end in religious insight but must be open to pastoral response.'[53] This process of reflection does not suggest that pastoral ministry is, in itself, revelatory of divine soteriological action. There are shadows of this more potent understanding of ministry. Ministerial effectivity is 'to celebrate God's saving presence and to contribute, by word and action and sacrament, to the fullness of this presence'.[54] Indeed, a 'goal of Christian ministry is the formation of reflective communities alive to the presence of God.'[55] However, within the overall context of the Whiteheads' research, these statements must be approached with caution. The real problem concerns their idea of experience: 'For us, experience refers to all those ideas, feelings, biases and insights that persons and communities bring to the reflection.'[56] Clearly, the starting point is not our understanding of pastoral experience developed in chapter eight of this study. This conviction remains, despite the assertion that revelation is 'the communication of God's love in Jesus Christ'[57] and 'God's self-disclosure which surprises us, overturns our certitudes and transcends our best imaginings – is *registered* in experience.'[58] The criticism is confirmed by their unequivocal acknowledgement of Browning's conviction that 'the contemporary function of the social sciences' is to act 'as 'coordinating models,' analogous to the pervading myths and theological images that supported a sense of shared meaning in previous cultures.'[59]

To some extent, a critique of these current methods was offered in the last chapter.[60] Furniss, in particular, understood theological reflection to be concerned with the acquisition of professional skills. These methods are more concerned with placing incidents of pastoral care under the laboratory microscope, than with allowing it to be viewed by a gathered audience on the dramatic stage. This can easily lead to a limited understanding of ministry. The drama of personal spiritual engagement tends to be marginalized. The full theological tradition is placed outside the reflective process. There is a danger of

53. Ibid. p.x
54. Ibid. p.3
55. Ibid. p.17
56. Ibid. p.43
57. Ibid. p.44
58. Ibid. p.45
59. Ibid. p.58
60. Especially with respect to the work of Pattison and Furniss.

reductionism, and disregard for the prophetic nature of ministry within a Christological symbol.

It is important to be critical of the methodologies often used in recent programmes of formation for pastoral ministry. According to Gerry O'Hanlon, who teaches theology at the Milltown Institute of Theology and Philosophy in Dublin, theological reflection is a means of bringing confessional doctrine and pastoral practice into a real conversation with each other.[61] Theological reflection, then, is the means of developing pastoral theology and its application to the ongoing formation of those involved in pastoral ministry. Thus, the methodological model is crucial. The methodology of some models of theological reflection uses the critical methods of liberation theology.[62] This raises some important issues about the nature of social analysis and the method's understanding of the Christian tradition. Some would argue the need for 'a proper social perspective'[63] in the practice of pastoral care. It is sometimes assumed that 'the character and methods of liberation theology' will provide this perspective.[64]

There are problems with this approach. Joseph Kroger, a Uruguayan liberation theologian, declares that 'liberation theology functions as a critical theory which *precedes and promotes* the praxis of faith'.[65] Therefore, pastoral ministry is understood within the context of a firmly imported agenda. Gustavo Gutiérrez, the Peruvian founder of liberation theology, does not believe that pastoral action results from theology. For him, the role of theology is simply to reflect on pastoral activity.[66] Within liberation theology, there *is* an action based on reflection upon previous activity. However, the locations of this reflection are always limited to situations of social oppression.[67] This leads to an incomplete understanding of the pastoral process. We should treat the use of liberation theological methods in pastoral theology with suspicion. Liberation theology lacks a theological critical evaluation. It does not involve the full Christian tradition. It is too focused on a Marxist notion of praxis and revolution.

---

61. Cf. O'Hanlon G. *Theological Reflection* in *The Furrow* vol.46 no.4, April 1995, p.232
62. Cf. ibid. p.234
63. E.g. Pattison, in Wright *Pastoral Care Revisited* (London: SCM Press Ltd., 1996) p.9
64. Ibid. p.8
65. Cf. Tilley T. *Postmodern Theologies* (Maryknoll: Orbis Books, 1995) p.119
66. Cf. ibid. p.120
67. Cf. ibid. p.122

Nouwen understands theological reflection in a very different way. He believes that 'strenuous theological reflection will allow us to discern critically where we are being led.'[68] The behavioural sciences or political considerations do not primarily inform this reflection. Rather, it is defined as 'thinking with the mind of Christ'.[69] There is a need for a critical theological analysis in which the student of pastoral ministry has training in prayer, which accompanies study 'to manifest the divine event of God's saving work in the midst of the many seemingly random events of their time.'[70] Interestingly, Nouwen does not find much evidence of this self-kenotic formation in modern seminaries.[71]

If theological reflection is the *opus operatum* of pastoral theology, we must now apply our methodological model to this tool of ongoing formation for the practice of pastoral ministry. If this model has remained faithful to the process of the Second Vatican Council, it will find a natural home in a mystagogical methodology. David Regan, who teaches mission theology to post-graduates in Brazil, correctly states that 'no comprehensive work exists on the topic of mystagogy as a whole.'[72] Our own investigation is a small attempt to make a contribution to such a reflection. Regan also suggests the appropriate nature of the mystagogical method for our purpose. The practice of pastoral care 'is the element which recommends the practice of mystagogy to pastoral concern' and if the exercise of ministry 'is more difficult to analyse than theological statements, it has more potential for uniting.'[73] Unfortunately, this crucial statement is not fully developed.

Regan has made an important contribution but does not fulfil the ambition of his book's sub-title *Pastoral Possibilities for Christian Mystagogy*. In his enthusiasm for mystagogy, he sets up an unnecessary tension between the intellectual operation of theology and the practice of pastoral care.[74] Framed within a context of Christological controversy, the ancient pastoral mystagogues were always concerned with doctrinal expression. Mystagogy, especially in a post-conciliar

---

68. Nouwen H. (1989) op.cit. p.65
69. Ibid. p.66
70. Ibid. p.68
71. Cf. ibid. pp. 69-70
72. Regan D. *Experience the Mystery* (London: Geoffrey Chapman, 1994) p.3
73. Ibid. p.7
74. Cf. ibid. p.27

framework, understands pastoral ministry to be experiential only when it is fully immersed within the Christological symbol. In the post-conciliar *Rite of Christian Initiation of Adults*, the mystagogia is placed after the catechumenate. Regan fails to understand the necessity for this, and argues for 'a much richer understanding of mystagogy'.[75] This means a mystagogical permeation of the whole of catechesis. In this, he misses the point completely. Mystagogy can take place only as a reflection on the life brought about by sacramental initiation.

There are further problems in Regan's thesis. These are seen most clearly in the chapter on *Mystagogy and Experience*. This begins with a mention of the events of salvation history. However, these events become experience only when their meaning is interpreted through faith and discernment. In this chapter, the word 'experience' is subjected to a variety of multi-disciplinary models. Authentic mystagogy is sacrificed in this process: 'To deal with religious experience, the post-Vatican II Church has not only adopted discernment in spiritual direction and pastoral planning, but has incorporated much of the wisdom of the psychological sciences into its spiritual theology.'[76] This causes confusion for Regan. He acknowledges a need to move beyond 'the modern culture of the Enlightenment' and 'what is merely rational'.[77] Experience cannot be 'imprisoned in a priori rationalist categories'.[78] Nevertheless, he also states that 'it is the element of rational reflection that gives experience its human quality and makes it different from simple sense perception.'[79] The practice of pastoral care must be subjected to 'discernment'.[80] However, the exact nature of this exercise is not fully defined. All this demonstrates a failure to understand mystagogy for what it is. We have already noted in this study how the fourth century mystagogical pastors focused their congregations on the visible elements of sacramental celebration.[81] Through liturgical celebration, these elements became vehicles of Christ's soteriological power. It is only faith that provides true meaning and interpretation to this liturgical action. And the same may be promulgated of pastoral ministry.

75. Ibid. p.111
76. Ibid. p.45
77. Ibid. p.45
78. Ibid. p.48
79. Ibid. p.46
80. Cf. ibid. p.49
81. E.g. bread, wine, water, oil etc.

Our reflection on contemporary pastoral theology suggests the possibility of a theological reflection that is conducted through the means of an authentic mystagogy. The Whiteheads' model of reflection was noted above: a methodology of attending, asserting and decision-making. A mystagogical method of theological reflection might adopt similar terminology: attending (or waiting), imagining (or analysing) and experience (or serving).

I. *An attending, that is a waiting upon the pastoral moment*
Attention is an important foundation for theological reflection. This is not primarily a focus on what is being *done* in a pastoral situation. Rather, it is the ability to *listen*, and to understand what is being communicated in the practice of pastoral ministry. It demands an attitude of contemplative attention to the pastoral moment. Only then, can the particular incident of pastoral care produce a lesson that is applicable to all pastoral ministry. In substance, this may be framed within a method of correlation, 'a dialectical relationship between divine revelation and human perception'.[82] This is not new, however, but has an ancient heritage. In platonic terms, such contemplative attending is named *theoria*. Andrew Louth, who teaches patristic theology at Goldsmith's College in the University of London, believes that this attention provides 'a fundamental, and fundamentally true, relationship to reality, or being.'[83] Charles Gerkin, a pioneer of pastoral reflection models, suggested that there is a need for 'careful listening and depth reflection' on the living documents of pastoral care practice, in order to 'yield profound and stimulating insights of a theological order.'[84]

This method of attending is valid only if there is an acceptance of the revelatory nature of pastoral ministry. William Hubert Vanstone, an Emeritus Canon of Chester Cathedral, indicates the dominant contemporary identification of the human person in the 'capacity for action'.[85] Thus, human dignity becomes inextricably connected to action, initiation and achievement.[86] Indeed, this would seem to be the

82. Vanstone W. *The Stature of Waiting* (London: DLT, 1982) p.ix
83. Louth A. *Discerning the Mystery* (Oxford: Clarendon Press, 1989) p.142
84. Eds. Couture P. and Hunter R. *Pastoral Care and Social Conflict* (Nashville: Abingdon Press, 1995) p.9
85. Vanstone W. (1982) op.cit. p.61
86. Ibid. p.61

impression given by the evangelists in their description of Jesus' public ministry. However, Vanstone notes the change once Jesus' passion begins in the Garden of Gethsemane. From this moment: 'Jesus is the grammatical subject of just nine verbs.'[87] From being the active subject, Christ becomes the receptive object of the action. Within a Christological symbol this provides a defining moment of mystagogical reflection. It is clearly the paradigmatic territory of the paschal mystery. The important point for authentic theological reflection is the response of the disciple. This is the attempt to enter into an attentive activity of gazing and pondering. This attitude may be applied to the exercise of contemporary pastoral ministry. It is that attending, which is also a waiting upon the mystery. Certainly, there is no attempt to dominate or control pastoral care. Instead, it is the striving to share the soteriological nature of true pastoral experience.

The issue for ongoing personal formation for ministry is not what the pastoral minister does in the pastoral situation, but instead, what the pastoral situation does to the one involved in pastoral care. Harmless believes that 'the first movement in liturgical catechesis is – or, at least, might be – a pedagogy of silence. In other words, the catechist recognizes that silence can teach; that the rite itself teaches'.[88] The same may be predicated of authentic pastoral care. This point may be illustrated in a further hagiographical incident from the life of Francis de Sales. Together with Jeanne de Chantal, he founded the religious Congregation of the Visitation at Annecy, in 1610. The project was not without difficulties. However, Francis was 'quite certain God would find a way, even when his creatures could not understand how it could be done.' There is an important pastoral response: 'So they agreed to do nothing for many long years, six or seven at the very least, and to keep the whole matter absolutely secret.'[89] Most situations in pastoral ministry do not involve the foundation of religious congregations. Nevertheless, a patient waiting may be a prudent response in order for pastoral care to become authentic experience.

Balthasar recognizes the importance of this attending.[90] He discusses

87. Ibid. p.20
88. Harmless W. (1995) op.cit. p.362
89. Ravier A. *Saint Jeanne de Chantal* (San Francisco: Ignatius Press, 1989) p.84
90. Balthasar H. *Presence and Thought* (San Francisco: Ignatius Press, 1995)

the matter in an essay on the religious philosophy of Gregory of Nyssa. Gregory was the Bishop of Nyssa towards the end of the fourth century. His theology uses elements of mystagogy. It is clearly situated within the Christian tradition, and is founded upon an 'attitude of intimate reflection'.[91] Gregory's anthropology is platonic and stoic.[92] This reflects a general note of patristic mystagogy, and has important epistemological implications. His theological concern is primarily mystical. In this sense, Balthasar recognizes the foundational image-centred expression of Gregory's thought. For this patristic theologian, the senses 'are signposts for penetrating deeper into the invisible from the visible'.[93] Within a mystical epistemology, this leads to a new spiritual knowledge. It is superior to that knowledge achieved by the senses alone.

This knowledge cannot be easily gained. There is a *diastasis* or 'spacing', which separates the created from the Creator. 'The abyss that separates the two forms of being is the fact of creation'.[94] This same concept of spacing may also be applied to any two created beings. In so many respects, two human beings can struggle to understand each other. Certainly, there are differences between the concerns of patristic theology and contemporary pastoral care. However, the philosophical ontology of Gregory enables some understanding of the difficulties involved in contemporary theological reflection. In other words, as suggested above, authentic attending to the data of pastoral care is not won easily. Pastoral theological reflection demands an ongoing development of the tools of reflection, in order that pastoral care can become an experience that is rooted in the paschal mystery.

For Gregory, 'spacing' creates a tension within space and time: 'This apparent contradiction is translated into the order of knowledge by a rending of consciousness with respect to a memory of the past and a prevision of the future'.[95] Our attending to the pastoral moment is therefore reduced and truncated. It sometimes fails to achieve the spiritual dynamic required in order for pastoral care to become experience. It also disables a subjective comprehensive knowledge: 'It

91. Ibid. p.12
92. Cf. ibid. p.16. Detailed analysis of Gregory of Nyssa's works is unnecessary in our own project. Balthasar has investigated these patristic texts, and compiled a useful summary of themes.
93. Ibid. p.49
94. Ibid. p.28
95. Ibid. p.31

always remains in itself. And whatever it perceives, it forms a perception of by itself. It is incapable of seeing a thing outside its own nature'.[96] Thus, the work of attention (within the process of theological reflection) demands nothing less than an epistemological state of conversion.

For Gregory of Nyssa, spiritual reflection 'escapes the multiplicity of the sensible so as to be a perfect unity, universal and concrete at the same time.'[97] The knowledge gained by this kind of attending is vital for pastoral theological reflection. It rises above fragmentation, and allows the pastoral minister to learn something which can be applied to every pastoral situation. Above all, 'Gregory loves to recognize humanity in that sheep that Christ took on his shoulders.'[98] This is surely the concrete and universal unity which has already been presented as an evangelical paradigm of pastoral care in the previous chapter of this study. This knowledge reflects the fundamental platonic notion of gazing rather than grasping: 'Human knowledge is therefore true only to the degree it renounces by a perpetual effort its own nature, which is to "seize" its prey.'[99] Here is a different world to the methodologies of modern clinical pastoral education. It is an epistemological method which does lead to authentic knowledge, but also continues further. It introduces an attitude of certain adoration and humility before the Mystery.

It may be tempting to deny the pastoral implications of this mystical theology. However, for Gregory of Nyssa, there is no true soteriological knowledge without *philanthropia* or love of humanity.[100] Above all, this term is applied to the basic moments in the economy of salvation. It is a divine initiative in Christ Jesus. *Philanthropia* provides the basis for understanding the Incarnation. Needless to say, if the disciple has truly received the nature of Christ, then there will be an obvious fruit in the Christian's relationship with others and their needs. If this configuration to Christ is an essential part of being a disciple, it is even more appropriate for the one involved in pastoral ministry. It demands an integrity that is clearly recognizable when attention is given to a moment of that ministry in the process of reflection. In this

96. Ibid. p.89
97. Ibid. p.50
98. Ibid. p.51
99. Ibid. p.93
100. Cf. ibid. p.143

manner: 'By belief in things that are accessible and comprehensible to us, we find ourselves guided toward the knowledge of inaccessible things.'[101] There is an awesome warning in all of this: 'If the mystagogue is not truly purified before beginning his ascent, he will not be able to undertake it. He will hear nothing.'[102] In a penetrating insight, Balthasar believes that art 'can die as a result of being looked at by too many dull (*geistlos*) eyes, and even the radiance of holiness can, in a way, become blunted when it encounters nothing but hollow indifference.'[103] This sentiment is even more applicable to the revelatory nature of pastoral ministry.

What are the lessons from this mystical study for the place of attending in contemporary theological reflection? Essentially, the one involved in pastoral care practice is seeking an understanding and a knowledge that is firmly situated within the divine plan of creation and salvation. Pastoral care is an ecclesial reality that unfolds in the context of this history. The difficulties inherent in attending are the problems of ontological becoming. This means that the pastoral minister is involved in a process of mystagogical reflection, which finds ultimate fulfilment only in an attitude of complete and utter service and discipleship. There can be no sense of skill-centred control or professional possession here. Through faith, the pastoral encounter is open to a different dynamic. Above all, attending means that the pastoral minister can learn from the pastoral situation, and the particular moment can contribute towards a general development of experience. This is vital if the words of one pastoral directory are correct: 'day-to-day parish ministry is such that the priest is constantly encountering new situations and problems for which no concrete norms or directives exist.'[104]

II. *An imagining, which produces authentic theological analysis*

What is meant by the word 'imagining'? In the context of theological method, Lonergan believes that reflective insight belongs to the third and highest level of consciousness. As an activity, insight is part of the stable structure of cognitional activity. However, the knowledge born

101. Ibid. p.149
102. Ibid. p.172
103. Balthasar H. *The Glory of the Lord vol.1: Seeing the Form* (Edinburgh: T. & T. Clark, 1982) p.23
104. Ed. Dalton W. *A Parish Pastoral Directory* (Blackrock: The Columba Press, 1995) p.15

of insight is without boundaries and cannot be so easily structured.[105] In the examination of this knowledge, according to Lonergan, there is a need for the subject to effect 'a personal appropriation of the concrete, dynamic structure immanent and recurrently operative in his own cognitional activities.'[106] Furthermore, insightful order is not won by 'logical or metaphysical priority, but by concrete motives of pedagogical efficacy.'[107] In any analysis of the knowledge gained in the process of pastoral ministry these insights must be kept in mind. That is why this second part of the theological reflection process is called imagining.

Terrence Tilley is the Professor of Religious Studies at the University of Dayton. In his introduction to *Postmodern Theologies*, Tilley declares that 'the erosion of the religious world has not been a destruction but a purification. The task now is to build a critical theology.'[108] This mentality underlies much contemporary reflection in many theological disciplines, including pastoral theology. Such an approach, however, does not produce the kind of imagination needed for authentic theological analysis of pastoral care. Tilley believes that many contemporary theologians possess a 'new and radical intellectual asceticism' which 'employs distilled and concentrated modern acids on religious and theological constructs.'[109] It is difficult to understand how this methodology is a purification of inherited tradition. It seems to be a total deconstruction. It is an utter violation of the necessary environment needed for theological imagination to take place.

In a world that is dominated by a technological mindset, there are no symbolic hierophanies pointing to the spiritual reality in the everyday moment.[110] There are obvious implications here for an understanding of the post-eighteenth century growth of secularism. Also, there is an obvious repercussion for pastoral care. It is increasingly difficult to use the imagination in the context of pastoral ministry. Any attending to the pastoral moment can easily lead to a clinical and fragmented analysis, instead of the insight and vision needed for incidents of pastoral care to become authentic experience.

105. Cf. Crowe F. *Lonergan* (London: Geoffrey Chapman, 1992) p.60
106. Cf. ibid. p.61
107. Cf. ibid. p.61
108. Tilley T. (1995) op.cit. p.vii
109. Ibid. p.viii
110. Cf. Thornhill J. *Christian Mystery in the Secular Age* (Maryland: Christian Classics Inc., 1991) p.11

Pamela Couture and Rodney Hunter teach pastoral care at the Candler School of Theology at Emory University. They suggest that the dominance of non-theological models has 'created conflict in the core identities of many persons in the pastoral care and counselling movement.'[111]

The imagination needed for authentic theological reflection may be situated in a mystagogical process. Ratzinger suggests that 'theology is born when the arbitrary judgment of reason encounters a limit, in that we discover something which we have not excogitated ourselves but which has been revealed to us.'[112] It is a moment of insight that lies within a different epistemological framework to the one in which we conduct ordinary every-day business. This theological method is not unreasonable or irresponsible. Indeed, it is a cognitional structure that contains a pleromatic attention to all detail. So often, pastoral care is framed within an aporia. It is understood as a problem-situation to be resolved by the application of learned technique. Imagination produces a new way of reflecting upon a pastoral situation. The insights gained are comparable to the new depth of knowledge found in the interpretation of a painting or musical composition. It is similar to the new understanding of human nature, arising from audience participation in a dramatic performance.

In order for imagination to produce this insight, there must be a dialogue within the pastoral process. The one engaged in ministry does not enter this conversation with anything but an all-consuming word of pastoral action. There is a need for imaginative listening. This is 'a capacity simply to be which puts in requisition the whole person.'[113] Without this imagination, the pastoral minister is only likely to hear the expression of a problem. In the language of Kasper, 'faith is open to something other, something new, something to come'.[114] If faith is needed to hear this new possibility, imagination is necessary to articulate the good news of salvation. Harmless' words about mystagogical catechesis may be applied to the imaginative element of theological reflection. This is 'less an explanation and more an exploration; it is less an explication and more an evocation.'[115]

111. Eds. Couture P. and Hunter R. (1995) op.cit. p.13
112. Ratzinger J. *The Nature and Mission of Theology* (San Francisco: Ignatius Press, 1995) p.8
113. Ibid. p.33
114. Cf. Thornhill J. (1991) op.cit. p.40
115. Harmless W. (1995) op.cit. p.365

Frank Wright, a Canon Emeritus of Manchester Cathedral, suggests that some pastoral theologians have sought the development of a pastoral care in the systematic combination of 'secular insights with the Christian doctrine of man'.[116] This has not really worked. Sometimes, there is the recognition of a temptation to 'concentrate on segments of people's lives and experience without exploring any further the ultimate goal of all pastoral care and counselling, and to see it as the growth to wholeness and the maturity of the other person.'[117] The focus on segmentation in this statement is important. However, the desired integrity is not necessarily gained by an alternative secular understanding of wholeness and maturity. This may be demonstrated by the confusion of language that can sometimes take place in the pastoral conversation. Wright is excited by 'the humanistic psychologist's description of the maturing or self-actualizing person', and the subsequent conclusion 'that there was a certain correspondence between the psychological goal of maturity and the Christian goal of sanctification.'[118] There is plenty of hagiographical evidence to suggest that the canonized would not achieve a modern psychologist's definition of psychological maturity.

Imagination, then, is the conscious heeding of the Christian tradition within the pastoral process. It is the unambiguous acknowledgement of a divine saving-presence in the pastoral encounter. This is the only environment in which the questions of theological and cultural understanding can be properly addressed. Imagination recognizes the typological nature of the pastoral moment: 'Where there is no vision the people get out of hand'.[119] Imagination is meant to develop in those involved in pastoral ministry, that life-giving vision which makes sense of individual and social drama in the pastoral situation. It provides a developing unity to the practice of pastoral care, and recognizes the place of human events within the economy of salvation.

Imagination restores the created and teleological purposes to the agenda of human life, after the rationalist attempts to destroy their credibility. Gerald Hanratty lectures in the Department of Philosophy

---

116. Wright F. *Pastoral Care Revisited* (London: SCM Press Ltd., 1996) p.7
117. Ibid. p.23
118. Ibid. p.24
119. Prov. 29:18. Another idea, contained in the Old Testament Wisdom literature, is that the people 'perish' without vision.

at University College, Dublin. His reflection on the pastoral insights of Cardinal Jean-Marie Lustiger of Paris suggests that in so many ways, 'facile optimism has been replaced by weary scepticism in many segments of contemporary Western societies.'[120] Imagination is the pastoral response to this post-Enlightenment philosophical fatigue. The modern mindset is so often defined within the false optimism that has replaced Christian hope. Against this, Cardinal Jean-Marie Lustiger focuses again on Gregory of Nyssa, and his formulation 'that the rational and free human being, created in the image and likeness of God, cannot be encompassed or comprehended in a definition.'[121] Imagination is needed to develop a pastoral care, large enough to breathe in this anthropological atmosphere. In this imagining, the pastor has the courage to invoke the One who shared our human nature with 'the glory that he has from the Father as only Son of the Father, full of grace and truth.'[122]

III. *An experience of serving*

The ultimate question offered within a mystagogical theological reflection, concerns human nature itself. Within any Christian anthropological definition of humanity there must be a radical content of service. This can be offered only within relationship. Therefore, the communitarian dimension of pastoral ministry still remains non-negotiable. Once again, attention to language and its use is crucial. John Foskett is a hospital chaplain and an accredited supervisor with the Association of Pastoral Care and Counselling. David Lyall lectures in the Department of Christian Ethics and Practical Theology at New College in the University of Edinburgh. Foskett and Lyall are convinced that 'at the most fundamental and basic level, the skills of attending, listening and responding are the raw material of all care'.[123] What do they mean by 'responding'? If this reflection process is truly theological, then it discovers a depth beyond solely human relationships. For an authentic mystagogical reflection, the apex of pastoral care is situated within a vision of that glory which is a revelation of saving mystery.

---

120. Hanratty G. *Light From Paris* (Blackrock: Four Courts Press, 1995) p.19
121. Ibid. p.25
122. John 1:14
123. Foskett J. and Lyall D. *Helping the Helpers* (London: SPCK, 1988) p.5

The Christological symbol achieves its full purpose within pastoral ministry, in the experience of serving. Angelo Scola, the Rector of the Pontifical Lateran University in Rome, suggests that Balthasar's Christology, as we have already seen, is built upon a total identification between Christ's personhood and mission.[124] Indeed, this truth determines the foundational place of Trinitarian doctrine in pastoral theology. Christ's mission can be understood only from the perspective of having been sent by the Father. God is defined as love, and this means 'a being-other which does not eliminate the unity of the divine Being.'[125] In the economy of salvation, the Trinity God chose to overcome the distance between the Creator and the created by the unity of Christ with human nature. This incarnation was not only ontological. It involved the service of saving love.

Scola asserts that the concept of mission is the foundational construction of Balthasar's theology.[126] Furthermore, within a Christocentric horizon, 'this signifies that our interest focuses primarily on method and not on content.'[127] Thus, the appointed mission to salvation is the means, as well as the substance, to understanding a ministry that is rooted within a Christological symbol. It is impossible to appreciate Jesus unless there is a pondering upon his relationship with the Father. Within an anthropology that is profoundly influenced by this symbol, it is necessary to understand the 'essence' of human nature in the midst of the 'dramatic performance of existence'.[128] Hence, the very nature of pastoral ministry is crafted within the theological reality of ecclesial communion.

The nature of communion indicates why this third part of theological reflection has been called an experience of serving. It is the idea of service that defines the pastoral relationship. Revelation is not only the presentation of a doctrinal word. It is a dynamic action, in which the created world 'can only respond, and hence "understand", through action on *its* part.'[129] There is a glory, 'which irradiates a beauty capable of enrapturing whoever perceives it.'[130] Within a

124. Cf. Scola A. *Hans Urs von Balthasar: A Theological Style* (Edinburgh: T & T Clark, 1995) p.73
125. Ibid. p.62
126. Cf. ibid. p.58
127. Ibid. p.45
128. Ibid. p.84
129. Ibid. p.41
130. Ibid. p.1

Johannine theology, as we have already noted in the last chapter, this glory is revealed above all in the movement of the paschal mystery. Thus, this vision of complete and unconditional service is appreciated only in the relationship of faith. Indeed, Balthasar believes that this mystery is never completely comprehensible. Mystery is often associated with divine ontology. However, that same sense of mystery pervades a reflection on the relationship between divine economy and the action of creation.[131]

Insofar as we are able to understand mystery, what does this mean for the practice of pastoral service? Balthasar describes his own sense of vocation: 'what suddenly entered my mind then was neither theology, nor the priesthood. It was simply this: you do not have to choose anything, you have been called! You will not serve, you will be taken into service.'[132] This personal statement provides a profound understanding of the idea of service in pastoral ministry. It is that manifestation of divine glory which alone makes sense of pastoral care, and invites us to become reflections of Christ's personal relationship with the Father. This is how 'grace does not denote something which would be added to an already completed man but is the form in which man is definitively himself.'[133] Thus, the ministry of pastoral serving is not merely functional. The notion of service provides an ontological dimension to the definition of Christian anthropology.

A pastoral ministry that is rooted within servanthood produces knowledge. Initiated into a relationship of service, the one who reflects on the practice of pastoral ministry is able to develop an ever-deepening knowledge of the mystery of salvation. It is truly mystagogical. Louth reflects on the philosophical distinction between the 'mysterious' and the 'problematic': 'A problem is something met with which bars my passage. It is before me in its entirety. A mystery, on the other hand, is something in which I find myself caught up, and whose essence is therefore not to be before me in its entirety.'[134] So often, as suggested above, certain pastoral care incidents can be understood as aporia rather than a moment of revelation. The relationship of service, viewed from within a Christological symbol,

131. Cf. Louth A. (1989) op.cit. p.3
132. Cf. Scola A. (1995) op.cit. p.9
133. Ibid. pp.47-48
134. Cf. ibid. p.68

provides the moving dynamic from problem to mystery. It also avoids the secular idea of skill acquisition, and tends towards 'the formation of pastoral identity'.[135]

The relationship between personal being and functional purpose is clearly an issue. In some models of pastoral care, there is conflict between a focus on the servant and the service he provides. In a therapeutic tradition, this dialectic is tentatively resolved in favour of the former: 'This is not to say that the pastoral therapeutic orientation is unconcerned with questions of right action, but only to say that it has shown greater concern for nurturing those qualities of personhood and interpersonal relationship'.[136] Our investigation of contemporary pastoral theological themes indicates the promotion of a pastoral service arising from a clearly theological understanding of the pastoral minister. Although cast within a largely psychological model, Hunter makes a necessary point: 'Religious symbols and rituals need to be integrated existentially into the personhood and personal relationships of the pastor.'[137] In the third chapter of this investigation, this integration was defined as configuration to Christ, within an ecclesiology of communion. Although the language of contemporary pastoral care models is very different, Couture and Hunter's survey suggests that the pastoral care movement is arriving at a similar place.[138] This leads to some important conclusions for the pastoral minister who wants to reflect upon pastoral care. First of all, there is a need to recognize that theological reflection is concerned with formation of pastoral theologians rather than counselling specialists. Secondly, there is an affirmation of the theological need for an understanding of service within pastoral care. And finally, we encounter the definitive need of an ecclesial context for the exercise of pastoral ministry.[139]

How is the one involved in pastoral ministry to understand the place of service within the practice of pastoral care? Hans-Georg Gadamer is a philosopher and concerned with textual hermeneutics. He reflects on the process of understanding from within a phenomenological position. Gadamer is determined that this 'is not to be thought of so

135. Foskett J. and Lyall D. (1988) op.cit. p.47
136. Eds. Couture P. and Hunter R. (1995) op.cit. p.23
137. Ibid. p.27
138. Cf. especially, eds. Couture P. and Hunter R. (1995) op.cit. chapter two
139. Cf. ibid. pp.178-179

much as an action of subjectivity, but as the placing of oneself within a process of tradition, in which past and present are constantly fused.'[140] Transposed into the pastoral action of service, this means the immersion of the pastoral minister into an ecclesial tradition of pastoral theology. The one involved in ministry will discover a fruitful reflection on the nature of service in the documents of the Second Vatican Council.

---

140. Cf. Jeanrond W. *Theological Hermeneutics* (London: SCM Press Ltd., 1994) p.65

General Conclusion

The documents of the Second Vatican Council were clearly influenced by non-theological disciplines. This has created a significant shift in theological agenda material. In the arena of pastoral theology, for example, there has been an unprecedented and laudatory dialogue with the behavioural sciences. The patristic development of mystagogy is a historical illustration of a similar inter-cultural conversation in the early Christian tradition. However, the more recent Second Vatican Council has also involved the unquestioning assimilation of non-theological methodologies. Contemporary pastoral theological reflection is now taking place in a redefined territory, with ambiguous boundaries. For the pastoral theologian, this has created a complex paradox and a confused theological hermeneutic. To some extent, the place of the theological tradition is no longer totally assured in some contemporary pastoral theological schools.

This investigation has sought the recovery of an explicitly theological content to the process of pastoral theological reflection. It is hoped that this pastoral theology will influence two aspects of any programme of reflection. First of all, pastoral ministers will begin to recognize the need for an exercise of ministry that is fully informed by the academic theological elements of the Christian tradition. In this respect, pastoral theology acts as the inter-face between other theological disciplines and pastoral ministry. Secondly, this study has attempted to develop a specifically theological methodological model for the necessary reflection on pastoral care practice. The principal fruit of this model has been applied to the process of theological reflection. This expressly theological methodology exposes the ambiguity of other reflection models currently used in the ongoing formation for ministry. It has also demonstrated the need for a critical vigilance in the employment of reflection models developed within clinical pastoral education.

This study has not attempted to design a systematic treatise on the priesthood or other forms of pastoral ministry within the communion

of disciples. A focus on post-conciliar developments in theology, however, necessarily presupposes a foundational notion of the priesthood. Therefore, this investigation h looked to the definitions of the Second Vatican Council, ir provide the theological basis for presbyteral ministry. Analy material, in chapter two of this investigation, indicates a lacl and full attention to the presbyteral ministry. In the Secon council's programme of theological renewal, the episco provided the paradigm for all ecclesial ministries.

There has also been a profound reappraisal of the laity. involved a new understanding of their nature and mission, o in the sacraments of initiation. The idea of collaborative m now firmly on the agenda. To some extent, this has created a tension, which remains largely unresolved in the post examination of presbyteral ministry. In the current th battleground, a number of dogmatic models for priestl clamouring for attention. There is a specific need to refle immediate tradition, developed in the post-Tridentine centurie the Second Vatican Council. This illustrates the constant obli situate presbyteral ministry within a clear dogmatic framewo suggests the need for an unequivocal attention to a pastoral n metaphor that encourages the fecundity of formation for mini

Therefore, this investigation has implied that the t communion is the most fitting metaphor for the pr contemporary pastoral care. The idea of communion is pa appropriate for those pastoral ministers who will exercise thei within a predominantly parish-based context. At this poi investigation, it was possible to recognize the massive infl the human sciences upon pastoral studies. This was especiall the derivative of communion, in the notion of community a for ministry and mission. Attention to the source documen Second Vatican Council, and post-conciliar developments, i a more theologically sound understanding of community Christological symbol.

This investigation leads to the assumption that the id sbyteral ministry, and all other ministries, is forged munitarian framework. Indeed, this is suggested of the hood and ministry itself. The theological perspective

assertion is discerned in the Trinitarian relationship of a genuine Christological symbol. In this study, this discernment involved a profound synthesis of ontological definition and functional purpose. Community is not only needed for the ministerial exercise of presbyteral service. This service can be understood only from within a radical concept of communitarian relationship.

Presbyteral identity and ministry, therefore, are discovered within a communitarian context. This calls for an attentive focus on the ecclesial communities in which presbyteral ministry is fashioned and exercised. The chapter on the parish suggested that an understanding of community is still in transition. Indeed, the whole notion of parish is fluxional. This is seen most clearly in the liturgical celebration of a parish community. There are signs of post-conciliar changes: language, ritual and even sanctuary furniture. Unfortunately, the essential reforms of the Second Vatican Council are still latent. Until the whole community is vibrant with a desire for evangelizing missionary activity, the renewal envisaged by the bishops of the Council cannot achieve its necessary maturity.

These statements about ecclesial communities are essential for an understanding of the pastoral minister's identity too. Modern candidates for ministry have complex and rich personalities. We can talk of a multi-cultural and diverse ethnic society. These people must breathe within an inherited recent tradition of changing and ambiguous models and methodologies. Their own personhood is a convergence of social influences and personal encounters, in a broader context of many different kinds of social relationships. In so many respects, this investigation has illustrated how all these forces come together in pastoral theological reflection. This study has made a unequivocal appeal to the Christian tradition. It has attempted design of a specifically mystagogical model of theological refl Finally, it is our hope that these means of investigation will programmes of formation and ongoing formation for past This is crucial. For thirty years after the Second Vatica programme is understood to be a pivotal element in Church to respond to ever-new demands upon th in pastoral ministry.

Bibliography

Church Documents:

Bishops' Committee on Priestly Formation *Pastoral Formation and Pastoral Field Education in the Catholic Seminary* (Washington: National Conference of Catholic Bishops, 1985)

Bishops' Working Party on Collaborative Ministry *The Sign We Give* (Bishops' Conference of England and Wales, 1995)

Commissions Justice et Paix d'Europe *Social Justice for All* (1994)

Committee for Ministerial Formation *The Charter for Priestly Formation* (The Bishops' Conference of England and Wales, 1990)

Committee for the World of Work *A New Community of Work* (1995)

Congregation for Catholic Education *Directives Concerning the Preparation of Seminary Educators* (Rome: Vatican Press, 1993)

Congregation for Catholic Education *Directives on the Formation of Seminarians Concerning Problems related to Marriage and the Family* (Rome: Vatican Press, 1995)

Congregation for the Clergy *Directory on the Ministry and Life of Priests* (London: CTS Publications, 1994)

Congregation for the Clergy *International Symposium Celebrating the anniversary of the promulgation of the Conciliar Decree Presbyterorum Ordinis* (Vatican City, 1995)

Congregation for the Doctrine of the Faith *Letter to the Bishops of the Catholic Church on some aspects of the Church understood as Communion* (London: Incorporated Catholic Truth Society, 1992)

ed. Flannery A. *Vatican Council II The Conciliar and Post Conciliar Documents* (New York: Costello Publishing Co., 1992)

John Paul II *Address to the Fiftieth General Assembly of the United Nations Organization* New York, 5 October 1995

John Paul II *Christifideles Laici* (London: CTS Publications, 1988)

John Paul II *Ecclesia in Africa in L'Osservatore Romano* 20 September 1995

John Paul II *Letter of the Holy Father Pope John Paul II to priests for Holy Thursday* (Vatican City: Libreria Editrice Vaticana, 1991)

John Paul II *Letter of the Holy Father Pope John Paul II to priests for Holy Thursday 1993* (Vatican City: Libreria Editrice Vaticana, 1993)

John Paul II *Letter of the Holy Father Pope John Paul II to priests for Holy Thursday 1994* (Vatican City: Libreria Editrice Vaticana, 1994)

John Paul II *Pastores Dabo Vobis* (London: The Incorporated Catholic Truth Society, 1994)

John Paul II *Redemptoris Missio* (London: CTS Publications, 1990)

John Paul II *Tertio Millennio Adveniente* (London: The Incorporated Catholic Truth Society, 1994)

John Paul II *Veritatis Splendor* (London: The Incorporated Catholic Truth Society, 1993)

National Conference of Catholic Bishops *Norms for Priestly Formation vols. 1 and 2* (Washington: United States Catholic Conference 1993)

New Jerusalem Bible (London: Darton, Longman & Todd, 1985)

Official report of the National Pastoral Congress *Liverpool 1980* (Slough: St Paul Publications, 1981)

Paul VI *Evangelii Nuntiandi* (London: CTS Publications, 1975)

US Catholic Conference *The Church in Our Day* (London: Catholic Truth Society, 1968)

Books:

ed. Alberigo G. et.al. *The Reception of Vatican II* (Tunbridge Wells: Burns & Oates, 1987)

Alison J. *Knowing Jesus* (London: SPCK, 1993)

tr. and ed. Allison Peers E. *The Complete Works of Saint John of the Cross, vol.2* (Wheathampstead: Anthony Clarke 1953)

Archer A. *The Two Catholic Churches* (London: SCM Press, 1986)

Balthasar H. *The Glory of the Lord vol.1: Seeing the Form* (Edinburgh: T. & T. Clark, 1982)

Balthasar H. *Does Jesus Know Us? Do We Know Him?* (San Francisco: Ignatius Press, 1983)

Balthasar H. *The Christian State of Life* (San Francisco: Ignatius Press, 1983)

Balthasar H. *Theo-Drama. Theological Dramatic Theory, vol.1: Prolegomena* (San Francisco: Ignatius Press, 1988)

Balthasar H. *Explorations in Theology vol.1* (San Francisco: Ignatius Press, 1989)
Balthasar H. *Explorations in Theology vol.2* (San Francisco: Ignatius Press, 1991)
Balthasar H. *Presence and Thought* (San Francisco: Ignatius Press, 1995)
Balthasar H. *Bernanos: An Ecclesial Existence* (San Francisco: Ignatius Press, 1996)
Baraúna W. *The Liturgy of Vatican II* (Chicago: Franciscan Herald Press, 1966)
Bausch W. *The Christian Parish* (Mystic: Twenty-Third Publications, 1980)
Bea A. *We who Serve* (London: Geoffrey Chapman, 1969)
Bernier P. *Ministry in the Church* (Mystic: Twenty-Third Publications, 1992)
Bertola C. *'I have called you friends' Sacramental, Theological and Existential Aspects of Priestly Fraternity* (New York: Alba House, 1989)
Blochlinger A. *The Modern Parish Community* (London: Geoffrey Chapman, 1965)
Bishop John Cuthbert Hedley *A Spiritual Man* (London: Burns & Oates, 1889)
Bishop John Cuthbert Hedley *A Bishop and his Flock* (London: Burns & Oates, 1903)
Bishop William Bernard Ullathorne *The Sermon delivered at the Consecration of the Bishops of Salford and Amycla* (London: Burns, Oates, & Co., 1872)
Bishop William Bernard Ullathorne *The Discourse delivered at the Opening Session of the Fourth Provincial Synod of Westminster* (London: Burns & Oates, 1873)
Bloom A. *The Closing of the American Mind* (London: Penguin Books, 1987)
Bosch D. *Transforming Mission Paradigm Shifts in Theology of Mission* (New York: Orbis Books, 1991)
Bouyer L. *The Church of God* (Chicago: Franciscan Herald Press, 1982)
Bouyer L. *The Liturgy revised* (London: Libra Books, 1965)
ed. Boyack K. *The New Catholic Evangelization* (New York: Paulist Press, 1992)

Brennan P. *Power in Rite* (Mill Hill: T. Shand Publications, 1986)
Browning D. *Practical Theology* (San Francisco: Harper & Row, 1983)
Bugnini A. *The Reform of the Liturgy 1948-1975* (Collegeville: The Liturgical Press, 1990)
Burghardt W. Preaching: *the Art and the Craft* (New York: Paulist Press, 1987)
Butler C. *The Vatican Council vol.1* (London: Longmans, Green & Co., 1930)
Campbell A. *Rediscovering Pastoral Care* (London: Darton, Longman & Todd, 1981)
Cardijn J. *Laymen into Action* (London: Geoffrey Chapman, 1964)
Cardinal H.E. Manning *The Eternal Priesthood* (London: Burns & Oates, fifth edition)
Cardinal H.E. Manning *The Pastoral Office* (Printed for Private Use Only, 1883)
Cardinal N. Wiseman *Lectures on the Principal Doctrines and Practices of the Catholic Church* (London: The Catholic Publishing & Bookselling Co., 1867)
Catechism of the Catholic Church (London: Geoffrey Chapman, 1994)
Chirico P. *Infallibility: The Crossroads of Doctrine* (London: Sheed & Ward, 1977)
Clarke J. *Story Of A Soul* (Washington D.C.: ICS Publications, 1976)
Congar Y. *Laity, Church and World* (London: Geoffrey Chapman, 1960)
Congar Y. *Lay People in the Church* (London: Geoffrey Chapman, 1965)
Congregation for Divine Worship *Rite of Christian Initiation of Adults* (London: Geoffrey Chapman, 1972)
Congregation for Divine Worship *The Divine Office vol.3* (London: Collins, 1974)
Congregation for Divine Worship *The Roman Missal* (Alcester: Goodliffe Neale, 1975)
Cooper N. *Collaborative Ministry* (New York: Paulist Press, 1993)
eds. Couture P. and Hunter R. *Pastoral Care and Social Conflict* (Nashville: Abingdon Press, 1995)
Cox H. *The Secular City* (Middlesex: Penguin Books, 1968)
Crichton J.D. *Changes in the Liturgy* (London: Geoffrey Chapman, 1965)

ed. Crichton J.D. et.al. *English Catholic Worship* (London: Geoffrey Chapman, 1979)

ed. Crowe F. *A Third Collection. Papers by Bernard J.F. Lonergan, S.J.* (London: Geoffrey Chapman, 1985)

Crowe F. *Lonergan* (London: Geoffrey Chapman, 1992)

ed. Dalton W. *A Parish Pastoral Directory* (Blackrock: The Columba Press, 1995)

Deeks D. *Pastoral Theology: An Inquiry* (London: Epworth Press, 1987)

de Lubac H. *The Christian Faith* (San Francisco: Ignatius Press, 1986)

de Lubac H. *The Motherhood of the Church* (San Francisco: Ignatius Press, 1982)

Donovan D. *What are they saying about the ministerial priesthood?* (New York: Paulist Press, 1992)

Drilling P. *Trinity and Ministry* (Minneapolis: Fortress Press, 1991)

Dubay T. *Faith and Certitude* (San Francisco: Ignatius Press, 1985)

Duffy E. *The Stripping of the Altars* (New Haven: Yale University Press, 1992)

Dulles A. *The Craft of Theology – From Symbol to System* (Dublin: Gill & Macmillan, 1992)

Duval A. *The Council of Trent and Holy Orders* in *The Sacrament of Orders* (London: The Aquin Press, 1962)

Edwards O. *Elements of Homiletic* (Collegeville: Pueblo Publishing Co., 1982)

Farley E. *Theologia* (Philadelphia: Fortress Press, 1983)

ed. Flanagan P. *A New Missionary Era* (Maryknoll: Orbis Books, 1979)

ed. Flannery A. *Evangelization Today* (New York: Costello Publishing Co., 1977)

ed. Flannery A. *Vatican II on the Church* (Dublin: Scepter Books, 1966)

eds. Finn P. and Schellman J. *Shaping English Liturgy* (Washington: The Pastoral Press, 1990)

Forde W. *Adventuring in Priesthood* (Dublin: The Columba Press, 1993)

Foskett J. and Lyall D. *Helping the Helpers* (London: SPCK, 1988)

Foster J. *Requiem for a Parish* (Westminster: The Newman Press, 1962)

Fowler J. *Faith Development and Pastoral Care* (Philadelphia: Fortress Press, 1987)

Frei H. *Types of Christian Theology* (Newhaven: Yale University Press, 1992)

Furniss G. *Sociology for Pastoral Care* (London: SPCK, 1994)
Geffré C. *A New Age in Theology* (New York: Paulist Press, 1974)
Geffré C. *The Risk of Interpretation* (New York: Paulist Press, 1987)
Gelineau J. *The Liturgy Today and Tomorrow* (London: DLT, 1978)
Gelpi D. *The Turn to Experience in Contemporary Theology* (New York: Paulist Press, 1994)
Gilley S. *Newman and his Age* (London: DLT, 1990)
ed. Goergen D. *Being a Priest Today* (Collegeville: The Liturgical Press, 1992)
Habgood J. *Church and Nation in a Secular Age* (London: DLT, 1983)
Hamer J. *The Church is a Communion* (London: Geoffrey Chapman, 1964)
Hanratty G. *Light from Paris* (Blackrock: Four Courts Press, 1995)
Häring B. *Sin in the Secular Age* (Slough: St Paul Publications, 1974)
Harmless W. *Augustine and the Catechumenate* (Collegeville: The Liturgical Press, 1995)
Hickey J. *Urban Catholics* (London: Geoffrey Chapman, 1967)
Hornsby-Smith M. *Roman Catholics in England* (Cambridge: Cambridge University Press, 1987)
Hornsby-Smith M. *The Changing Parish* (London: Routledge, 1989)
Hovda R. Strong, *Loving and Wise* (Collegeville: The Liturgical Press, 1976)
Jeanrond W. *Theological Hermeneutics* (London: SCM Press Ltd., 1994)
ed. Jedin H. *History of the Church vol.viii The Church in the Age of Liberalism* (London: Burns & Oates, 1981)
Kasper W. *Theology and Church* (London: SCM, 1989)
Kasper W. *Transcending all Understanding: The Meaning of Christian Faith Today* (San Francisco: Ignatius Press, 1989)
Kemp R. *A Journey in Faith* (New York: Sadlier, 1979)
ed. Komonchak J. et.al. *The New Dictionary of Theology* (Dublin: Gill and Macmillan, 1987)
Lane T. *A Priesthood in Tune* (Dublin: The Columba Press, 1993)
ed. Latourelle R. *Vatican II Assessment and Perspectives vol.1* (New York: Paulist Press, 1989)
ed. Latourelle R. *Vatican II Assessment and Perspectives vol.3* (New York: Paulist Press, 1989)
Lonergan B. *Method in Theology* (London: Darton, Longman & Todd, 1971)

Louth A. *Discerning the Mystery* (Oxford: Clarendon Press, 1989)
Lynch P. *Awakening the Giant* (London: DLT, 1980)
Lyons E. *Partnership in Parish* (Blackrock: The Columba Press, 1987)
Martin R. *The Catholic Church at the End of an Age* (San Francisco: Ignatius Press, 1994)
Mazza E. *Mystagogy* (New York: Pueblo Publishing Co., 1989)
McClelland V.A. *Cardinal Manning His Public Life and Influence 1865-1892* (London: Oxford University Press, 1962)
McDonald K. *Communion and Friendship: A Framework for Ecumenical Dialogue in Ethics* (Rome: Pontifical University of St Thomas, 1989)
eds. McGregor B. and Norris T. *The Formation Journey of the Priest* (Blackrock: The Columba Press, 1994)
tr. McHugh J. and Callan C. *Catechism of the Council of Trent for Parish Priests* (New York: Joseph F. Wagner, 1923)
ed. McNamara K. *Vatican II: The Constitution on the Church* (London: Geoffrey Chapman, 1968)
Michonneau G. *Revolution in a City Parish* (London: Blackfriars, 1949)
Michonneau G. *The Missionary Spirit in Parish Life* (Cork: Mercier Press, 1952)
Mick L. *RCIA Renewing the Church as an Initiating Assembly* (Collegeville: The Liturgical Press, 1989)
ed. Milner P. *The Ministry of the Word* (London: Burns & Oates, 1967)
Monnin A. *Life of the Blessed Curé D'Ars* (London: Burns, Oates & Washbourne, Ltd.)
ed. Murphy J. *New Beginnings in Ministry* (Blackrock: The Columba Press, 1992)
ed. Neuner J. and Dupuis J. *The Christian Faith* (London: Collins, 1983)
Newbigin L. *The Gospel in a Pluralist Society* (London: SPCK, 1989)
Newbigin L. *The Open Secret* (London: SPCK, 1995)
ed. Newman J. *The Christian Layman* (Dublin: Scepter Books, 1966)
Nichols A. *Yves Congar* (London: Geoffrey Chapman, 1989)
Nichols A. *From Newman to Congar* (Edinburgh: T & T Clark, 1990)
Nichols A. *Holy Order* (Dublin: Veritas, 1990)
Norman E. *The English Catholic Church in the Nineteenth Century* (Oxford: Clarendon Press, 1984)
Nouwen H. *In the Name of Jesus* (London: DLT, 1989)

Olin J. *Catholic Reform from Cardinal Xinenes to the Council of Trent 1495-1563* (New York: Fordham University Press, 1990)

O'Collins G. *Retrieving Fundamental Theology* (London: Geoffrey Chapman, 1993)

O'Meara T. *Theology of Ministry* New York: Paulist Press, (1983)

Osborne K. *Ministry: Lay Ministry in the Roman Catholic Church* (New York: Paulist Press, 1993)

Osborne K. *Priesthood* (New York: Paulist Press, 1988)

O'Shea J. et.al. *Parish Project* (London: Harper Collins Religious, 1992)

Ostdiek G. *Catechesis for Liturgy* (Washington DC: The Pastoral Press, 1986)

Oster H. *The Paschal Mystery in Parish Life* (London: Burns & Oates, 1967)

Pattison S. *A Critique of Pastoral Care* (London: SCM Press Ltd., 1993)

Polanyi M. *Personal Knowledge: Towards a Post-Critical Philosophy* (London: Routledge & Kegan Paul, 1958)

Rademacher W. *Lay Ministry* (Slough: St Paul Publications, 1991)

Rahner K. *Theology of Pastoral Action* (London: Burns & Oates, 1968)

ed. Rahner K. et.al. *Sacramentum Mundi – An Encyclopedia of Theology* (London: Burns and Oates, 1969)

Rahner K. and Ratzinger J. *The Episcopate and the Primacy* (Edinburgh: Nelson, 1962)

Ramshaw E. *Ritual and Pastoral Care* (Philadelphia: Fortress Press, 1987)

Ratzinger J. *Feast of Faith* (San Francisco: Ignatius Press, 1986)

Ratzinger J. *Principles of Catholic Theology* (San Francisco: Ignatius Press, 1987)

Ratzinger J. *The Nature and Mission of Theology* (San Francisco: Ignatius Press, 1995)

Ravier A. *Saint Jeanne de Chantal* (San Francisco: Ignatius Press, 1989)

Ravier A. *Francis de Sales Sage and Saint* (San Francisco: Ignatius Press, 1988)

Regan D. *Experience the Mystery* (London: Geoffrey Chapman, 1994)

ed. Richard L. et.al. *Vatican II The Unfinished Agenda* (New York: Paulist Press, 1987)

Rikhof H. *The Concept of Church* (London: Sheed & Ward, 1981)
Ritschl D. *The Logic of Theology* (London: SCM Press Ltd., 1986)
Ryan D. *The Catholic Parish* (London: Sheed & Ward, 1996)
tr. and ed. Ryan J. *Introduction to the Devout Life by St Francis de Sales* (New York: Image Books, 1972)
eds. Scherer J. and Bevans S. *New Directions in Mission and Evangelization 2* (New York: Orbis Books, 1994)
Schiefen R. *Nicholas Wiseman and the Transformation of English Catholicism* (Shepherdstown: Patmos Press, 1984)
Scola A. *Hans Urs von Balthasar A Theological Style* (Edinburgh: T & T Clark, 1995)
Sofield L. and Juliano C. *Collaborative Ministry Skills and Guidelines* (Notre Dame: Ave Maria Press, 1987)
Shaw R. *To Hunt, To Shoot, To Entertain: Clericalism and the Catholic Laity* (San Francisco: Ignatius Press, 1993)
Stacpoole A. *Vatican II by those who were there* (London: Geoffrey Chapman, 1986)
Tavard G.A. *Theology for Ministry* (Dublin: Dominican Publications, 1983)
The Year of Preparation for the Vatican Council (London: Burns, Oates, & Co., 1869)
Thornhill J. *Christian Mystery in the Secular Age* (Maryland: Christian Classics Inc., 1991)
Tilley T. *Potmodern Theologies* (Maryknoll: Orbis Books, 1995)
ed. Tracy D. et. al. *Toward Vatican III The Work that needs to be done* (Dublin: Gill and Macmillan, 1978)
Trochu F. *The Curé D'Ars* (Rockford: Tan Books and Publishers, Inc., 1977)
Vanier J. *Community and Growth* (London: DLT, 1989)
Vanstone W. *The Stature of Waiting* (London: DLT, 1982)
ed. Vorgrimler H. *Commentary on the Documents of Vatican II vol.1* (London: Burns & Oates, 1967)
ed. Vorgrimler H. *Commentary on the Documents of Vatican II vol.2* (London: Burns & Oates, 1968)
ed. Vorgrimler H. *Commentary on the Documents of Vatican II vol.3* (London: Burns & Oates, 1969)
ed. Vorgrimler H. *Commentary on the Documents of Vatican II vol.4* (London: Burns & Oates, 1969)

ed. Vorgrimler H. *Commentary on the Documents of Vatican II vol.5* (London: Burns & Oates, 1969)

Ward C. *Priests and People* (Liverpool: Liverpool University Press, 1965)

Whitehead J. and E. *Method in Ministry: Theological Reflection and Christian Ministry* (London: Sheed & Ward, 1995)

Whitehead E. and J. *Community of Faith* (Minneapolis: The Winston – Seabury Press, 1982)

Whitehead E. and J. *Christian Life Patterns* (New York: Doubleday & Company Inc., 1982)

Wicker B. *Culture and Liturgy* (London: Sheed & Ward, 1963)

ed. Wilde J. Parish *Catechumenate: Pastors, Presiders, Preachers* (Chicago: Liturgy Training Publications, 1988)

Wilson A. *Blessed Dominic Barberi, C.P.* (London: Sands & Co., 1967)

Winter M. *Mission or Maintenance* (London: DLT, 1973)

Wright F. *Pastoral Care Revisited* (London: SCM Press Ltd., 1996)

Zizioulas J. *Being as Communion* (London: DLT, 1985)

Periodical Articles:

Amalorpavadass D. *Evangelization and Culture* in *Concilium* no.114 *Evangelization in the World Today* (New York: The Seabury Press)

Barron R. *The Priest as Bearer of the Mystery* in *The Furrow* vol.46 no.4 April 1995

Browne M. *Collegiality: the nota praevia* in *Doctrine and Life* vol.16 January 1966.

Boyd I. *What are the clergy for?* in *Theology* May/June 1995.

Corecco E. *The Bishop, Head of the Local Church and Discipline* in *Concilium* vol.8 no.4 *Order and the Sacraments* (London: Burns & Oates, 1968)

Crichton J.D. *Worshipping with Awe and Reverence* in *Priests and People* vol.9 no.12 December 1995.

Davis C. *The Parish and Theology* in *The Clergy Review* vol.49 no.5 May 1964.

Doepfner J. *The Liturgy and the World* in *Doctrine and Life* vol.14 December 1964.

Duggan R. *Pastoral Care from a Roman Catholic Perspective* in *Concilium* no.5 *Catholic Identity* (London: SCM Press, 1994)

Dulles A. *Vatican II and the Church's Purpose* in *Theology Digest* vol.32 no.4 Winter 1985.

Dupuy B. *Is there a Dogmatic distinction between the function of Priests and the function of Bishops?* in *Concilium* vol.4 no.4 *Apostolic by Succession?* (New Jersey: Paulist Press, 1968)

Estévez J. *Catechism highlights centrality of sacraments* in *Christian life in L'Osservatore Romano* 5 May 1993.

Famerée J. *Collegiality and communion in the church* in *Theology Digest* vol.42 no.1 Spring 1995.

Final relation of the Synod in *L'Osservatore Romano* 16 December 1985, Vatican City.

Fischer B. *The Rite of Christian Initiation of Adults: Rediscovery and New Beginnings* in *Worship* vol.64 no.2 March 1990.

Frohnes H. *Mission in the Light of Critical Historical Analysis* in *Concilium* no.114 *Evangelization in the World Today* (New York: The Seabury Press)

Gaillardetz R. *In Service of Communion: A Trinitarian Foundation for Christian Ministry* in *Worship* vol.67 no.5 September 1993.

Gastgeber K. *Adapting the Life and Ministry of Priests to the Pastoral Situation* in *Concilium* vol.8 no.4 *Order and the Sacraments* (London: Burns & Oates, 1968)

Ganoczy A. *The Absolute Claim of Christianity: The Justification of Evangelization or an Obstacle to it?* in *Concilium* no.114 *Evangelization in the World Today* (London: The Seabury Press)

Hinze B. *Johann Sebastian Drey's critique of Friedrich Schleiermacher's theology* in *The Heythrop Journal* vol.37, no.1 January 1996.

Hollenweger W. *The Aims of Evangelization* in *Concilium* no.114 *Evangelization in the World Today* (New York: The Seabury Press)

Hornsby-Smith M. *Priests, People and Parishes in Change: Reflections of a Sociologist* in *New Blackfriars* vol.65 no.766 April 1984.

Houtart F. and Remy J. *A Survey of Sociology as Applied to Pastoral Work* in *Concilium* vol.3 no.1 *The Pastoral Mission of the Church* (New Jersey: Paulist Press, 1965)

Imbelli R. and Groome T. *Signposts towards a Pastoral Theology* in *Theological Studies* vol.53 no.1 March 1992.

Johnstone B. *The European Synod: The Meaning and Strategy of Evangelization* in *Gregorianum* vol.73 no.3 1992.

Karlic E. *Catechism beautifully illustrates the nature of liturgical action* in *L'Osservatore Romano* 28 April 1993.

Kasper W. *A New Dogmatic Outlook on the Priestly Ministry* in *Concilium* vol.3 no.5 *The Ministry and Life of Priests Today* (London: Burns & Oates, 1969)

Kavanagh A. *What is participation? – or, participation revisited* in *Doctrine and Life* vol.23 July 1973.

Kress R. *Theological Method: praxis and liberation* in *Communio* vol.vi, no.1 Spring (1979).

Lamb M. *Modernism and Americanism* in *Communio* vol.xxi, no.4 Winter (1994).

Lawler M. and Shanahan T. *The Church is a Graced Communion* in *Worship* vol.67 no.6 November 1993.

Macquarrie J. *Existentialism and theological method* in *Communio* vol.vi, no.1 (1979).

Madges W. *Faith, Knowledge and Feeling: Towards an Understanding of Kuhn's appraisal of Schleiermacher* in *The Heythrop Journal* vol.37, no.1 January 1996.

Martini C. *Catechism responds to desire and needs of Church today* in *L'Osservatore Romano* 31 March 1993.

McBrien R. *Church and Ministry: the achievement of Yves Congar* in *Theology Digest* vol.32 no.3 Autumn 1985.

McClelland V.A. Review of *The Convert Cardinals: John Henry Newman and Henry Edward Manning* by David Newsome, in *The Heythrop Journal* vol.36 no.1 January 1995.

McNicholl A. *The Lay Apostolate* in *Doctrine and Life* vol.14 December 1964.

Mette N. *Evangelization and the Credibility of the Church* in *Concilium* no.114 *Evangelization in the World Today* (New York: The Seabury Press)

ed. Milburn D. *Impressions of an English Bishop at the First Vatican Council* in *The Wiseman Review* no.493 Autumn 1962.

Mulvihill M. *The Liturgy of Christian Initiation* in *Liturgy* vol.17 no.1 October-November 1992.

Murphy C. *Collegiality: An Essay toward better understanding* in *Theological Studies* vol.46 no.1 March 1985.

Noujeim G-P. *Eastern tradition reflected in new catechism's spirituality* in *L'Osservatore Romano* 24 March 1993.

O'Connell L. *Collegiality: theology and practice for the 80s* in *Theology Digest* vol.29 no.4 Winter 1981.

O'Gara M. *Listening to forgotten voices: the French minority bishops of Vatican I and infallibility* in *Theology Digest* vol.37 no.1 Spring 1990.

O'Grady C. *The Secular City* in *Doctrine and Life* vol.20 July 1970.

O'Hanlon G. *Theological Reflection* in *The Furrow* vol.46 no.4, April 1995.

O'Leary D. *Water in the Wilderness – the Challenge of Collaborative Ministry* in *The Furrow* vol.46 no.10 October 1995.

Ratzinger J. *The Pastoral Implications of Episcopal Collegiality* in *Concilium* vol.1 no.1 *Dogma* (New Jersey: Paulist Press, 1965)

Scola A. *The event of Jesus Christ today* in *Communio* vol.xxi, no.4 Winter (1994).

Schillebeeckx E. *The Priest and the Synod of 1971* in *Doctrine and Life* vol.22 February 1972.

Schonborn C. *The divine economy interwoven through new catechetical work* in *L'Osservatore Romano* 17 March 1993.

Schuster H. *the Nature and Function of Pastoral Theology* in *Concilium* vol.3 no.1 *The Pastoral Mission of the Church* (New Jersey: Paulist Press, 1965)

Semple G. *An Open University for Theology* in *The Furrow* vol.46 no.10 October 1995.

Stack G. *An Outline Catechumenate* in *Liturgy* vol.3 no.2 December 1978-January 1979.

Starkloff C. *Inculturation and Cultural Systems* in *Theological Studies* vol.55 no.1 March 1994.

Talec P. *Evangelization and Christendom in the Countries of the West* in *Concilium* no.114 *Evangelization in the World Today* (New York: The Seabury Press)

Thiel J. *Schleiermacher as 'Catholic': A change in the rhetoric of modern theology* in *The Heythrop Journal* vol.37, no.1 January 1996.

Tomko J. *Catechism shows God's salvific will requires Church to be missionary* in *L'Osservatore Romano* 3 March 1993.